NORTH CAROLINA
LAND GRANTS
in
SOUTH CAROLINA

Brent H. Holcomb

First published by A. Press, Inc., 1980
Reprinted by Genealogical Publishing Company
3600 Clipper Mill Rd., Suite 260
Baltimore, Maryland 21211-1953
1986, 1999, 2009
Library of Congress Catalogue Card Number 86-81689
ISBN 978-0-8063-1164-7
Made in the United States of America

INTRODUCTION

The border between North and South Carolina was a point of controversy for many years. Finally, in 1764, the border east of the Catawba River was surveyed. However, it was not until 1772 that it was surveyed west of that river. Before these surveys, over 1,000 land grants were issued by North Carolina in territory which is now South Carolina. These grants are in the present counties of Marlboro, Chesterfield, Lancaster, York, Chester, Union, Cherokee, Spartanburg, Greenville, Laurens and Newberry. As most researchers know, these counties did not come into existence until many years after the border was surveyed. In the period just after the survey, these grants were considered in Craven or Berkeley Counties, and St. Mark's or St. David's Parish, South Carolina. The North Carolina counties from which these land grants were issued were Bladen, Anson, Mecklenburg, and Tryon. Bladen County was formed in 1734; Anson was formed from Bladen in 1748 or 1749; Mecklenburg, from Anson in 1763; Tryon, from Mecklenburg in 1769. Of course, if land could be granted, it could be sold or inherited. Therefore, the other records of these North Carolina counties should be consulted, especially deeds and probate records. Conveniently for the researcher, all of these records are published in abstract form, and are easily accessible. Records of these grants after the border survey can be found in the South Carolina Land Memorials, the Charleston Deeds until 1785, and the deeds of the various counties involved.

Some explanation of the North Carolina land grants is necessary. Actual copies of grants were not kept by North Carolina, but "Minutes or Dockets" (abstracts). Plats and warrants are often not extant for these early grants. Some lands were entered, but for some reason, grants were not issued. (All such lands are indicated by a file number beginning in "0.") Some have warrants extant; some, plats; and even one has an original grant already made out. Abstracts of all extant plats and warrants are contained in this volume. If no plat or warrant is extant, the grant was abstracted. Copies of any instrument are available from the Land Grant Clerk, Secretary of State, Raleigh, N.C. 27603, for $.50 each. The file and book numbers in parentheses are duplicate grants for the same tract. The abbreviations CB, SC Bear, etc., signify chain bearers and are important personages, as they are often close neighbors or relatives of the grantee. One female chain bearer has been found (see p. 106, grant of Abraham Read).

This volume is a combination of the two volumes published in 1975. There have been a number of corrections and additions made for this edition. Hopefully, this work will help locate some missing links for the pioneers of the Carolina frontier. Some relationships are stated in the warrants, particularly in the Kuykendall and Neely families.

Brent H. Holcomb, C.A.L.S.
P.O. Box 21766
Columbia, South Carolina 29221
January 4, 1980

TABLE OF CONTENTS

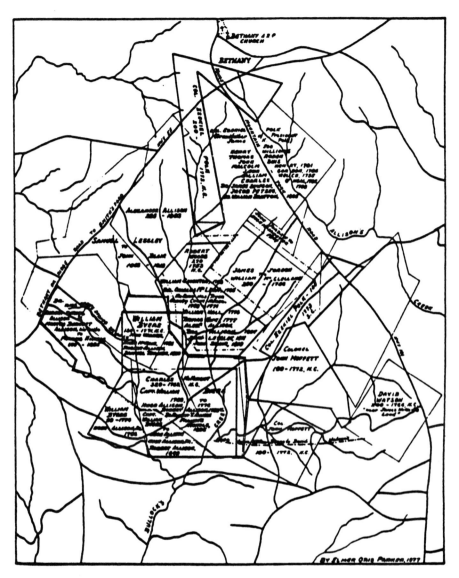

North Carolina Land Grants on the Headwaters of Bullock's and Allison's Creeks in present York County, South Carolina.

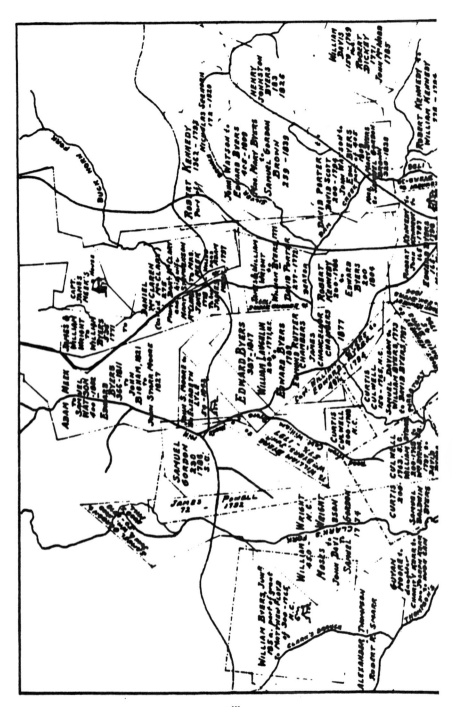

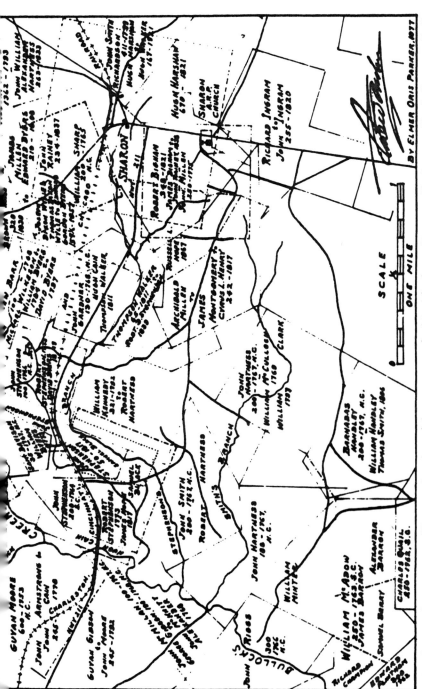

Bullocks Creek Area near Sharon showing eighteen grants in Mecklenburg County, N. C., now York County, S. C.

ix

CLARK, JOHN File no. 312; Bk. 5, p. 363
  300 A on S side Great P.D. River beginning on an Island 28 Sept 1745 Gab. Johnston

HICKS, JOHN File no. 505; Bk. 2, p. 102
  640 A about 9 miles above the Great Cheraws . . . mouth of Rocky Creek May 22 1741 Issued by J.M. Gab. Johnston

HINSON, PHILIP File no. 1000; Bk. 10, p. 163
  640 A on NE side Pee Dee adj. John Hixes 2 May 1741 Gab. Johnston

KING, JASPER File no. 878; Bk. 10, p. 134
  400 A on SW side of Peedee River opp. to Rockey Creek . . . John Westfield's line 22 May 1741 Gab. Johnston

McMANUS, JAMES File no. 387; Bk. 5, p. 431
  998 A on both sides Lynches creek . . . 6 Apr 1750 Gab Johnston

TOMPKINS, THOMAS File no. 999; Bk. 10, p. 163
  400 A on SW side Pee Dee . . . William Dinkins corner . . . 2 May 1741 Gab Johnston

ALEXANDER, JOHN File no. 1718 (1206); Gr. no. 1115; Bk. 15, p. 40 (13, 35)
200 A on S side Broad River on Crooked Creek below Robt. McAfersons . . . 24 Sept 1754 Matt Rowan

ALEXANDER, JOHN File no. 939 (306); Gr. no. 672; Bk. 10, p. 421 (2, 101)
400 A on S side Broad River on N fork Thicketty Creek . . . 23 Feb 1754 Matt Rowan

ALISON, ROBERT File no. 427 (2197); Gr. no. 292; Bk. 2, p. 146 (16, 73)
Plat: 15 July 1754, tract on a branch of Fishing Creek on S side Catawba . . . Andrew Woods' line . . . 157 A . . . By Jas. Carter D.S. [No CB]
To Robert Palmer, Esqr., Surveyo. General. Iss. 15 Oct. 1755

ARMOR, JAMES File no. 2138 (367); Gr. no. 88; Bk. 16, p. 23 (2, 125)
Plat: May 9, 1753, Surved for James Armour 300 A on a fork of Allisons Creek . . . adj. William Dickeys Saml Young [surv.] [No CB]. Iss 27 Mar 1755

ARMSTRONG, ARCHIBALD File no. 08
Warrant: unto Archbald [sic] Armstrong 200 A on a North branch of fishing creek called the beaverdam branch about 3 miles from Casper Culps's place 28 Mar 1753 Matt: Rowan

ARMSTRONG, JAMES File no. 844 (222); Gr. no. 340; Entry no. 117; Bk. 10, p. 386 (2, 67)
Warrant: unto James Armstrong 350 A on N side Broad River on N fork Bullocks Creek . . . 28 Mar 1753
Grant: 320 A on N side Broad, N side Bullocks Creek . . . 30 Aug 1753 Matt Rowan.

ARTHAUD, ISAAC File no. 395 (2166); Gr. no. 163; Bk. 2, p. 133 (16, 41)
Warrant: unto Isaac Arthaud, 200 A upon Thompsons Creek near Banjamin Jackson Below where the Catawba Path Crosses on both sides of the Creek . . . 26 Mar 1755 Arthur Dobbs
Plat: May 5th 1755, Surved for Isaac Arthurd [sic] . . . 202 A on Thomsons Creek near Benjaben [sic] Jacksons below the path that leads to the Cataba Nation . . . P Saml Young, Sep: Surveyor Mattw & Wm Rushing, C B. Iss. 3 Oct 1755

BAIRD, WILLIAM File no. 010
Warrant: unto William Baird 300 A on N side Cataba River

2

on the Waxhaw Creek near to William Nutt at an Indian Path
. . . 4 Apr 1752 Gab Johnston.

BAKER, SAMUEL Entry no. 367; File no. 012
Warrant: to Saml Baker 600 A above John Wilson's . . . 11
May 1753 Matt Rowan directed to Mr. Sam Young Dep Sur.

BAKER, SAMUEL File no. 013
Warrant: to Saml Baker 600 A on the Golden Grove above
his other survey . . . 11 May 1753 Matt: Rowan

BALAM, HONES File no. 166 (788); Gr. no. 275; Bk. 2, p. 56
(10, 375)
400 A on S side Broad River on Thicketty Creek . . . below
McPeters land . . . 11 May 1753 Matt Rowan

BARKLEY, JOHN File no. 1159 (1673); Gr. no. 1056; Bk. 15, p.
18 (13, 17)
300 A on S side Bear Creek . . . 17 May 1754 Matt Rowan

BARNES, JOHN Entry no. 325; File no. 020
Warrant: unto John Barns 300 A on the north fork of fishing
creek about 3 miles from Moses Dickeys place . . . 14 Oct
1752 Nath Rice

BARNET, JOHN Entry no. 585; File no. 018
Warrant: unto JOHN BARNET 300 A on N side Catawba adj.
WILLIAM McKee, Alexander Nesbit, William Moor including
an old Cabin & a peach orchard . . . 30 Aug 1753 Matt:
Rowan

BARNETT, JOHN File no. 918 (286); Gr. no. 796; Bk. 10, p. 417
(2, 96)
430 A on N side Broad River on Moores Creek . . . 1/2 survey
made formerly to Guyan Moore . . . 23 Feb 1754 Matt
Rowan

BARNITT, JOHN File no. 912 (280); Gr. no. 677; Bk. 10, p. 416
(2, 95)
599 A on N side Cataba adj. William McKee, near Alexander
Neesbit, and including an old cabbin . . . 23 Feb 1754 Matt
Rowan

BARNITT, WILLIAM File no. 916 (284); Gr. no. 800; Entry no.
575; Bk. 10, p. 416 (2, 96)
Warrant: unto William Barnett, 300 A on N side of Cataba in
branches of Cane Creek, adj. Thomas Mackilheny's Survey
. . . 29 Aug 1753 Matt: Rowan
300 A on N side Cataba on Branches of Cain Creek adj.
Thomas McKennys Survey 23 Feb 1754 Matt: Rowan

BARNITT, WILLIAM File no. 938 (305); Gr. no. 797; Bk. 10, p. 421 (2, 100)
Warrant: unto William Barnet 450 A on S side Cataba adj. Wm Henry, the place formerly surveyed for Thos Robinson ... 31 Aug 1753 Matt Rowan
450 A on S side Cataba adj. Henry's & John Turners, formerly surveyd for Thomas Robinson 23 Feb 1754 Matt Rowan

BARR, JOHN File no. 679 (58); Gr. no. 151; Bk. 10, p. 331 (2, 24)
600 A in the County of Anson ... 28 Mar 1753 Matt Rowan

BARR, JOHN File no. 96 (718); Gr. no. 149; Bk. 2, p. 32 (10, 343)
640 A on S side Cataba on N branch of Ellisons Creek near William Dickies 31 Mar 1753 Matt Rowan

BETTY, CHARLES File no. 351 (2122); Gr. no. 108; Bk. 2, p. 118 (16, 4)
Plat: February 15th 1755, Surd for Charles Betty 302 A including the south forks of fishing creek below John Kuykindals Land ... Pr Saml Young, Dep: Surveyor Saml Cobron & Thomas Betty, C. B. Iss. 28 Mar 1755

BETTY, THOMAS File no. 392 (2163); Gr. no. 93; Bk. 2, p. 128 (16, 31)
Plat: Decemr 19th 1752, Surd for Thomas Betty 290 A on ye South side of the Cataba River on a Branch of fishing Creek to the North of William Prices survey ... Pr Saml Young Dep Sur Plotted by me March 26th 1755 [no CB] Iss. 28 Mar 1755

BOLE, SHUSANA File no. 934 (301); Gr. no. 668; Bk. 10, p. 421 (2, 100)
192 A on N side Broad on the fork of Turkey Creek adj. James Love ... 23 Feb 1754 Matt Rowan

BOLE, SUSANNAH File no. 045
Warrant: unto Susanah Bole 400 A on N side Broad River, on Love's Creek above Moore land including the inden Camps ... 3 Apr 1752 Gab Johnston

BOYLE, EDWARD File no. 047
Warrant: unto Edward Boyle 300 A on S side Catabo on a branch of fishing Creek between Moses Dickeys Survey & John Kerkindale ... 28 Mar 1753 Matt: Rowan

BROWN, ALEXANDER File no. 1238 (1740); Bk. 13, p. 42 (15, 48)
320 A on S fork Fishing Creek above David Lewis land ... 24 Sept 1754 Matt Rowan

BROWN, BARTLETT File no. 791 (169); Gr. no. 278; Bk. 10, p. 375 (2, 56)

600 A on S side Pacolet on both sides Kings River . . . 11 May 1753 Matt Rowan

BROWN, BARTLETT File no. 792 (170); Gr. no. 280; Bk. 10, p. 376 (2, 57)
400 A on S side Pacolet on Kings River . . . his lower survey . . . 11 May 1753 Matt Rowan

BROWN, BARTLETT File no. 793 (171); Gr. no. 280; Bk. 10, p. 376 (2, 57)
600 A on both sides Kings River below Samuel Gilkeys land . . . 11 May 1753 Matt Rowan

BROWN, GABRIEL File no. 632 (12); Gr. 10, p. 305 (2, 6)
200 A on S side Broad River at the mouth of a long creek . . . known as Rangers Lodge . . . 3 Apr 1752 Gab Johnston

BROWN, JACOB File no. 1208 (1720); Gr. no. 1170; Bk. 13, p. 36 (15, 40)
300 A on the So side of Broad River on a fork of Browns Creek below the great Shoals September 24th 1754 Matt Rowan

BROWN, JOHN File no. 1218 (1730); Gr. no. 1164; Bk. 13, p. 38 (15, 43)
300 A on S side Broad, main fork of Browns Creek . . . Edward McNeils Land . . . 24 Sept 1754 Matt Rowan

BULLOCK, JAMES Entry no. 42; File no. 050
Warrant: unto James Bullock, 400 A on South Side Broad River, on Thickety Creek . . . above McPeter . . . 3 Apr 1752 Gab Johnston
Plat: Suryd James Bollock [sic] a plantation containing 400 A on ye south side of Broad River on thicketty . . . above McPeters . . . Francs Mackilwean Dept Sur. [No CB]

CALWELL, ROBERT File no. 876 (254); Gr. no. 696; Bk. 10, p. 410 (2, 88)
517 A on N side Waxhaw Creek, adj. Samuel Mailveney [sic] corner . . . 23 Feb 1754 Matt Rowan

CAMBLE, JAMES File no. 935 (302); Gr. no. 655; Bk. 10, p. 421 (2, 100)
Plat: July 7th 1752; Surved for James Camble 400 A on S side Cataba 2 or 3 miles North of Crowders Creek . . . [No CB] . . . Pr Fran: Mackilwean Dep Sur. Iss. 23 Feb 1754

CAMPBELL, PATRICK File no. 0134
Warrant: Unto Patrick Campbell, 600 A on Campbell's Creek, a fork of Lawsons Creek . . . 5 Oct 1752 Nath Rice

CAMPBELL, PATRICK File no. 0135
> Warrant: Unto Patrick Campbell 400 A in the fork of Campbells Creek . . . 5 Oct 1753 Nath Rice

CAMPBELL, MARGARET File no. 1807; Bk. 15, p. 127
> Plat: Surved for Margret Camble 376 A on the South Side of Broad River on ye No fork of Paclat River above ye midle Cherakee path . . . March 1d 1753 Pr Fan [sic] Mackilwean Dep Sur. [No CB] Iss. 19 Mar 1756

CARE, ROBERT File no. 1754; Gr. no. 1120; Bk. 15, p. 49
> 400 A on little River . . . 25 Sept 1754 [No Gov. signature]

CARRUTH, WALTER File no. 2159 (388); Gr. no. 107; Bk. 16, p. 30 (2, 128)
> 300 A on S side Enoree below Benjaben Gordons Survey . . . 28 Mar 1755 Arthur Dobbs

CARTER, OWEN File no. 163 (786); Gr. no. 273; Bk. 2, p. 55 (10, 374)
> 200 A on S side Broad River in the forks of Pacolet [and Broad River] 11 May 1753 Matt Rowan

CARTER, ROGER File no. 0131; Entry no. 509
> Warrant: Unto Roger Carter, 400 A on So fork Fishing Creek, betwixt John Kuykindale & William Henry 29 Aug 1753 Matt Rowan

CARTHY, GEORGE JUNR File no. 695 (74); Gr. no. 163; Bk. 10, p. 336 (2, 27)
> 800 A on S side Catawba in forks of Fishing Creek . . . 3 Apr 1753 Matt Rowan

CASE, WILLIAM File no. 0126
> Plat: Decemr 18th 1753, Surveyed for William Case, 100 A at the mouth of Litle River where he now lives . . . Pr Sam Young, Dep. Sur. [No CB]

CATHEY, ALEXANDER File no. 349; Gr. no. 160; Bk. 2, p. 116
> Plat: Decemr. 19th 1754, Survd for Alexander Cathey, 300 A on the South side of Pacalate River on a Branch of Clarks Mill Caled [sic] the Jumping Run including the faireforest [sic] path. Pr Saml Young, Dep Sur. Saml Gilkey & Alex Locart, CB Iss. 28 Mar 1755

CLARK, JOHN File no. 2115 (343); Gr. no. 91; Bk. 16, p. 2 (2, 117)
> Plat: Jan 3, 1754, Survd for John Clark 200 A on ye S side Broad River, on Beaver Dam Creek, about 4 miles from old Turners including path to Indian Creek . . . Saml Young Iss. 28 Mar 1755

6

CLARK, JOHN File no. 2117 (345); Gr. no. 115; Bk. 18, p. 3 (2, 117)
Plat: March 26, 1754, Surveyed for John Clark, 800 A on Pacalet River, including the place where he now lives . . . Pr Saml Young, Dept. Sur. Iss. 28 Mar 1755 [No CB]

CLARK, JOHN File no. 1635 (1121); Gr. no. 1015; Bk. 15, p. 11 (13, 11)
300 A on S fork Sandy River . . . 17 May 1754 Matt Rowan

CLARK, JOHN File no. 787 (165); Gr. no. 274; Bk. 10, p. 274 (2, 56)
400 A on S side Broad River . . . William Loves corner . . . 11 May 1753 Matt Rowan

CLARK, JOHN File no. 638 (18); Bk. 10, p. 307 (2, 7)
600 A on S side Broad River, where Clark was settled . . . 3 Apr 1752 Gab Johnston

CLARK, JOSEPH File no. 699 (77); Bk. 10, p. 337 (2, 28)
640 A on Allisons Creek below the fork . . . George Rennix line . . . 29 Mar 1753 Matt Rowan

CLEMENTS, MATT File no. 676 (55); Bk. 10, p. 331 (2, 23)
400 A on N side S fork Fishing Creek below the Bufflow [sic] lick 31 Mar 1753 Matt Rowan

COOK, ISAAC File no. 1644 (1130); Gr. no. 1024; Bk. 15, p. 12 (13, 12)
250 A on S side Broad on Cane Creek adj. Joseph Holonsworth [sic] Land . . . 17 May 1754 Matt Rowan

COUSARD, RICHARD File no. 1192 (1704); Gr. no. 1146; Bk. 13, p. 32 (15, 36)
302 A on N side Cataba on Gills Creek . . . about 1 mile sd. Cousard . . . 24 Sept 1754 Matt Rowan

COUSARD, RICHARD File no. 1143 (1657); Gr. no. 1038; Bk. 13, p. 14 (15, 15)
115 A on Gills Creek betwixt Black river path . . . adj. his own survey . . . on N side Cataba . . . 16 May 1754 Matt Rowan

COWAN, JOHN File no. 1116 (1630); Gr. no. 996; Bk. 13, p. 7 (15, 8)
270 A on N side Cataba being the place he now lives on 17 May 1754 Matt Rowan

COX, ISAAC File no. 0147
Plat: Decemr 13th 1753, Surved for Isaac Cox, 300 A on S side Broad River, on Cain Creek, including the lowest fork of sd. creek . . . Pr Saml Young Dep Sur. [No CB]

COX, ISAAC File no. 0148
Plat: Decemr 12th, 1753, Surved for Isaac Cox, 383 A on S

side Broad River on N fork Cain Creek that Runs into the Beaver Dam . . . Pr Saml Young [No CB]

COX, THOMAS File no. 911 (279); Gr. no. 659; Bk. 10, p. 416 (2, 95)

400 A on S side Broad River on Cam [sic] Creek about 1 1/2 miles below Joseph Hollingsworths survey . . . 23 Feb 1754 Matt Rowan

CRAWFORD, OLIVER File no. 236 (858); Gr. no. 354; Bk. 2, p. 70 (10, 359)

455 A on N side Broad River on Turkey Creek above James Lewis survey . . . 30 Aug 1753 Matt Rowan

CRESWELL, ANDREW File no. 1974 (1465); Bk. 15, p. 336 (13, 261)

120 A on N side Waxaw Creek adj. Robert Caldwell, James Waughope . . . 10 Apr 1761 Arthur Dobbs

CROSBEY, DENNIS File no. 789 (167); Gr. no. 276; Bk. 10, p. 375 (2, 56)

600 A on N side Broad adj. his own line . . . 11 May 1753 Matt Rowan

CROSBEY, DENNIS File no. 790 (168); Gr. no. 277; Bk. 10, p. 375 (2, 56)

600 A on N side Broad, mouth of Sandy River . . . 11 May 1753 Matt Rowan

CULP, CASPER File no. 1230 (1742); Gr. no. 1187; Bk. 13, p. 40 (15, 46)

987 A on S side Cataba . . . 25 Sept 1754 Matt Rowan

CULP, CASPER File no. 965 (331); Gr. no. 839; Bk. 10, p. 433 (2, 112)

250 A on W side Cataba adj. Casper Sleager adj. his own line . . . 20 Feb 1754 Matt Rowan

DAVIDSON, GEORGE File no. 0103

Warrant: Unto George Davison, 400 A on the So side of Broad River in the Beaverdam Creek . . . 5 Oct 1752 Nath Rice

DAVIDSON, GEORGE File no. 0104; Entry no. 895

Warrant: Unto George Davison 640 A on Moses Dickies Creek and So side Catauba taking in the forks of sd. creek . . . 28 Mar 1751 Gab: Johnston

DAVIDSON, THOMAS File no. 329 (962); Gr. no. 838; Bk. 2, p. 11 (10, 433)

640 A on a fork of Fishing Creek . . . 20 Feb 1754 Matt Rowan

DAVIS, WILLIAM File no. 080
Warrant: Unto William Davis 300 A on the So side Waxsaw [sic] . . . an Indian Old field . . . 4 Oct 1751 Gab: Johnston

DAVIS, WILLIAM File no. 029; Entry no. 906
Warrant: Unto William Davis, 600 A on south side Fishing Creek about half a mile above Abraham Stover's . . . 20 Feb 1754 Matt: Rowan

DeROSSET, MOSES JOHN File no. 339; Bk. 2, p. 116
Warrant: Unto Moses John DeRosset 400 A on a branch of EnoRee below John Gordons [torn] ("Patent to be made out of Lewis DeRosset")
400 A on S side Enoree, Duncans Creek above his second survey 9 Mar 1754 Matt Rowan

DeROSSETT, MOSES JOHN File no. 0107; Entry no. 607
Warrant: Unto Moses John DeRosset 400 A on N side Enoree River, above John Gordon's . . . 1 Sept 1753 Matt: Rowan

DeROSSET, MOSES JOHN File no. 1741 (1229); Gr. no. 1201; Bk. 15, p. 46 (13, p. 40)
Warrant: Unto Moses John DeRosset on S side Broad on a branch of little River about 4 miles above the mouth . . . 1 Sept 1753 Matt Rowan
400 A on S side Enoree River on Duncans Creek above his first survey 24 Sept 1754 Matt Rowan

DICKEY, JOHN File no. 910 (278); Gr. no. 656; Bk. 10, p. 416 (2, 95)
Warrant: Unto John Dickey 400 A on a branch of Fair Forest call'd Sugar Creek above John Hickcock land . . . 4 Sept 1753 Matt Rowan
200 A on S side Fairforrest on Sugar Creek, above John Hitchcock . . . 23 Feb 1754 Matt Rowan

DICKSON, WILLIAM File no. 075; Entry no. 193
Warrant: Unto William Dickson, 500 A on waters of Broad River . . . 3 Apr 1752

DICKSON, WILLIAM File no. 101 (723); Gr. no. 193; Bk. 2, p. 37 (10, 340)
250 A on S side Tiger River alias Sonvills River . . . 6 Apr 1753 Matt Rowan

DICKSON, WILLIAM File no. 1127 (1641); Gr. no. 1021; Bk. 13, p. 12 (15, 12)
300 A on Bush River below John Dixsons survey . . . 17 May 1754 Matt Rowan

DILL, PHILLIP File no. 2326 (2385); Gr. no. 60; Bk. 17, p. 42 (18, 37)
300 A on SW side PD . . . land granted to Thos Tomkins . . . Dinkins upper line . . . 22 Feb 1764 Arthur Dobbs

DIXON, DAVID File no. 1151 (1666); Gr. no. 1047; Bk. 13, p. 15 (15, 16)
Warrant: Unto David Dixon 300 A on Bush River, a branch of Broad River . . . 15 Nov 1752
[N. B. Bush River is actually a branch of Saluda River, instead of Broad]
300 A on S side Broad River, S fork Tinkers Creek . . . 10 May 1754 Matt Rowan
[This grant apparently does not belong with the warrant, but they are indexed together in the Land Grant Office]

DICKINSON, ADAM File no. 077
Warrant: Unto Adam Dickinson 600 A on the No side Broad River . . . dividing ridge Between Buffalo & Kings Creek . . . 30 Aug 1753 Matt Rowan

DICKSON, JOHN File no. 864; Bk. 10, p. 397
Warrant: Unto John Dickson 500 A on waters of Broad River . . . 3 Apr 1752 Gab Johnston

DICKSON, JOHN File no. 242 (864); Gr. no. 593; Bk. 2, p. 76 (10, 397)
244 A on E side Fairforrest . . . 15 Nov 1753

DICKSON, JOHN File no. 724; Gr. no. 194; Bk. 10, p. 349
Warrant: Unto John Dickson 500 A on waters of Broad River . . . 3 Apr 1752 Gab Johnston
208 A on E side Fair Forrest 6 Apr 1753 Matt Rowan
[There is some confusion with the warrants and grants for John Dickson.]

DIXON, MICHAEL File no. 1304; Entry no. 449; Bk. 13, p. 109
Warrant: Unto Michael Dixon 250 A on Buck [sic] River Joyning William Dixons Land . . . 3d Oct. 1755 Arthur Dobbs
Plat: Jenuary [sic] 8th 1756, Surved for Michal [sic] Dixon . . . 250 A on Bush River Including the forks . . . Pr Saml Young, Dep: Surveyor
Thomas Durrumple & Lewis Johns, Chain Cariers Iss. 13 ___ 1756 [S.C. Land Memorials, Vol. XII, p. 179 gives issue date as 13 Mar 1756]

DIXON, WILLIAM File no. 079; Entry no. 1021
Warrant: Unto William Dixon land on Bush River, a branch

of Broad River 15 Nov 1752 Nath Rice

DOBBS, GEORGE File no. 569 (512); Bk. 10, p. 171 (5, 331)
Warrant: Unto George Dobbs, 150 A on S side PD & both
sides Thompson Creek . . . 5 Apr 1749 Gab Johnston
150 A on S side Great Pee Dee on both sides Thompsons
Creek . . . 13 Apr 1749 Gab: Johnston

DONLOP, SAMUEL File no. 4 (624); Bk. 2, p. 3 (10, 301)
Warrant: Unto Samuel Donlap, 300 A on N side Catauba on
both sides of the Catoba branch between Ramseys & the
river . . . 26 Sept 1751 Gab Johnston
240 A on N side Cataba between Ramsey & the river . . . 3
Apr 1752 Gab Johnston

DOUGLAS, GEORGE File no. 1209 (1721); Gr. no. 1134 (?); Bk.
13, p. 36 (15, 40)
Warrant: Unto George Douglas 300 A on Cain Creek between
Robert Ramsays & John Dugloss's land . . . 15 May 1754
Matt Rowan
302 A on No side Cataba River on Cain Creek above William
Moors Land 24 Sept 1754 Matt Rowan

DUMAS, BENJAMIN File no. 2248 (478); Bk. 16, p. 212 (2, 199)
140 A on NE side P. D. Philip Howsons lower corner . . . 1
July 1758 Arthur Dobbs

DUNLAP, SAMUEL File no. 086; Entry no. 713
Warrant: Unto Saml Dunlap 350 A on N side Cataba River,
Joyning Andrew Pickings, Will Davis, & William Hood Includ-
ing an Improvement . . . 14 Oct 1752 Nath Rice

DUNLAPE, WILLIAM File no. 084; Entry no. 517
Warrant: Unto William Donlope 200 A on South side Broad
River, including the mouth of Fannings Creek . . . 29 Aug
1753 Matt: Rowan

ELLIOTT, JOHN File no. 909 (277); Gr. no. 666; Bk. 10, p. 416
(2, 95)
350 A on N side Broad adj. his own lines & James Fanning
. . . 23 Feb 1754 Matt Rowan

ERWIN, CHRISTIAN File no. 219 (841); Gr. no. 337; Bk. 2, p. 67
(10, 386)
400 A including the Cataba River & the Waggon ford at the
Cataba Nation . . . 30 Aug 1753 Matt. Rowan

ERWIN, THOMAS File no. 2125 (354); Gr. no. 70; Bk. 16, p. 5
(2, 118)
Warrant: Unto Thomas Ervine 600 A on the Golden Grove

11

above Saml Bakers Landing . . . 11 May 1753 Matt Rowan
Plat: Decemr 17th 1754, Survd. for Thomas Erwine, 600 A
on the No Bank of Enoree at the upper end of the fork
[fort?] Shoal about four or five Miles Below Bartlet Browns
Land . . . Saml Young D. Sur. Bartlet Brown, Saml. Gilkey,
Chain carriers Iss. 26 Mar 1755

EWART, ROBERT File no. 1757 (1246); Gr. no. 1218; Bk. 15, p.
50 (13, 43)
400 A on N side Broad River on a Branch of Turkey Creek
about 2 miles from William Prices . . . 25 Sept 1754 Matt
Rowan

FIELDS (FEALDS), JEAN Entry no. 1285; File no. 0268
Warrant: Unto Jean Fields, 200 A on S side Broad on Low S
fork of Browns Creek including the place where she now lives
. . . 24 Sept 1754 Matt Rowan "unexecuted"

FINLEY, SAMUEL File no. 1217 (1729); Gr. no. 1119; Bk. 13, p.
38 (15, 42)
300 A on N side Broad River on main fork of Kings Creek
. . . 24 Sept 1754 Matt Rowan

FISHER, MUHAM [MALCOLM] File no. 956 (323); Gr. no. 831;
Bk. 10, p. 432 (2, 111)
330 A on an Island in the Cataba . . . 20 Feb 1754 Matt
Rowan

FLOID, MATHEW File no. 2142 (371); Gr. no. 68; Bk. 16, p. 24
(2, 125)
Plat: Dec 17, 1754, Surd for Mathew Floid 450 A on N side
Broad River, adj. James Fanning . . . P Saml Young, Dep Sur.
Benjaben Love & Bryan McChan, C.C. Iss. 26 Mar 1755

FERGUSON, WILLIAM File no. 1750; Gr. no. 1171; Bk. 15, p. 48
400 A on S side Broad River on Kings River including his
own Improvements . . . 24 Sept 1754 Matt Rowan

FORSTER, HENRY File no. 418 (2188); Gr. no. 235; Bk. 2, p.
140 (16, 60)
Plat: July 28th 1755, Surved for Henrey Foster . . . 200 A on
mitchols Creek on the South side of fairforest . . . Pr Saml
Young Dep: Surveyor Cormick McChachoy & Henry foster,
Chain Bearers.
200 A on Mitchells Creek, on the So side of Fairforrest . . .
along sd. Thos Mitchells line . . . 3 Oct 1755 Arthur Dobbs

FORSTER, HENRY File no. 419 (2189); Gr. no. 236; Bk. 2, p.
141 (16, 50)
240 A on the No side of Fairforrest including James McKil-

wains old Cabbin . . . James McKilwains line . . . 3 Oct 1755 Arthur Dobbs

GAMBLE, JAMES File no. 0273; Entry no. 1188
Warrant: Unto James Gamble 350 A on S branch of fishing Creek about one mile South of Thomas Davidsons Land . . . 15 May 1754 Matt: Rowan

GAMBLE, JAMES File no. 0274; Entry no. 1187
Warrant: Unto James Gamble 700 A on S side Catabo, Rockey Creek, on both sides of the creek . . . 15 May 1754 Matt: Rowan

GILKEY, SAMUEL File no. 1266 (1777); Bk. 13, p. 61 (15, 71)
600 A on S side Broad about 3 miles below Gabriel Browns . . . 18 Nov 1752 Nath Rice

GILKEY, SAMUEL File no. 161 (783); Gr. no. 270; Bk. 2, p. 55 (10, 374)
600 A on S side Broad on both sides Kings River . . . 11 May 1753 Matt Rowan

GILKEY, SAMUEL File no. 162; Gr. no. 271; Bk. 2, p. 55
600 A on S side Broad on Gilkeys Creek . . . 11 May 1753 Matt Rowan

GILL, THOMAS File no. 119 (741); Gr. no. 207; Bk. 2, p. 40 (10, 354)
130 A in County of Anson . . . 6 Apr 1753 Matt Rowan

GILLESPY, GEORGE File no. 275 (907); Gr. no. 665; Bk. 2, p. 94 (10, 415)
427 A on S side Fairforest . . . Black oak level . . . little River path . . . 23 Feb 1754 Matt Rowan

GORDON, BENJAMIN File no. 933 (300); Gr. no. 7981; Bk. 10, p. 421 (2, 100)
300 A on S side Enowe [sic] on Rockey Creek . . . 23 Feb 1754 Matt Rowan

GORDON, JOHN File no. 1115 (1629); Gr. no. 993; Bk. 13, p. 7 (15, 5)
465 A on S side Teager River . . . 17 May 1754 Matt Rowan

GORDON, JOHN File no. 1201 (1713); Gr. no. 1152; Bk. 13, p. 34 (15, 38)
640 A on head of little River on N side Broad River . . . 24 Sept 1754 Matt Rowan

GORDON, JOHN File no. 843 (221); Gr. no. 339; Bk. 10, p. 386 2, 67)
300 A on N side Tigar River on beaverdam creek below James Ottersons 30 Aug 1753 Matt Rowan

GORDON, JOHN File no. 920 (287); Gr. no. 663; Bk. 10, p. 417 (2, 96)
300 A on N side River adj. where to sd. Gordon now lives . . .
23 Feb 1754 Matt Rowan

GORDON, THOMAS File no. 1628 (1114); Gr. no. 992; Bk. 15, p. 7 (13, 7)
200 A on Long Lick . . . 20 May 1754 Matt Rowan

GORDON, THOMAS File no. 949 (316); Gr. no. 823; Bk. 10, p. 431 (2, 110)
300 A on S side Tiger on Fishing Creek . . . 25 Feb 1754 Matt Rowan

GORDON, THOMAS File no. 891 (259, 936, 303); Gr. no. 664; Bk. 10, p. 411 (2, 90; 2, 100)
300 A on S side Enoree on Dunchans Creek 23 Feb 1754 Matt Rowan

GRAHAM, RICHARD File no. 1139 (1653); Gr. no. 1033; Bk. 13, p. 13 (15, 14)
400 A on N side Broad River on Clarks Creek below Gayin Moors land . . . formerly surveyed for James Moor . . . 16 May 1754 Matt Rowan

GRAHAM, RICHARD File no. 1637 (1123); Gr. no. 1017; Bk. 13, p. 11 (15, 11)
300 A on S side Cataba . . . mouth of Dutchmans Creek opposite to the Nation . . . 17 May 1754 Matt Rowan

GREEN, WILLIAM File no. 713 (91); Bk. 10, p. 431 (2, 31)
350 A on S side Broad River on thickety creek . . . 31 Mar 1753 Matt Rowan

GREGG, FREDERICK File no. 1164 (1253); Gr. no. 1202; Bk. 15, p. 56 (13, 49)
302 A on N fork Pacalet known as Bettys place . . . 25 Sept 1754 Matt Rowan

GUILKEY, SAMUEL File no. 780 (158); Gr. no. 268; Bk. 10, p. 373 (2, 54)
600 A on Guilkeys Creek . . . 11 May 1753 Matt Rowan

GUILKEY, SAMUEL File no. 785; Gr. no. 272; Bk. 10, p. 374
510 A on S side Broad on McDowels Creek . . . McDowels line . . . 11 May 1753 Matt Rowan

GUILKEY, SAMUEL File no. 784; Gr. no. 271; Bk. 10, p. 374
600 A on S side Broad on Gilkeys Creek . . . 11 May 1753 Matt Rowan

HAGGARDY, WILLIAM File no. 225 (847); Gr. no. 343; Bk. 2, p. 68 (10, 387)
300 A on So side Cataba on a branch of Fishing Creek below Robert Leepers Survey . . . 30th Aug 1753 Matt Rowan

HAMBLETON, ARCHIBALD File no. 1640 (1126); Gr. no. 1020; Bk. 15, p. 12 (13, 11)
400 A on Doncans Creek on the So side of Enore about three miles above Thomas Gordons Land . . . 17 May 1754

HARDEN, BENJABEN File no. 1160; Gr. no. 1041; Bk. 15, p. 15
396 A on So side Broad River on a fork of Bullocks Creek . . . May 17th 1754 Matt Rowan

HARNET, CORNL. File no. 0293; Entry no. 610
Warrant: Unto Corrl Harnet, 400 A on S fork of Golden Grove above John Wilsons upper Survey . . . 1 Sept 1753

HARRIS, JAMES File no. 0297
Warrant: Unto James Harris, 600 A on So side Packelot River on a creek called Fairforrest . . . John McDoweles Land . . . 4 Apr 1752 Gab Johnston

HARRIS, CHARLES File no. 1305 (1815); Bk. 13, p. 109 (15, 132)
Plat: Surveyed for Charles Harris, 500 A on N side of a fork of Browns Creek, S side Broad River . . . 23 May 1753 Chrisr. Neale, Dep Sur. [No CB] Iss. 13 Mar 1756

HARRIS, JAMES File no. 0298
Warrant: Unto James Harris 600 A on So side Packlet on a Creek called Harris Creek . . . 4 Apr 1752 Gab Johnston

HICHCOCK, JOHN File no. 232 (854); Gr. no. 350; Bk. 2, p. 69 (10, 389)
790 A on N side Broad on N fork Sandie River . . . 30 Aug 1753 Matt Rowan

HICHCOCK, JOHN File no. 849 (227); Gr. no. 345; Bk. 10, p. 387 (2, 68)
600 A on N side Broad adj. George Cowens survey . . . including John Hitchcocks Improvement . . . 30 Aug 1753 Matt Rowan

HITCHCOCK, JOHN File no. 856 (234); Gr. no. 352; Bk. 10, p. 389 (2, 69)
270 A on S side Broad on a branch of Fairforrest called Sugar Creek . . . including some large Indian Cabbins . . . 30 Aug 1753 Matt Rowan

15

HITCHCOCK, JOHN File no. 233; Gr. no. 351; Bk. 2, p. 69
200 A on N side Broad River on N side N fork Sandie River about 2 miles below the other survey . . . 30 Aug 1753 Matt Rowan

HOOD, WILLIAM File no. 947 (314); Gr. no. 820; Bk. 10, p. 431 (2, 109)
275 A at the Waxhaws . . . 20 Feb 1754 Matt Rowan

HOWARD, JAMES and PETER File no. 0313
Plat: Decembr 2d, 1753, Surved for James & Peter Howard . . . 800 A on the No fork of Golden Grove River nixt above James Mackilwains Land . . . Saml Young Dep Sur [No CB]

HOWARD, JOHN File no. 159; Gr. no. 267; Bk. 10, p. 373
300 A on a Branch of Broad River called Thicketty Creek . . . 11 May 1753 Matt Rowan

HOWELL, JOHN File no. 376; Gr. no. 73; Bk. 3, p. 126
Plat: Novemr 25th 1754, Surd. for John Howel 202 A on Black Walnut otherwise Caled Mitchels Creek, it Being a Branch of fairforest above James Mitchols Land . . . Pr Saml Young Dep Sur: Henrey Foster & James Means, C.B. Iss. 26 Mar 1755

HUTCHINS, ANTHONY File no. 1538; Bk. 13, p. 343
300 A on N side Pee Dee . . . Hicks Creek . . . 24 Apr 1762

JACKSON, BENJAMIN File no. 1366; Gr. no. 345; Bk. 13, p. 151
Warrant: Unto Benjn Jackson, 300 A on SW side Pee Dee, on path from Thompson Creek to Jones Creek including Norway Improvement . . . 24 May 1757 Arthur Dobbs
300 A on SW side Pee Dee, N side Thompson Creek above the half moon . . . 25 May 1757 Arthur Dobbs

JOHNSTON, JAMES File no. 1518; Bk. 13, p. 321
Plat: Survey'd for James Johnston 250 A on both side Camp Creek, joyning James Dunns line . . . crossing the Waggon Road . . . By Francis Beaty, Dep: Sur. David Kerr, James Dunn, CB Iss. 23 Apr 1762

KELSEY, JOHN File no. 420; Gr. no. 237; Bk. 2, p. 141; Entry no. 168
Warrant: Unto John Kelsey 200 A on a Branch of fair forest Including a Buffelow Lick near John Wilsons Land . . . 26 Mar 1755 Arthur Dobbs Iss. 3 Oct. 1755

KELSEY (KELSO), JOHN File no. 1616 (1102); Gr. no. 976; Bk. 15, p. 4 (13, 4)
345 A on S side Waxaw Creek . . . 17 May 1754 Matt Rowan

KENNEDY, GEORGE File no. 1795 (1284); Gr. no. 246; Bk. 13, p. 87 (15, 110)
Plat: Augt 8th, 1755, Surved for George Kennedy 300 A on the South side of Broad River on Browns Creek including the forks of said Creek and his own Improvement . . . Pr Saml Young, Dep: Surveyor Augustus & John Brown, CB Iss. 3 Oct 1755

KELSO, JOHN File no. 2190; Gr. no. 237; Bk. 16, p. 60
Plat: July 24th 1755, Surved for John kellso 200 A on the north fork of fair forest Below John Willsons Land . . . Henrey foster & Joseph Kelso, CB Pr Saml Young Dep: Surveyor Iss. 3 Oct 1755
[This is apparently a duplicate to the grant to JOHN KELSEY, File no. 420, p. 11]

KER, JOHN File no. 218 (840); Gr. no. 336; Bk. 2, p. 67 (10, 386)
Warrant: Unto John Kerr, 300 A on S side Broad River on a Creek . . . 14 Oct 1752 Nath Rice
275 A on S side Broad on N fork Golden Grove . . . 30 Aug 1753 Matt Rowan

KER, JOHN File no. 839; Gr. no. 335; Bk. 2, p. 67 (10, 386)
300 A on S side Broad on N fork Golden Grove above his other Survey . . . 30 Aug 1753 Matt Rowan

KERRAL, JOSEPH File no. 0337
Plat: Surved for Joseph Kerral 100 A on S side Cataba River, on a branch of Fishing Creek . . . Samuel Young's corner . . . Pr Saml Young, Dep. Sur. March 1, 1755 [No CB]

KERRAL, JOSEPH File no. 0338
Plat: Survd for Joseph Kerral, 100 A on a branch of Fishing Creek . . . adj. Samuel Youngs corner . . . Pr Saml Young March 1, 1755 Charles Betty & Saml Cobrun, Chain Bearers

KILLPATRICK, JAMES File no. 0346
Plat: Surveyed for James Killpatrick 400 A on S side Catabo River adj. James Leonards Line on waters of fishing Creek . . . 22 8ber 1759, . . . adj. Jno. Armstrong, Alex. Ruteree [?] . . . Pr Edwd Nugent, Dep Sur. Jno Armstrong, Alexr Ruteree, chain carriers

KILLPATRICK, JAMES File no. 0347
Warrant: Unto James Killpatrick, 400 A on So side Catabo adj. James Lenards line . . . waters of fishing creek . . . 20 Feb 1754 Matt Rowan

KILLPATRICK, JAMES File no. 0348
Warrant: Unto James Kilpatrick, land on N side of Broad River adj. Robert Love's including his own improvement . . . 20 Feby 1754

KILLPATRICK, JAMES File no. 1701 (1189); Gr. no. 1132; Entry no. 1194; Bk. 15, p. 36 (13, 32)
Warrant: Unto James Kilpatrick, on Turkey Creek nigh to his other Entry . . . 15 Jan 1754 Matt: Rowan
400 A on N side Broad River on a fork of Turkey Creek . . . 24 Sept 1754 Matt Rowan

KILLPATRICK, JAMES File no. 1708 (1196); Gr. no. 1135; Bk. 13, p. 33 (15, 37) Entry no. 890
Warrant: Unto James Kilpatrick, 200 A on N side Broad River, N side Turkey Creek . . . James Loves land . . . 20 Feb 1754 Matt Rowan
160 A on N side Broad River on a N branch of Turkey Creek about one mile below his other survey . . . 24 Sept 1754 Matt Rowan

KILLPATRICK, JAMES File no. 1709 (1197); Gr. no. 1136; Bk. 13, p. 33 (15, 37)
790 A on N side Broad River including the place where sd. Kilpatrick now lives . . . Robert Loves corner . . . 24 Sept 1754 Matt Rowan

KING, WILLIAM File no. 0350
Warrant: Unto William King 300 A on So side Waxaw Creek . . . 4 Oct 1751 Gab: Johnston

KING, WILLIAM File no. 0351
Warrant: Unto William King, 200 A on mouth of 12 mile creek joyning Saml Burnets & John Whites line . . . N side Cataba . . . 24 Sept 1754 Matt: Rowan

KING, WILLIAM File no. 948 (315); Gr. no. 822; Bk. 10, p. 331 (2, 109)
355 A adj. Samuel Mcleaveneys . . . 20 Feb 1754 Matt Rowan

KUYKENDAL, PETER File no. 2078; Bk. 15, p. 461
200 A on Fishing Creek adj. Kuykendales, Woods & McDowels . . . N side Dickeys fork of sd. Creek . . . 15 Nov 1762 Arthur Dobbs

KUYKENDAL, ABRAHAM File no. 0355
Warrant: Unto Abrham Kukendall, 600 A on N side Broad River on Sandy River . . . 4 Apr 1752 Gab. Johnston

KUYKENDALL, PETER File no. 1504; Bk. 13, p. 373
Plat: Surveyed for Peter Kuykendall, 200 A on Fishing Creek joining Kuykendals, Woods & McDoweles . . . Frans Beaty D. Sur. William Armstrong, James Armstrong, CB Iss. 15 Nov 1752
[This is apparently a duplicate to the above entry for Peter Kuykendal]

LAND, THOS File no. 2194 (424); Gr. no. 180, Bk. 16, p. 164 (2, 142)
496 A on E side Burns Creek . . . 16 Oct 1755 Arthur Dobbs

LARIMORE, JAMES File no. 2143 (372); Gr. no. 72; Bk. 16, p. 25 (2, 125)
Plat: April 2, 1754, Surd for James Larimore 239 A adj. John Hoods Corner . . . Pr Saml Young, D Sur. Plotted by me, March 26, 1754 [No CB]. Iss. 26 Mar 1755.

LARIMORE, JAMES File no. 1687 (1173); Gr. no. 1090; Bk. 15, p. 25 (13, 23)
400 A on Camp Creek, on E side Cataba . . . 17 May 1754 Matt Rowan

LASON, SAMUEL File no. 0360
[Envelope Empty — see David Palmer]

LAWSON, HUGH File no. 937 (304); Gr. no. 689; Bk. 10, p. 421 (2, 100)
600 A on S side Broad River on Lawsons Creek [n.d.] Matt Rowan

LAWSON, ROGER File no. 929 (296); Gr. no. 690; Bk. 10, p. 420 (2, 99)
600 A on S side Broad River on S side Pacolet on a Large Creek now called Lawsons Creek . . . 23 Feb 1754 Matt Rowan

LEEPER, ROBERT File no. 842 (200); Gr. no. 338; Bk. 10, p. 386 (2, 67)
800 A on S side Cataba below the mouth of S fork of Sd. river . . . including his own improvement . . . 30 Aug 1753 Matt Rowan

LEWIS, ALEXANDER, File no. 120; Bk. 2, p. 40
400 A on E side Fishing Creek below Cobus Kirkendalls . . . 9 Apr 1753 Matt Rowan

LEWIS, BENJAMIN File no. 678 (53); Bk. 10, p. 331 (2, 23)
450 A on head of S fork Fishing Creek Metias [sic] Clements corner . . . 31 Mar 1753 Matt Rowan

LOCKART, ALEXANDER File no. 903 (271); Gr. no. 802; Bk. 10, p. 414 (2, 93)
300 A on S side Broad on Kings River above William Forguisons land . . . Great Cain Bottom . . . 23 Feb 1754 Matt Rowan

LOVE, JAMES File no. 0369
Plat: Decemr 16, 1754: ReSurved. for James Love, 300 A on N side Broad River . . . mouth of turkie creek, place where he now lives . . . Pr Saml Young, Dep. Sur. Benjaben Love & Jas. Kilpatrick, Chain Bearers

LOVE, JAMES File no. 0370
Plat: December 6, 1754: Re Surved for James Love, 300 A on N side Broad including the mouth of turkie creek, the place where he now lives . . . Pr Saml Young Benjaben Love, James Kilpatrick, CB

LOVE, ROBERT File no. 1811 (1300); Bk. 15, p. 131 (13, 108)
Plat: Jan. 19, 1754, Surd. for Robert Love 400 A on N side Broad, ye place where he now lives . . . adj. Benjaben Loves . . . Pr Saml Young, Dep. Sur. [No CB] Iss. 13 Mar 1756

LOVE, ROBERT File no. 1135 (1649); Gr. no. 1029; Bk. 13, p. 13 (15, 13)
700 A on N side Broad River on Bullocks Creek . . . 17 May 1754 Matt Rowan

LOVE, WILLIAM File no. 774 (152); Gr. no. 261; Bk. 10, p. 371 (2, 53)
400 A on N side Broad River, both sides Moores Creek, Being the place he now lives on . . . 11 May 1753 Matt Rowan

LUCKIE, JOHN File no. 0373
Warrant: Unto John Luckie, 400 A on Kings River adj. Samuel Luckys lower line . . . 11 May 1753 Matt: Rowan

LUCKIE, ROBERT File no. 0374
Warrant: Unto Robert Luckie, 400 A adj. Luckies upper line . . . 11 May 1753 Matt Rowan

LUCKIE, SAMUEL File no. 0375
Warrant: Unto Samuel Luckie, 400 A on Kings River, a branch of Broad River . . . 11 May 1753 Matt: Rowan

LUCKEY, WILLIAM File no. 0372
Warrant: Unto William Luckey, 400 A on S side Broad, on middle fork of Little River, about a mile above the mouth . . . 29 Aug 1753 Matt: Rowan

LYNN, ANDREW File no. 1171 (1685); Gr. no. 1084; Bk. 13, p. 22 (15, 24)
91 A on both sides of Gills Creek, waters of Cataba River . . . John Phillips Line. 17 May 1754 Matt Rowan

LYNN, JOHN File no. 1643 (1129); Gr. no. 1023; Bk. 15, p. 12 (13, 12)
302 A on N side Camp Creek, N side Cataba about half a mile above Thomas Lees Land . . . 17 May 1753 Matt Rowan

LYNN, JOHN File no. 770 (148); Gr. no. 181; Bk. 10, p. 361 (2, 46)
200 A on N side Waxhaw Creek, E side Cataba . . . 6 Apr 1753 Matt Rowan

LYNN, JOHN & JAMES CARTER File no. 135 (757); Gr. no. 224; Bk. 2, p. 43 (10, 358)
938 A on E side Catabo on the path from Indian Nation to McDowells . . . 9 Apr 1753 Matt Rowan

LYON, JOHN File no. 971 (337); Gr. no. 861; Bk. 10, p. 438 (2, 115)
600 A on S side Enoree, on Rockey Creek . . . [n.d.] Matt Rowan

LYON, JOHN File no. 1768 (1257); Gr. no. 1161; Bk. 15, p. 61 (13, 53)
400 A on the So branch of Gillshott Thomas's Creek below James Woods Survey . . . 27 Sept 1754 Matt Rowan

LYON, RICHARD File no. 974 (252); Gr. 10, p. 409 (2, 87)
402 A on a branch of Beaverdam above Thomas Clarks . . . Silver Ridge . . . 2 Mar 1754 Matt Rowan

LYON, RICHARD File no. 1620 (1106); Gr. no. 983; Bk. 15, p. 5 (13, p. 5)
400 A on S fork Pacalet River . . . Maiden Meadow . . . 17 May 1754 Matt Rowan

LYON, RICHARD File no. 1105 (1619); Gr. no. 982; Bk. 13, p. 5 (15, 5)
400 A on N side Broad . . . head drafts of Little River . . . 17 May 1754 Matt Rowan

McBRIDE, JOHN File no. 2211 (441); Bk. 16, p. 92 (2, 155)
Plat: April 22, 1756, Surveyed for John McBride, land on N side P.D. . . . beginning in a reedy marsh above his house . . . adj. Jacob Lipham . . . 191 A . . . _____ Heron, Dept. Sur. John Jones, Thos. Morgan, Chainors. Iss. 26 May 1757

McCLEALAN, JAMES File no. 1168; Gr. no. 1080; Bk. 13, p. 21
300 A on N side Cataba adj. John Brevards & Robt Tinings
. . . 17 May 1754 Matt Rowan

McCLELAN, ROBERT File no. 2123 (352); Gr. no. 114; Bk. 16,
p. 5 (2, 118)
250 A adj. Robt Davis on N side Waxaw Creek . . . 28 Mar
1755 Arthur Dobbs

McCORCALE, ROBERT File no. 1740 (1228); Gr. no. 1114; Bk.
15, p. 46 (13, 40)
224 A on both sides of a branch that runs into Cain Creek on
N side of sd. creek . . . 24 Sept 1754 Matt Rowan

McCOWN, ANDREW File no. 0408
Plat: July 4, 1753, Surveyed for Andrew McCown, on both
sides Camp Creek waters of Cuttaba on Jno arnel Pender line
. . . Pr Jas Carter, D. S. [No CB]

McCULLOH, JOHN File no. 925 (292); Gr. no. 684; Bk. 10, p.
418 (2, 97)
350 A lying on main branch of Fishing Creek about 2 miles
below James Kuykendalls plantation . . . 23 Feb 1754 Matt
Rowan

McDONALD, HUGH File no. 0413
Plat: Surveyed for Hugh McDonald on N side Thomas Gills
Creek . . . Feb. 14, 1753 Pr Alexr Lewis, D. S. [No CB]

McDOWELL, CHARLES File no. 2 (622); Bk. 2, p. 1 (10, 299)
200 A on S side Broad River, on the second Big Creek that
runs into sd. river above the mouth of Pacolate . . . 4 Apr
1751 Gab Johnston

McDOWELL, JOHN File no. 0415
Plat: April 1, 1754, Surveyed for John McDowele, 300 A on
main fork of Kings Creek adj. Jno Adenton . . . Pr Saml
Young, Dep Sur. Jno Kickendal & Charles Dunlap, Ch. Ca.

McKANE, JOHN File no. 1464; Bk. 13, p. 261
Plat: Survey'd for John McKane, 220 A on N side Waxaw
Creek, adj. Robt Caldwell, Wm King Snr., Robert McClellan
. . . dated 8 Sept 1757 Thos Patton & Wm King, C.B. Iss. 10
Apr 1761

McKNIGHT, CHARLES File no. 199 (821); Gr. no. 316; Bk. 10,
p. 384 (2, 64)
320 A on No side Broad, on a head fork of Bullocks Creek,
Wt from William Watsons survey . . . 30th August 1753 Matt:
Rowan

McKNIGHT, CHARLES File no. 703 (81); Gr. no. 37A; Bk. 10, p. 338 (2, 29)
400 A on S· side Cataba on lower No fork of Fishing Creel called Wild Cat Branch . . . below George Rennix survey . . . 3 Apr 1753 . . . Matt Rowan

MacKNIGHT, JAMES File no. 198 (820); Gr. no. 315; Bk. 10, p. 384 (2, 64)
300 A on So side Broad River, on the No fork of Pacolet River, below Charles Beaty's survey . . . 30th Aug 1753 Matt: Rowan

McKNIGHT, JOHN File no. 826 (204); Gr. no. 321; Bk. 10, p. 284 (2, 65)
340 A on N side Broad on a fork of Turkey Creek above Clarks path 30 Aug 1753 Matt Rowan

McKNIGHT, WILLIAM File no. 827 (205); Gr. no. 322; Bk. 10, p. 385 (2, 65)
300 A on S side Cataba on a path between James Sharps survey & the Cataba Nation . . . 30 Aug 1753

McLANE, ARCHIBALD File no. 1488; Bk. 13, p. 287
200 A on waters of Long Creek, E side Catauba near his other land . . . 10 Apr 1761 Arthur Dobbs

McLEAN, ARCHIBALD File no. 1178; Gr. no. 1101; Bk. 13, p. 24
500 A on W side Broad on S fork Sandy River including the place where David Dunbar lately lived adj. Caleb Douds Survey . . . 20 May 1754 Matt Rowan

McLELAN, ROBERT File no. 0457
Plat: November 5, 1754, Surd for Robert McClelan, 250 A adj. Robert Daves line . . . N side Waxaw Creek . . . Pr Saml Young, Dep Sur. Moses Davis, Robert McClelan, C.B.

McMANUS, JAMES File no. 1338 (1848); Bk. 13, p. 135 (15, 195)
Plat: Surveyed for James McManus, 400 A between Turkie Creek & Wild Cat upon S side Lynches Creek about 1 mile from where he now lives . . . May 8, 1755 Pr Saml Young Wm & Mathew Rushing, CB Iss. 13 Oct 1756

McMANUS, JAMES File no. 1337 (1847); Bk. 13, p. 135 (15, 194)
Plat: Surd for James McManess, 400 A on Thompson Creek above Robert Palmers Esqr Surv . . . May 7, 1755 Saml Young, Dep Sur. Mathew & William Rushing, CB Iss. 13 Oct 1756

McMANUS, JAMES File no. 1339 (1849); Bk. 13, p. 135 (15, 195)
Plat: Surved for James McManus, 300 A on So fork Wild Catt Creek ... Saml Young Dep Surveyor, May 8, 1755 Iss. 13 Oct 1756 Matthew and William Rushing, chain carriers

McMANUS, JAMES File no. 1493 (2003); Gr. no. 13, p. 309 (15, 384)
Plat: Surveyed for James McManus, 300 A on N side Lynches Creek in the upper line of sd. McManus' flat Rock Survey ... _____ March 1759 [No Surv.] John Little [?] & Hugh Manough, C. B. Iss. 8 Jan 1760

McMANUS, JAMES File no. 2004; Bk. 15, p. 384
150 A adj. 300 A survey on Wild Cat ... 8 Jan 1760 Arthur Dobbs

McMANUS, JAMES File no. 1494; Bk. 13, p. 309
Plat: March 1759, Surveyed for Jas McManus ... comer of his upper 300 Survey on Wild Catt ... Frederick Islers Land ... 150 A ... [No Surv.] Iss. 8 Jan 1760 John Till [?] and Hugh Manough, chain carriers

McMANUS, JAMES File no. 1495 (2005); Bk. 13, p. 309 (15, 384)
500 A on NE side Lynches Creek about 1/2 mile above mouth of Kills [Hills?] Creek ... his lower survey ... 8 Jan 1760 Arthur Dobbs

McNABB, ANDREW File no. 748 (126); Gr. no. 175; Bk. 10, p. 355 (15, 384)
457 A in County of Anson ... 6 Apr 1753

McNEAL, EDWARD File no. 0453
Plat: March 5th, 1753, Surved for Edward McNeal, 570 A on ye S side Broad River, on ye forks of Browns Creek ... Pr Fran Mackilwean, Dep Sur. [No CB]

McPETERS, DANIEL File no. 819 (197); Gr. no. 314; Bk. 10, p. 383 (2, 63)
600 A on N side Chickety Creek ... 30 Apr 1753 Matt Rowan [should read Thickety Creek]

McPHERSON, ROBERT File no. 1793; Gr. no. 244; Bk. 15, p. 110
Plat: 14 July 1755, Survd. for Robert McPherson, 200 A on N fork Sandy River Including Ducars [?] Improvement ... Pr Saml Young, Dep Surveyor. Adam McCole, Robert Mcferson, CB Iss. 3 Oct 1755

McVENEY, SAMUEL File no. 140 (762); Gr. no. 223; Bk. 2, p. 44 (10, 359)
528 A adj. Andrew Pickins on N side Waxhaw Creek ... 9 Apr 1753 Matt Rowan

McFARSON, ROBERT File no. 1120 (1634); Gr. no. 1014; Bk. 15, p. 11 (13, 10)
300 A on S side Broad on Bush River ... 17 May 1754 Matt Rowan

MAINS [MEANS], HUGH File no. 2435 (2376); Bk. 18, p. 342 (17, 374)
335 A on S side Fair Forrest Creek ... 18 Nov 1752 Nath Rice Rec. by Order of Council April 28, 1767

MACKILWEAN, JAMES File no. 1791 (1280); Gr. no. 242; Bk. 15, p. 109 (13, 86)
Plat: Surved for James Mackilwain 540 A ... South side fairforest Creek including the place where he now Lives Joyning George Storeys Lines ... Pr Saml Young, Dep Surveyor Henry foster & Joseph Kellso, Surveyor Chain Bearers. Plat dated July 24, 1755 Iss. 3 Oct 1755

MEANS, JAMES File no. 901 (267); Gr. no. 661; Bk. 10, p. 414 (2, 93)
200 A on Fairforest being the place where he now lives ... William Mitchells line ... 23 Feb 1754 ... Matt Rowan

MEEK, ADAM File no. 1654 (1140); Gr. no. 1034; Bk. 15, p. 14 (13, 13)
400 A on N side Broad River on McGees Creek ... formerly surveyed for Robert McGee ... 16 May 1754 Matt Rowan

MEEK, ADAM File no. 1663 (1149); Gr. no. 1045; Bk. 15, p. 16 (13, 15)
350 A joyning James Ormonds survey on the Lower end of the S fork Cataba on Long Creek ... 17 May 1754 Matt Rowan

MIDDLETON, JOHN File no. 851 (229); Gr. no. 347; Bk. 10, p. 387 (2, 68)
600 A on N side Broad on main N fork of Kings Creek ... 30 Aug 1753 Matt Rowan

MILLER, RICHARD File no. 1650 (1136); Gr. no. 1030; Bk. 15, p. 13 (13, 13)
400 A on thickley [sic] Creek below William Greens land ... 17 May 1754

MILLER, ROBERT File no. 421 (2191); Gr. no. 238; Bk. 2, p. 141 (16, 61)

Plat: July 31, 1755, Surved for Robert Miller 300 A on fork of Little River below David Davis's land . . . by the Indean [sic] path . . . Pr Saml Young, Dep Surveyor John Brown & Robert Millar, Chain Bearers. Iss. 3 Oct 1755

MITCHOL, JAMES File no. 2134; Gr. no. 63; Bk. 16, p. 22
Plat: November 27th 1754, Surd. for James Mitchol 287 A on the South Side of Broad River on Mitchols Creek near Robert Wilsons Corner . . . Pr. Saml Young, Dep: Survr. William Mitchel and Thos Mitchel, Chain Bearers. Iss. 26 Mar 1755

MITCHELL, JAMES File no. 857; Gr. no. 353; Bk. 10, p. 389
300 A on So side of Broad River Joining William Michells Survey . . . 30 Aug 1753 Matt Rowan

MOORE, GEYAN, File no. 20 (640); Bk. 2, p. 7 (10, 307-8)
600 A on N side Broad River on the Beaverdam Creek . . . by the Beauty Spott 3 Apr 1752 Gab Johnston

MOORE, GEYAN File no. 634 (14); Bk. 10, p. 306 (2, 6)
600 A on N side Broad River on Beaverdam Creek above the mouth . . . 3 Apr 1752 Gab Johnston

MOORE, GEYAN File no. 3127; Gr. no. 464; Bk. 23, p. 81
600 A on N side Broad River on Loves Creek, a branch of Moores Creek . . . 3 Sept 1753 Matt Rowan Recorded by Order of Council 14 Oct 1767

MOORE, GUYAN, File no. 3128; Bk. 23, p. 81
800 A on both sides of Broad River known as Mount Pleasant 3 Apr 1752 Gab. Johnston Recorded by Order of Council 14 Oct 1767

MOORE, GYGAN File no. 3129; Gr. no. 466; Bk. 23, p. 81
600 A on N side Broad River on Clarks Creek . . . 3 Sept 1753 Matt Rowan

MOORE, JOHN File no. 2135 (364); Gr. no. 78; Bk. 16, p. 22˚(2, 124)
Plat: Aug. 1, 1753, Surveyed for John Moore, 580 A on N side of a Branch of Turkey Creek, called Moores Creek . . . A. J. Smith, D Sur. [No CB] Iss. 26 Mar 1755

MOORE, SAMUEL File no. 0394
Plat: Surveyed for Samuel Moore . . . N side S fork Fishing Creek . . . Dec. 15, 1752 Alexr Lewis [surv.]

MOORE, WM File no. 0548
Plat: April 8, 1754, Surveyed for William Moore, 300 A on ye South fork of fishing Creek adj. branches of turkie creek

... Pr Saml Young, Dep Sur. Jas. Kukindal & Samuel Young, Ch. Ca.

MURRAY, JAMES ESQR. File no. 873 (251); Gr. no. 863; Bk. 10, p. 409 (2, 87)
400 A on a branch of Golden Grove called Beaverdam Creek ... Silver ridge 2 Mar 1754 Matt Rowan

NEELY, SAMUEL File no. 0446; Entry no. 447
Warrant: Unto Saml Neely 200 A on S side Cataba, on a branch of fishing Creek two miles below Gasper Slegers ... 3 Oct 1755 Arthur Dobbs
Plat: Sept 8, 1756, Surveyed for Saml Neely, 200 A on a branch of fishing creek about 2 miles below Gasper Sleekers Land ... Francis Beaty, D Surv. Saml Neely & William Neely, C. Bear.

NEELY, SAMUEL File no. 0447; Entry no. 1281
Warrant: Unto Samuel Neely, 300 A on main fishing creek, including the third path 24 Sept 1754 Matt: Rowan

NEELY, SAMUEL File no. 1731 (1219); Gr. no. 1165; Entry no. 89; Bk. 15, p. 43 (13, 38)
Warrant: Unto Samuel Neely 300 A adj. his Brother Thomas Neely ... 28 Mar 1753
300 A below the Seludy Path on the Et side Branch that runs into Fishing Creek ... 24 Sept 1754 Matt Rowan

NEELY, SAMUEL File no. 1889 (1379); Bk. 15, p. 243 (13, 176)
200 A on N side Cataba on a branch of fishing creek about two miles below Gasper Sleekers land including sd. Neelys improvement ... 20 Nov 1757 Arthur Dobbs
[This grant may well be the one that belongs with the warrant and plat above, File no. 0446]

NEELY, SAMUEL File no. 2126 (355); Gr. no. 64; Bk. 16, p. 6 (2, 118)
Plat: Nov. 16, 1754, Surd for Samuel Neeley, 400 A on S side Cataba, on N side Fishing Creek, below Siludy Waggon Road ... William Neely & Henrey McKeney, CB. Saml Young [surv.] Iss. 26 Mar 1755

NEELY, THOMAS File no. 1203 (1715); Gr. no. 1166; Bk. 13, p. 35 (15, 39)
300 A on W side Fishing Creek ... 24 Sept 1754 Matt Rowan

NEELY, WILLIAM File no. 1397 (2287, 2470, 1906); Entry no. 499; Bk. 13, p. 222 (18, 431; 16, 254; 15, 288)
Warrant: Unto William Nailey, 400 A on W side Cataubar on

both sides Fishing Creek adj. Philip Walkers line . . . 18 Nov 1757 Arthur Dobbs

400 A on both sides Fishing Creek on W side Cataubar 21 Oct 1758 Arthur Dobbs

Plat: Surveyed for William Neely 400 A on both sides Fishing Creek [n.d.] Francis Beaty, Dep Sur. James Neely & Samuel Neely, C.B.

NEELY, WILLIAM File no. 1234 (1746); Gr. no. 1169; Bk. 13, p. 41 (15, 47)

Warrant: Unto William Neely 300 A adjoyning his Brother Samuel Neelys. 28 Mar 1753 Matt: Rowan

140 A on N fork Fishing Creek below the Seludy path . . . 24 Sept 1754

NESBITT, ALEXANDER File no. 0444

Warrant: Unto Alexander Nessbet, 400 A on a branch of Cain Creek . . . 20 Feb 1754 Matt: Rowan

NISBET, ALEXANDER File no. 377; Gr. no. 78; Bk. 2, p. 126

390 A adj. Alexander McMahams on waters of Cain Creek, E side Cataba . . . [n.d.] Arthur Dobbs

NISBET, ALEXANDER File no. 2148; Gr. no. 78; Bk. 16, p. 26

Plat: Surveyed for Alexand Nisbet . . . Alexr McMehans Corner . . . on the waters of Cain Creek on the E side Cataba . . . David Strains line . . . William Moores line . . . Surd 20 Feb 175 _____, plotted by me March 26th 1755, Pr Saml Young D Sur. [No CB, No iss. date].

NUTT, ANDREW File no. 879 (257); Gr. no. 691; Entry no. 163; Bk. 10, p. 411 (2, 89)

Warrant: Unto Andrew Nutt, 200 A adj. his own lines on N side Cataba, waters of Cain Creek . . . 26 Mar 1755 Arthur Dobbs

200 A on N side Cataba, S side Waxaw Creek . . . 23 Feb 1754 Matt Rowan

NUTT, WILLIAM File no. 766 (144); Gr. no. 180; Bk. 10, p. 360 (16, 58)

Warrant: Unto William Nutt, 300 A adj. James McCorkills . . . 14 Oct 1752 Nath Rice

190 A on N side Waxhaw Creek . . . 5 Apr 1753 Matt: Rowan

NUTT, ANDREW File no. 414 (2184); Gr. no. 231; Bk. 2, p. 140 (16, 58)

Plat: May 13, 1755, Surved for Andrew Nutt, 150 A on N bank Catauba, below the mouth of 12 Mile Creek . . . adj. McCorcal, Samuel Burnet, William Nutt . . . Pr Saml Young . . . Hugh McCain, William Nutt, CB Iss. 3 Oct 1755

OAR, WILLIAM File no. 0426; Entry no. 347
Warrant: Unto William Oarr, 300 A on S side Broad River . . .
on a branch of Little River . . . 25 Sept 1754 Matt Rowan
Plat: December 19, 1754, Surd. for William Oar, 302 A on S
side Pacalet, N side Sandy Run . . . Pr Saml Young, Dep Sur.
Jno Clark, Saml Gilkey, C.B.

OARR, WILLIAM File no. 1728 (1216); Gr. no. 1172; Bk. 15, p.
42 (13, 37)
Warrant: Unto William Orr, 400 A on S side Broad including
his own Improvements . . . 3 Sept 175 _____ Matt Rowan
402 A on Kings River, opposite to the great Shoals including
his own improvements . . . 24 Sept 1754 Matt Rowan

OATES, JOHN File no. 380 (2151); Gr. no. 79; Bk. 2, p. 127 (16,
27)
Plat: April 25, 1754, Surveyed for John Oats . . . 202 A on N
side Broad, being the place where William Case now lives . . .
Saml Young [surv.] Thos Case & William Case, CH. C. Iss. 26
Mar 1755

OATES, JOHN File no. 230 (852); Gr. no. 348; Bk. 2, p. 69 (10,
387)
Warrant: Unto John Oates 400 A on S side Broad River
about 1/4 mile below Hollinsworth . . . 6 Oct 1752 Nath Rice
360 A on S side Broad River, on upper Fishdam Creek above
John Clarks survey 30 Aug 1753 Matt Rowan

OATS, JOHN File no. 0425; Entry no. 635
Warrant: Unto John Oates 200 A adj. his own line . . . 4 Sept
1753 Matt Rowan

PALMER, DAVID File no. 1354 (1864); Gr. no. 13, p. 142 (15,
203)
Plat: Surved for Samuel Lason, 400 A on S side Broad, Beaver Dam Creek joyning Philip Smith . . . Aug 1, 1755, Pr Saml
Young, Dep Sur. George Sanders & John Clark, CB Iss. 7 Oct
1756

PARK, DAVID File no. 913 (281); Gr. no. 658; Bk. 10, p. 416 (2,
95)
200 A on S side Pacolet above the place where Col. Clark
now lives . . . 23 Feb 1754 Matt Rowan

PARK, DAVID File no. 915 (283); Gr. no. 657; Bk. 10, p. 416 (2,
95)
300 A on middle fork of little river, 3 miles above Robert
Miller plantation 23 Feb 1754 Matt Rowan

PATTON, THOMAS File no. 1247 (1758); Gr. no. 1139; Bk. 13, p. 43 (15, 50)
300 A on S side Broad on Duncans Creek above Moses John Derosetts survey including Carrays Cabbin . . . 24 Sept 1754 Matt Rowan

PAUL, ABRAM File no. 612 (554); Bk. 10, p. 288 (15, 50)
200 A on S side Pee Dee on both sides Thompsons Creek . . . Drys line . . . 4 Apr 1750 Gab. Johnston

PAUL, WILLIAM File no. 914 (282); Gr. no. 651; Bk. 10, p. 416 (2, 95)
300 A on N side Broad River on the ridg between Bullochs and Moors branch . . . Clarks path . . . 23 Feb 1754 Matt Rowan

PICKINS, ANDREW File no. 649 (28); Bk. 10, p. 312 (2, 11)
551 A on N side Waxhaw Creek . . . 13 Apr 1752 Gab Johnston

PICKINS, MARTHA File no. 1692 (1180); Gr. no. 1103; Bk. 15, p. 28 (13, 25)
514 A on N side Cane Creek being a branch of the Cataba 20 Mar 1754 Matt Rowan

PICKENS, WILLIAM & GRIFFITH RUTHERFORD File no. 2180 (410); Gr. no. 183; Bk. 16, p. 46 (2, 135)
362 A on W side Cataba on Rockey Creek . . . 3 Oct 1755 Arthur Dobbs

POPWELL, JOHN File no. 0419; Entry no. 1287
Warrant: Unto John Popwell, 300 A on the South Side of Broad River on Browns Creek above John Browns Land 24 Sept 1754. Matt: Rowan
"Not Executed Dropt for fear of the Indians"

RAMSEY, ROBERT File no. 0476
Warrant: Unto Robert Ramsey, 500 A adj. William Beards corner on the Waxhaw Creek . . . 7 Apr 1752 Gab Johnston

RAMSEY, ROBERT File no. 0477
Warrant: Unto Robert Ramsey, 200 A on the Waxhaw Creek . . . 7 Apr 1752 Gab Johnston

RAMSEY, ROBERT File no. 2017 (1522); Bk. 15, p. 398 (13, 322)
Plat: Surveyed for Capt Robert Ramsey, 100 A adj. N side Kane Creek and NE side of his own land where he now dwells . . . Francis Beaty D Sur [n.d.] Robert Dunlop, Robt Ramsey, C.B. Iss. 23 Apr 1762

RAMSEY, ROBERT File no. 5 (625); Bk. 2, 3 (10, 302)
Warrant: Unto Robert Ramsey, 300 A on N side Catauba on head of Cain Creek 26 Sept 1751 Gab Johnston
300 A on N side Catauba, both sides Cane Creek . . . 3 Apr 1752 Gab Johnston

RAMSEY, ROBERT File no. 7 (627); Bk. 3, pp. 3-4 (10, 302)
400 A on N side Cataba, both sides Cane Creek . . . 3 Apr 1752 Gab Johnston

RAMSEY, ROBERT File no. 671 (49); Gr. no. 6; Bk. 10, p. 329 (2, 21)
Warrant: Unto Robert Ramsey, 400 A on Waxhaw or the 12 mile Creek above the upper Indian path . . . 7 Apr 1752 Gab Johnston
310 A on N side Catawba on S fork 12 mile Creek above an Indian path . . . 31 Mar 1753 Matt Rowan

RENNICKS, GEORGE File no. 83 (705); Gr. no. 114; Bk. 2, p. 29 (10, 339)
Warrant: Unto George Renick, 400 A on a fork of fishing Creek opsit to Cataba Nation, commonly called Wild Cat branch . . . 5 Oct 1752 Nath Rice
400 A on S side Cataba on N fork Fishing Creek called Wild Cat branch . . . 28 Mar 1753 Matt Rowan

RENNICK, GEORGE File no. 0468
Warrant: Unto Robert Shaw & George Rennick, 800 A on S side Cataba River on Rockey Creek 5 Oct 1752 Nath Rice
March 31, 1753 . . . altered to the mouth of Ellisons Creek . . . Matt: Rowan

REYNOLDS, RICHARD File no. 2156; Gr. no. 80; Bk. 16, p. 29
600 A on S side S fork Catauba on Renold Creek including the place where he now lives . . . Thomas Renols line . . . 28 Mar 1755 Arthur Dobbs

REYNOLDS, THOMAS File no. 799 (177); Gr. no. 294; Bk. 10, 381 (2, 60)
Warrant: Unto Thos Rennels, 300 A on ye Branches of Kings Creek . . . 28 Sept 1750 Gab Johnston
300 A on Kings Creek that runs into Broad River 30 Aug 1753 Matt Rowan

REYNOLDS, THOMAS File no. 801 (170); Gr. no. 296; Bk. 10, 381 (2, 61)
Warrant: Unto Thomas Rennils, 600 A on Buffelow Creek about 4 miles above the fork . . . 4 Oct 1751 Gab Johnston

500 A on Buffelow Creek that runs into Broad River 30 Aug 1753 Matt Rowan

REYNOLDS, THOMAS File no. 800 (178); Gr. no. 295; Bk. 10, p. 381 (2, 60)
Warrant: Unto Thomas Rennels 600 A on Buffelow Creek . . . 4 Oct 1751 Gab Johnston
400 A on Bufflow Creek about 4 miles above the fork 30 Aug 1753 Matt Rowan
[The above two warrants are placed with the wrong grants.]

RIVERS, JOSEPH File no. 0464; Entry no. 90
Warrant: Unto Joseph Rivers, 400 A on S side Broad River on a fork of Golden Grove adj. John Clarks . . . 3 Apr 1753 Matt Rowan

ROBINSON, WILLIAM File no. 0512
Warrant: Unto William Robinson, 400 A on the Grove below John Wilson including the Indian Camp 4 Sept 1753 Matt: Rowan

ROBINSON, TOWNSEND File no. 405 (2175); Gr. no. 176; Bk. 2, p. 134 (16, 44)
183 A on Beaverdam Branch of Rockey Creek . . . 3 Oct 1755 Arthur Dobbs

ROE, GODFREY File no. 357; Gr. no. 125; Entry no. 1082; Bk. 2, p. 123
Warrant: Unto Godfrey Roe, 300 A on S side Broad River on the N side Little River above the mouth of Cain Creek . . . 26 Feb 1754 Matt Rowan
Plat: [torn] . . . April 24, 1754 . . . 302 A . . . Pr Saml Young, Dep Sur. [No CB] Iss. 28 Mar 1755

ROE, GODFREY, File no. 2128; Gr. no. 126; Bk. 16, p. 18
302 A on S side Broad on N side Little River above the mouth of Cain Creek 28 Mar 1755 Arthur Dobbs
[The above grants to Godfrey Roe may be duplicates, but they are numbered 125 and 126.]

ROGERS, DANIEL File no. 104 (726); Gr. no. 188; Bk. 10, p. 350 (2, 37)
Warrant: Unto Daniel Rogers, 300 A on fishing creek including the place where he now lives . . . 14 Oct 1752 Nath Rice
300 A on Fishing Creek which runs through the midst thereof . . . 6 Apr 1753 Matt Rowan

ROGERS, HUGH File no. 0502
Warrant: Unto Hugh Rogers, 300 A on S side Cataba . . . Be-

tween John Larys & John Bettys on Lantis Creek . . . 28 Mar 1753 Matt: Rowan

ROUTLEDGE, GEORGE File no. 0499
Warrant: Unto George Routledge, 300 A on Pacalet River . . . 28 Mar 1753 Matt Rowan

RUSSELL, JAMES File no. 1241; Gr. no. 1173; Bk. 13, p. 42
400 A on S side Broad River on Kings River including his own improvements . . . William Forguisons line . . . 24 Sept 1754 Matt Rowan

RUSSELL, JAMES File no. 2217 (447); Entry no. 181; Bk. 16, p. 117
310 A on S side Little River on Antiquoram Creek . . . Alexander Forguisons Creek . . . 26 Nov 1757 Arthur Dobbs [This grant is recorded with plat in S.C. Land Grant Vol. 40, pp. 90-91. Volume is titled "Georgia Grants."]

RUSSELL, ROBERT File no. 1869 (1359: Bk. 13, p. 146 (15, 208)
317 A on So side Little River in the fork of Antiquorum Creek adj. James Russels . . . 23 Oct 1756 Arthur Dobbs

RUTLIDGE, GEORGE File no. 1714 (1202); Gr. no. 1117; Bk. 15, p. 39 (13, 34)
400 A on S side Enoree River on Rockey Creek below David Templetons land 24 Sept 1754 Matt Rowan

SHENAN, THOMAS File no. 0158; Entry no. 1284
Warrant: Unto Thomas Shenan 200 A joyning James Fanning, S side Broad River . . . 24 Sept 1754 Matt: Rowan

SHERILL, WILLIAM File no. 34 (655); Bk. 2, p. 15 (10, 318)
200 A on N side Broad River on a creek thereof . . . 13 Apr 1752 Gab Johnston

SIMMONDS, HENRY File no. 0166; Entry no. 620
Warrant: Unto Henry Simmonds 400 A on Reedy River below the great Falls. 3 Sept 1753 Matt: Rowan
Plat: Decemr 29, 1753, Survd for Henery Simonds 400 A on S side Enoree on Duncans Creek above John Mirrucks Pr Saml Young, Dep Sur.

SIMONTON, ROBERT File no. 959 (236); Bk. 10, p. 432
Warrant: Unto Robert Simonton, 500 A on waters of Broad River . . . 3 Apr 1752 Gab Johnston
500 A on S side Cataba River on Simontons Creek . . . 20 Feb 1754 Matt Rowan

SLEAGER, GOSPER File no. 1232 (1744); Gr. no. 1188; Bk. 13, p. 41 (15, 46)
768 A between waters of Cataba and fishing Creek . . . 25 Sept 1754 Matt Rowan

SMITH, JOHN File no. 777 (155); Gr. no. 264; Bk. 10, p. 372 (2, 54)
300 A on N side Broad River below the Hickory Level . . . 11 May 1753 Matt Rowan

SMITH, ROGER File no. 1891 (1381); Gr. no. 435; Bk. 15, p. 244 (13, 176)
Warrant: Unto Roger Smith, 150 A on S side Waxaw Creek adj. Jno White & WM Kees [McKees] Land . . . 30 Oct 1755 Arthur Dobbs
150 A on S side Waxaw Creek near John Whites and Mc McKees lands &c. 26 Nov 1757 Arthur Dobbs
Plat: Sept 9, 1756, Surveyed for Roger Smith, 150 A on S side Waxaw Creek, near Jno Whites & William McKees . . . Francis Beaty, Dep Sur. Wm Douglas, WM Hood, Sworn Chain Bearers.

STEAN, JAMES File no. 1205 (1717); Gr. no. 1167; Bk. 13, p. 35 (15, 40)
400 A on S side Broad River on Neals Creek above Neals Survey . . . 24 Sept 1754 Matt Rowan

STORY, GEORGE File no. 0191
Warrant: Unto George Storey, 600 A on S side Broad River . . . above John Clarkes Entrey . . . 3d April 1752 Gab Johnston

STEEL, THOMAS File no. 1160; Gr. no. 1057; Bk. 13, p. 7
Warrant: Unto Thomas Stell [sic], 400 A on both sides Fishing Creek, including the place he lives on . . . 26 Feb 1754 Matt Rowan
400 A on S side Fishing Creek . . . 17 May 1754 Matt Rowan

TATE, ROBERT File no. 223 (845); Gr. no. 341; Bk. 2, p. 68 (10, 387)
300 A on S side Broad on N fork Golden Grove above George Parks survey 30 Aug 1753

TAYLOR, JACOB File no. 111 (733); Gr. no. 205; Bk. 2, p. 39 (10, 352)
370 A on N fork Fishing Creek . . . 6 Apr 1753 Matt Rowan

TAYLOR, WILLIAM File no. 1231 (1743); Gr. no. 1186; Bk. 13, p. 40 (13, 46)

334 A on W side Cataba adj. Casper Culps . . . 25 Sept 1754 Matt Rowan

TAYLOR, WILLIAM File no. 117 (739); Bk. 2, p. 40 (10, 353)
428 A on E side of the Cataba River . . . 6 Apr 1753 Matt Rowan

TEMPLETON, DAVID File no. 848 (226); Gr. no. 344; Bk. 10, p. 287 (2, 68)
300 A on S side Cataba 4 or 5 miles from the river on the path from the Cataba Nation to George Cartheys [sic] upon Fishing Creek . . . 30 Aug 1753

TEMPLETON, DAVID File no. 1668 (1153); Gr. no. 1049; Bk. 15, p. 17 (13, 16)
400 A on S side Enoree adj. Walter Carruths Survey on Ducans [sic] Creek about 2 miles below Benjamin Gordons Land . . . 16 May 1754 Matt Rowan

THOMAS, GILL SHAW File no. 0279; Entry no. 637
Warrant: Unto Gill Shaw Thomas . . . 400 A at or near Burch's line . . . 4 Sept 1753 Matt Rowan

THOMAS, JOHN File no. 350; Gr. no. 100; Bk. 2, p. 118
Plat: Surd for John Thomas 600 A on the So side Cataba on a small creek Between Crowders Creek and Alisons Joyning Cambles Land, it Being the land formerly surved. for sd. John Thomas . . . 1 Feb 1755 Hugh Keley & Daniel OCain CB Iss. 28 Mar 1754

THOMAS, JOHN File no. 1124 (1638); Gr. no. 1018; Bk. 13, p. 11 (15, 11)
448 A on S side Cataba including the place where he now lives . . . Largers line . . . 17 May 1754 Matt Rowan

THOMSON, BENJAMIN File no. 1122 (1636); Gr. no. 1016; Bk. 13, p. 11 (15, 11)
200 A on N side Cataba on both sides Rum Creek . . . Bairels line . . . Thomas Simsons line . . . 17 May 1754 Matt Rowan

THOMPSON, SAMUEL File no. 0199
Plat: Survey'd for Samuel Thompson 900 A on S side Broad River on a Big Creek running into Little River otherwise Called Gastaway [?] or Litle River or fair forrest 6 or 7 miles above the Great Lick . . . [appears to be a plat by Alexander Lewis]

TOOMER, JOSHUA File no. 1766 (1255); Gr. no. 1199; Bk. 15, p. 60 (13, 52)
402 A on S side Broad River on Duncans Creek above Mitchells improvement 25 Sept 1754 Matt Rowan

TOOMER, JOSHUA File no. 1354 (1765); Gr. no. 1198; Bk. 13, p. 52 (15, 60)
402 A on S side Enoree on Duncans Creek below Mitchells improvement 25 Sept 1754 Matt Rowan

TURNER, JOHN File no. 824 (202); Gr. no. 319; Bk. 10, p. 384 (2, 64)
340 A on S side Cataba adj. Thomas Robinsons survey 30 Aug 1753 Matt Rowan

TOWNSEND, ROBERT File no. 0202
Warrant: Unto Townsend Robinson, 600 A on N side S fork Fishing Creek below the Indian path to Sandy River . . . formerly David Lewis . . . 17 Nov 1753 Matt: Rowan

TOWNSEND, ROBERT File no. 0203
Warrant: Unto Townsend Robinson, 300 A on the N side Cataba, about a mile or two above the forks formerly for Alexr Dobbins . . . 17 Nov 1753. Matt Rowan
[The preceding two warrants are indexed under the name of Robert Townsend, but were actually to Townsend Robinson.]

WALKER, PHILIP File no. 1745 (1333); Gr. no. 1168; Bk. 15, p. 46 (13, 41)
Warrant: Unto Philip Walker, 300 A on Fishing Creek below the Seludy path 28 Mar 1753 Matt Rowan
300 A on N branch of Fishing Creek . . . 24 Sept 1754 Matt Rowan

WALKER, PHILIP File no. 413 (2183); Gr. no. 229; Bk. 2, p. 140 (16, 58)
300 A on S side Cataba, S side Fishing Creek, near Jacob Taylors line . . . 3 Oct 1755 Arthur Dobbs

WALKER, SAMUEL File no. 0213
Warrant: Unto Samuel Walker 360 A on N side Broad . . . 3 Apr 1752 Gab Johnston
Plat: Survey'd for Samuel Walker 250 A on N side Broad River on the Creek where James Bullock formerly Liv'd & sold to Samuel Chew, otherwise called Clarks Creek . . . June ye 6 1752 Alexr Lewis D: S [No CB]

WALKER, THOMAS File no. 0214; Entry no. 487
Warrant: Unto Thomas Walker, 400 A on S side Broad River on Kings Rivers above Gilkies Land . . . 29 Aug 1753 Matt: Rowan

WALKER, THOMAS File no. 860 (238); Gr. no. 356; Bk. 10, p. 389 (2, 70)

356 A on S side Cataba, N branch Fishing Creek adj. Mathew Tools survey 30 Aug 1753 Matt Rowan

WATKINS, JOHN File no. 822 (200); Gr. no. 317; Bk. 10, p. 384 (2, 64)
274 A on S side Cataba adj. Thomas Robinson adj. John Turners corner 30 Aug 1753 Matt Rowan

WATSON, WILLIAM File no. 213 (835); Gr. no. 330; Bk. 2, p. 6 (10, 385)
400 A on a N branch of Fishing Creek about one mile above John Humphries . . . 30 Aug 1753 Matt Rowan

WATSON, WILLIAM File no. 823 (201); Gr. no. 318; Bk. 2, p. 64 (10, 384)
Warrant: Unto William Watson 400 A on S side Cataba, and head of Allisons Creek above James Wilson 3 Apr 1752 Gab Johnston
400 A on S side Cataba at head of Allisons Creek above James Wilsons survey 30 Aug 1753 Matt Rowan

WATSON, WILLIAM File no. 333 (967); Gr. no. 649; Bk. 2, p. 64 (10, 435)
400 A on N side Cataba . . . George Renicks line . . . 28 Feb 1754 Matt Rowan

WAUGHOPE, JAMES File no. 1964 (1455); Bk. 15, p. 334 (13, 259)
Plat: Survey'd for Jas Waughope, 135 A adj. his own, Robert Caldwells, & Moses Davies on waters of Waxaw Creek . . . Francis Beaty, D Sur. 27 Mar 1759, John Davies & John Nutt, CB Iss. 10 Apr 1761

WHITE, JOHN File no. 1223 (1735); Gr. no. 1151; Entry no. 882; Bk. 13, p. 39 (15, 45)
Warrant: Unto John White 300 A on N side Cataba adj. Joseph White 20 Feb 1754 Matt Rowan
300 A on N side Cataba adj. William White, Joseph White . . . 24 Sept 1754 Matt Rowan

WHITE, JOHN File no. 1665; Gr. no. 1056; Entry no. 884; Bk. 15, p. 16
Warrant: Unto John White, 200 A on N side Cataba, S side Waxaw Creek adj. John Kelseys land . . . 20 Feb 1754
250 A on N side Cataba and S side Waxaw Creek between Joseph Whites, William McKees, & John Keillys [sic] land . . . 16 May 1754 Matt Rowan

WHITE, JOSEPH File no. 1693 (1181); Gr. no. 1104; Bk. 15, p. 28 (13, 25)

632 A on N side Waxhaw Creek . . . 21 May 1754 Matt Rowan

WHITE, STEPHEN File no. 1236 (1748); Gr. no. 1157; Entry no. 1230; Bk. 13, p. 41 (15, 47)
491 A on N side Waxsaw Creek . . . Andrew Pickings line . . . 24 Sept 1754 Matt Rowan

WHITE, STEPHEN File no. 763 (141); Gr. no. 228; Bk. 10, p. 359 (2, 44)
Warrant: Unto Stephen White, 400 A on N side Cataba where he now lives 7 Apr 1752 Gab Johnston
325 A on E bank Catawba . . . 9 Apr 1753 Matt Rowan

WHITESIDE, HUGH File no. 1450 (1959); Bk. 13, p. 250 (15, 333)
Plat: Survey'd for Hugh Whiteside, 200 A on Fishing Creek adj. Samuel & William Neelys lines [n.d.] FRANCIS BEATY [surv.] Samuel Neely & William Neely, CB Iss. 10 Apr 1761

WILSON, FRANCIS File no. 1137 (1651); Gr. no. 1031; Bk. 13, p. 13 (15, 14)
1000 A on N fork Little River about Six miles above Robert Millers Land 16 May 1754 Matt Rowan

WILLSON, JAMES File no. 0242; Entry no. 908
Warrant: Unto James Wilson, 300 A on S side Broad & N side Thicketty Creek including the place claimed by Richard Carroll . . . 20 Feb 1754 Matt: Rowan

WILSON, JAMES File no. 2119 (347); Bk. 16, p. 3 (2, 117)
Plat: Aug 16, 1754, Survd for James Willson 302 A on a branch of Thicketty Creek opposite to Richd Millers, known as Richard Kerals . . . Saml Young Will Green & Jno Stewart, C.C. Iss. 28 Mar 1755

WILSON, JOHN File no. 75 (696); Gr. no. 33; Bk. 2, p. 28 (10, 337)
300 A on S side Broad on N fork Pacolet River below Margaret Campbells place . . . 31 Mar 1753 Matt Rowan

WILLSON, JOHN File no. 237 (859); Gr. no. 355; Bk. 2, p. 70 (10, 389)
540 A on Golden Grove above his second survey 30 Aug 1753 Matt: Rowan

WILLSON, JOHN File no. 216 (838); Gr. no. 334; Bk. 2, p. 67 (10, 386)
400 A on S side Broad on each side Golden Grove . . . 30 Aug 1753 Matt Rowan

WILSON, JOHN File no. 0243
  Warrant: Unto John Wilson 600 A above James Mitchells above the Falls on Big Creek of Little River or Fair Forrest being the Waters of Broad River . . . 3 Apr 1752 Gab. Johnston

WILSON, JOHN File no. 0244
  Warrant: Unto John Wilson 600 A above Arthur McClures Entry on Big Creek of Little River or Fair Forrest it being on Waters of Broad River on the So side of the Creek 3d Apr 1752 Gab Johnston

WILLSON, JOHN File no. 0245
  Warrant: Unto John Wilson 400 A on Packlet on S side of Broad 3 Apr 1752 Gab Johnston

WILLSON, JOHN File no. 0246
  Warrant: Unto John Wilson 600 A on Little River, waters of Broad River above the mouth of Little River . . . 3 Apr 1752 Gab Johnston

WILLSON, JOHN File no. 0247
  Warrant: Unto John Wilson 400 A on Packlet waters of Broad River . . . 3 Apr 1752 Gab Johnston

WILLSON, WILLIAM File no. 1775 (1264); Bk. 15, p. 71 (13, 60)
  600 A on N side Broad River on Kings Creek . . . 18 Nov 1752 Nath Rice

WILLSON, WILLIAM File no. 776 (154); Gr. no. 263; Bk. 10, p. 372 (2, 54)
  400 A on S side Broad River, below McNiells . . . 11 May 1753 Matt Rowan

WILLSON, WILLIAM File no. 1204 (1716); Gr. no. 1141; Bk. 13, p. 35 (15, 39)
  302 A on S side Broad River in the fork of Browns Creek being the place formerly surveyed for Edward McNeile . . . 24 Sept 1754 Matt Rowan

WILLSON, WILLIAM File no. 2187 (417); Gr. no. 234; Bk. 16, p. 59 (2, 140)
  300 A on N side Broad on Dry Creek below James Fannings Survey . . . 3 Oct 1755 Arthur Dobbs

WILLSON, WILLIAM File no. 1265 (1776); Bk. 13, p. 60 (15, 71)
  Warrant: Unto Wilm Wilson, 300 A on N side Broad on the place he now lives on called Hickory Levell . . . 4 Apr 1752 Gab Johnston

300 A on N side Broad called the hicory level 18 Nov 1752 Nath Rice

WINNEHAM, FRANCIS File no. 2395 (2336); Gr. no. 207; Bk. 18, p. 107 (17, 119)
Plat: 1 Jan 1764, Then surveyed for Fras. Winneham on SW of P.D. on N side Westfields Creek including his Improvement containing 100 A B Heron DS [No CB] Iss. 16 Nov 1764

WOODS, ANDREW File no. 666 (44); Gr. no. 30; Bk. 10, p. 328 (2, 20)
Warrant: Unto Andrew Wood 400 A on S side Cataba on waters of Fishing Creek, near Geo. Carthy . . . 5 Oct 1752 Nath Rice
400 A on S side Cataba on a branch of Fishing Creek adj. George Carthy 31 Mar 1753 Matt Rowan

WOOD, BARTHOLOMEW File no. 846 (224); Gr. no. 342; Bk. 10, p. 387 (2, 68)
300 A including the mouth of Duncans Creek . . . 30 Aug 1753 Matt: Rowan

WOOD, CARTUS File no. 861 (239); Gr. no. 357; Bk. 10, p. 389 (2, 68)
300 A on S side Tigar River including an Improvement where old Mr. Timmings now lives, now claimed by Stephen Holston . . . 30 Aug 1753 Matt Rowan

WOODS, ROBERT File no. 0254; Entry no. 26
Warrant: Unto Robert Woods 400 A on S side Broad River . . . 14 Oct 1752

WOODS, JAMES File no. 0251
Warrant: Unto James Woods, 300 A on Reedy River above Alexr Carthys Entry. 17 May 1754 Matt: Rowan

WOODS, JAMES File no. 356 (2127); Gr. no. 129; Bk. 1, p. 123 (16, 18)
Plat: Aug 3, 1754, Surd for James Woods, 302 A on Gilshot Thomas Creek, branch of S fork Broad River . . . nigh the Chriakee path . . . Saml Young, Dep Sur
302 A on Gillshot Thomas Creek, a branch of S fork Broad River . . . [No CB] 28 Mar 1755 Arthur Dobbs

YOUNG, CHARLES File no. 0260; Entry no. 1256
Warrant: Unto Charles Young, 400 A on the So side of Enoree about 2 or 3 miles above Gordons Survey . . . 20th May 1754 Matt Rowan

YOUNG, SAMUEL File no. 206 (828); Gr. no. 323; Bk. 2, p. 65 (10, 385)

520 A on Fairforrest below James Means 30 Aug 1753 Matt Rowan

YOUNG, SAMUEL & THOMAS GORDEN File no. 258 (890); Gr. no. 719; Bk. 2, p. 89 (10, 411)
450 A on S side Enoree on Indian Creek above Abraham Anderson . . . part of great Swamp . . . 25 Feb 1754 Matt Rowan

ROBINSON, GEORGE File no. 1349 (1859); Bk. 13, p. 138 (15, 198)
Warrant: Unto George Robison [sic], 300 A on So side of Teague [sic] River Joyning Gordons Land . . . 27 Mar 1755 Arthur Dobbs
Plat: Augt 2d, 1755, Surved for George Robison 310 A on South Side of Broad River including Peters Cabin adj. John Gordons line . . . Pr Saml Young, Dep Surveyor. Jno Brown, Thos Gordon, Chain Bearers Iss. 13 Oct 1756

ADAIR, ROBERT File no. 731 (1459); Gr. no. 300; Bk. 17, p. 334 (18, 306)
Plat: Survey'd for Robert Adair, 280 A on waters of Turkey Creek including his own Improvements . . . 28 Augt. 1765 William Dickson Survr. Robert Adair & James Hamilton, Cha. Bear. Iss. 26 Sept 1766

ALEXANDER, BENJAMIN File no. 290 (1022); Gr. no. 88; Bk. 17, p. 92 (18, 86)
Plat: Survd. for Benjamin Alexander 400 A on the South Branch of Fishing creek adj. Benjamin Lewises Land . . . [n.d.] By George Alexander D. Surv. Nathaniel Alexander & Benjamin Alexander, Ch: Bearers. Iss. 9 Nov 1764

ALEXANDER, BENJAMIN File no. 733 (1461); Gr. no. 320; Bk. 17, p. 334 (18, 306)
Plat: Survey'd for Benjamin Alexander a Plantation Containing 200 A on Waters of Bullocks Creek on the head-branches of Bells Creek . . . Shearers line . . . William Hartgroves line . . . 30 July 1765 Wm Dickson Sur. Thomas Gillham & Charles Gillham, Cha. Bear. Iss. 26 Sept 1766

ALEXANDER, EBENEZER File no. 546 (1272); Gr. no. 102, Bk. 17, p. 208 (18, 190)
Plat: Survey'd for Ebenezer Alexander 300 A on No fork of Packolett River . . . George Alexander's lower Corner . . . 19 Augt 1765 William Dickson, Surv. William Ross & Joseph White, Cha. Bear. Iss. 30 Oct 1765

ALEXANDER, GEORGE File no. 545 (1271); Gr. no. 101; Bk. 17, p. 208 (18, 190)
Plat: Surveyed for George Alexander 200 A on both sides Packolett River South Side Broad River, adj. below his other Survey . . . 19 Augt 1765 William Dickson, Sur. William Ross & Archd. McDowell, Cha. Bear. Iss. 30 Oct 1765

ALEXANDER, GEORGE File no. 547 (1273); Gr. no. 103; Bk. 17, p. 209 (18, 190)
Plat: Survey'd for George Alexander 200 A on both sides of the No Fork of Packolett River, joining between his own and Ebenezer Alexanders lines . . . 19 Augt 1765. William Dickson, Survr. William Ross, Archd McDowell, CB. Iss. 30 Oct 1765

ALEXANDER, GEORGE File no. 548 (1274); Gr. no. 104; Bk. 17, p. 209 (18, 190)

Plat: Surveyed for George Alexander, 150 A on waters of Bullocks Creek between Wades and Laferty's lines . . . 26 Augt 1765. William Dickson Sur. William Sims & Patrick Laferty, Cha. Bear. Iss. 30 Oct 1765

ALEXANDER, GEORGE File no. 909 (1630); Gr. no. 154; Bk. 17, p. 407 (18, 372)
Plat: July the 21st, 1766, Surveyed for George Alexander 150 A on both sides Turkey Creek . . . P Zach Bulloch, Sur. William Ross, John Miller, CB. Iss. 25 Apr 1767

ALEXANDER, GEORGE File no. 661 (1388); Grant no. 61; Bk. 17, p. 288 (18, 261)
Plat: Surveyed for George Alexander 300 A on both sides of the No fork of Packolet including the Mouth of Mill Creek . . . 19 Augt 1765 William Dickson, Sur. William Ross, Archd McDowel, CB. Iss. 25 Sept 1766

ALEXANDER, HEZEKIAH File no. 1032 (300); Gr. no. 103; Bk. 18, p. 89 (17, 95)
Plat: Survey'd for Hezekiah Alexander 180 A on both sides Allisons Creek on ye W side Catawba . . . adj. William Patrick . . . By George Alexander [n.d.] Mathew Patton & John Davies, CB. Iss. 9 Nov 1764

ALEXANDER, HEZEKIAH File no. 1522 (801); Gr. no. 476; Bk. 18, p. 341 (17, 372)
Plat: Surveyed for Hezekiah Alexander 200 A on a Branch of Mill Creek, a Branch of Turkey Creek including the forks of sd. creek upon both sides the New Cut Road leading from Milles's to Gorrels [n.d.] Jno. Mck. Alexander. Rob & Alexander Harp., C.C. Iss. 27 Sept 1766

ALEXANDER, JOHN File no. 2431; Gr. no. 297; Bk. 23, p. 241
Plat: Survey'd for John Alexander 200 A on both sides of Lawsons fork of Packelet above John Wottens [?] Land . . . 5th Jany 1768 By Wm Sharp, Survr. Jos. Jones & David Davis, C: Bear. Iss. 28 Apr 1768

ALEXANDER, JNO. McKNIT File no. 1029 (297); Gr. no. 100; Bk. 18, p. 88 (17, 95)
Plat: [n.d.] Surveyed for John McKnitt Alexander 300 A on both sides Allisons Creek adj. the Waggon Road, Including Pean's Cabbin & Mill Seats . . . George Alexander, D.S. James Campbell & Joseph Bradner, CB Iss. 9 Nov 1764

ALEXANDER, JOHN McKNIT File no. 2067; Grant no. 36; Bk. 23, p. 87
Plat: Surveyed for John McKnit Alexander, 300 A on Ridge

Between Thicketty and Gilkeys Creek including some Springs of Steens branch . . . 1 June 1767. Wm Sharp, Sur. Robt Lusk, John Sharp, CB Iss. 24 Oct 1767

ALEXANDER, JOHN McKNIT File no. 556 (1282); Gr. no. 112; Bk. 17, p. 210 (18, 191)
Plat: 26 July 1765, Surveyed for John McKnitt Alexander, 300 A on waters of Bullocks Creek, head of Tius branch . . . John Brandons line . . . William Dickson, Sur. William Sharp, John Brandon, CB. Iss. 30 Oct 1765

ALEXANDER, JNO. McKNIT File no. 1198 (470); Gr. no. 91; Bk. 18, p. 150 (17, 165)
Plat: Surveyed for John McKnitt Alexander, 138 A on David Watsons Spring Branch . . . Including Stuarts old Camp . . . George Alexander, D Sur. Jeremiah Potts, Archibald McDowell. Iss. 6 Apr 1765

ALEXANDER, JNO. McKNIT File no. 1027; Gr. no. 98; Bk. 18, p. 88
220 A on W side Cataba between Crowders and Allisons Creek on Beaver Dam Creek . . . near Joseph Bradners line . . . 9 Nov 1764 Arthur Dobbs

ALEXANDER, JNO. McKNIT File no. 728 (1456); Gr. no. 297; Bk. 17, p. 333 (18, 305)
Plat: Surveyed for John McKnitt, 150 A on waters of Susy Bowles Branch about a mile above the fork . . . 24 July 1765. WILLIAM DICKSON, Sur. Robert Harper & William Sharp, CB. Iss. 26 Sept 1766

ALEXANDER, JOHN McKNITT File no. 1533; Gr. no. 12; Bk. 18, p. 345
250 A on Bullocks Creek . . . John Riggs . . . Fultons line . . . 22 Apr 1767 Wm Tryon

ALEXANDER, JOHN McKNITT File no. 800 (1521); Gr. no. 474; Bk. 18, p. 341 (17, 372)
Plat: [n.d.], Surveyed for John McKnitt Alexander, 100 A on Stony fork of Fishing Creek above Hugh McClellands Land . . . Jno McK. Alexander Sur.
Samuel Porter, John McEllily, C.B. Iss. 27 Sept 1766

ALEXANDER, JOHN McKNITT File no. 558 (1284); Gr. no. 114; Bk. 17, p. 211 (18, 192)
Plat: 25 July 1765, Surveyed for John McKnitt Alexander, on both sides Susy Bowles branch including Stephen Wrights old Impvt . . . William Dickson, Sur. Robert Lusk, John Miles, C.B. Iss. 30 Oct 1765

ALEXANDER, JNO. McKNIT File no. 1520 (799); Gr. no. 473; Bk. 18, p. 340 (17, 372)
Plat: [n.d.], Surveyed for John McKnitt Alexander, 200 A on a small branch of S fork Susah. Bowls Creek . . . 2 miles above Lackey land . . . By Jno. Mck. Alexander, Sur. Robt & Alexander Harper, C.B. Iss. 26 Sept 1766

ALEXANDER, JNO. McKNIT File no. 1281 (555); Gr. no. 111; Bk. 18, p. 91 (17, 210)
Plat: Surveyed for John McKnitt Alexander, 200 A on waters of Turkey Creek . . . Morris's Mill branch . . . by a small Grave yard . . . 19 Aug 1765 WILLIAM DICKSON, Sur. Robert Adair, Barnabas Henley, C.B. Iss. 30 Oct 1765

ALEXANDER, JNO. McKNIT File no. 292 (1024); Gr. no. 95; Bk. 17, p. 93 (18, 87)
Plat: [n.d.], Surveyed for John McKnitt Alexander 500 A upon Allisons Creek adj. George Rennex, Davies, Andrew Allison, near the Waggon Road . . . By George Alexander, D.S., Will: Cleghorn & John Alexander Junr, C.B. Iss. 9 Nov 1764

ALEXANDER, JOSEPH File no. 2080; Gr. no. 50; Bk. 23, p. 90
Plat: Surveyed for Joseph Alexander 200 A on both sides a branch of s branch of No fork Tyger about 1/2 mile above Alexander McCarters . . . 24 May 1767 . . . Wm Sharp, Sur. Joseph Jones, John Sharp, C.B. Iss. 26 Oct 1767

ALEXANDER, JOSEPH File no. 2081; Gr. no. 51; Bk. 23, p. 90
Plat: Surveyed for Joseph Alexander 200 A on N side Tygar on both sides Wards Creek adj. John Miller . . . 26 May 1767 Wm Sharp Surv. Charles Moore & John Sharp, C.B. Iss. 26 Oct 1767

ALLEN, DAVID File no. 2226; Gr. no. 381; Bk. 23, p. 152
Plat: 30 Dec 1766, Surveyed for David Allen, 200 A on both sides Goathers Creek . . . Zach Bullock [Surv.]. Moses Jone [sic], William Richards, C.B. Iss. 26 Oct 1767

ANDERSON, DAVID File no. 2398; Gr. no. 196; Bk. 23, p. 220
Plat: Surveyed for David Anderson, 250 A on So side So of Tygar River on both sides Bens Creek . . . 25 May 1767 Peter Johnston, Surv. Charles Moore, Jno. Anderson, C.B. Iss. 28 Apr 1768

ANDERSON, JOHN File no. 016
Plat: Surveyed for John Anderson, 150 A on S side S fork Tygar on both sides Bens Creek . . . David Lewis' line . . . 25 Nov 1767 . . . Peter Johnston, Surv. Willm Anderson & David Anderson, C.B.

45

ANDERSON, JOHN File no. 1347 (620); Gr. no. 20; Bk. 18, p. 254 (17, 280)
Plat: Surveyed for John Anderson 600 A . . . including the Indian camps and large Kane brake on Enoree . . . 26 Feb 1766 William Dickson Survr. Frances Dodds & Thomas Collins, Cha. Bear. Iss. 25 Sept 1766

ANDERSON, JNO. File no. 1364 (637); Gr. no. 37; Bk. 18, p. 251 (17, 283)
Plat: Surveyed for John Anderson, 200 A on Stoney fork of Fishing Creek including crab Tree Bottom . . . Thomas McClellands line . . . Robert McClellands line . . . 30 Apr 1766 William Dickson Sur. William Neeley, Thomas McClelland, C.B. Iss. 25 Sept 1766

ARMSTRONG, JAMES File no. 1091 (359); Gr. no. 268; Bk. 17, p. 135 (18, 121)
Plat: 22 Mar 1764, Surveyed for James Armstrong, 240 A on waters of Fishing Creek adj. Abraham Kuykendall . . . By George Alexander. James Young & Moses Cotter, C.B. Iss. 16 Nov 1764

ARMSTRONG, MARTIN File no. 018
Plat: May 14, 1767, Surveyed for Martin Armstrong 200 A on branches of Fishing Creek including his own improvement adj. SW corner of Indian land . . . adj. William Millers line, Peter Kuykendalls line . . . P William Sims. John Fondren & Meseck [sic] Stallions, C.B.

ARMSTRONG, MARTIN File no. 675 (1402); Gr. no. 75; Bk. 17, p. 290 (18, 264)
Plat: Surveyed for Martin Armstrong, 260 A on main fork of Fishing Creek called Humphreys branch . . . adj. Mr. Palmers . . . near Lanhams line . . . 21 Sept 1765. William Dickson, Sur. Abraham Kuykendall & Martin Armstrong, C.B. Iss. 25 Sept 1766

ATKINS, ALEXANDER File no. 019
Plat: Surveyed for Alexr Akins, 223 A including his improvement adj. Wm Patricks lines . . . 13 May 1767. Peter Johnston, Surv.
John McCormick, Wm Akins, C.B.

BAALS, RICHARD File no. 1079 (347); Gr. no. 255; Bk. 18, p. 118 (17, 131)
300 A on ridge between Turkey Creek & Fishing Creek . . . 16 Nov 1764 Arthur Dobbs

BALM, HONES File no. 023
> 3 July 1767, Agreeable to an Order of Council to me directed I have Resurvey'd and run the lines of a tract of Land Granted to Haunas Balm on both sides of Thicketty Creek, in Anson, now Mecklenburg County . . . in the presence of·Mr. John Clark who was personally present with Mr. Francis Mackilwean, the Deputy Surveyor who formerly run the same Land for the said Haunas Balm in the Year 1752. Wm Dickson Sur. North Carolina, Mecklenburg County. This day came John Clark, before me one of His Majesties Justices of the peace . . . and swore that he was present with Frances Mackilwean when he Survey'd the above Tract of Land for sd. Haunas Balm . . . there was no tree marked except the beginning tree . . . the sd. John Clark was present with William Dickson when he Resurvey'd the same . . . the Beginning Tree which he believes is destroy'd or decay'd that it cannot be found . . . Jno Clarke, Before me 6 Nov 1767, John Thomas, J.P.

BARNES, CHARLES File no. 2359; Gr. no. 110; Bk. 23, p. 204
> Plat: July 31, 1765, Survey'd for Charls Barns 81 A on W side Broad River P William Sims, S.M.C. John Barns, Wm McKown, C.B. Iss. 28 Apr 1768

BARNETT, HUGH File no. 792 (1514); Gr. no. 467; Bk. 17, p. 371 (18, 339)
> Plat: 27 Feb 1766, Surveyed for Hugh Barnet 300 A on S fork Tyger River above Joseph Mayes . . . by the side of the middle Cherokee Path . . . P Zac Bullock Thomas Clark, Joseph Thompson, CB Iss. 27 Sept 1766

BARNETT, ROBERT File no. 022
> Warrant: Unto Robert Barnet 200 A on waters of Tyger River above the forks and below the mountain . . . 24 Oct 1765 Wm Tryon
> Two identical plats: Feb 28, 1766, Surveyed for Robert Barnet, 200 A on main S fork Tyger adj. Hugh Barnet P Zach Bullock, Sur. Thomas Clark, Joseph Thomson, CB

BEATY, FRANCIS File no. 999 (267); Gr. no. 27; Bk. 18, p. 68 (17, 71)
> Plat: Surveyed for Francis Beaty, 250 A on N side Allisons Creek, 1 1/2 miles below Cedar flatt . . . branch of Crowders Creek [n.d.] By Hugh Beaty, D. Surv. John Slone, John Beaty, CB Iss. 21 Apr 1764

BELL, ZACHARIAH File no. 2135; Gr. no. 186; Bk. 23, p. 114
> Plat: Survey'd for Zachariah Bell 100 A on Turkey Creek in-

cluding Richard Walters Improvement . . . 25 Dec 1767 Jno McK Alexander Ezekiel & Thomas Gilham, CB Iss. 26 Oct 1767

BELL, ZACHARIAH File no. 543 (1269); Gr. no. 99; Bk. 17, p. 208 (18, 189)
Plat: 26 July 1765, Surveyed for Zachariah Bell, 150 A on Tius branch of Bullocks Creek . . . Charles Tius corner . . . land Bell bought of John Wherry . . . William Dickson, [Surv.] William Sharp & Charles Tius, CB Iss. 30 Oct 1765

BELL, ZACHARIAH File no. 721 (1449); Gr. no. 290; Bk. 17, p. 332 (18, 304)
Plat: [n.d.], Surveyed for Zachariah Bell, 150 A between Bullocks Creek and Broad River . . . Dunlaps line . . . By Jno. McK. Alexander, Sur. Wm Bean, Wm Bell, CB Iss. 26 Sept 1766

BELL, ZACHARIAH File no. 713 (1441); Gr. no. 282; Bk. 17, p. 330 (18, 302)
Plat: Surveyed for Zachariah Bell, 200 A upon the dividing Ridge between Bullocks & Turkey Creeks adj. Benjamin Alexander, Walter Burison, Clark . . . [n.d.] By Jno. Mck. Alexander, Sur. John Brandon, William Bell, C.C. Iss. 26 Sept 1766

BERRY, RICHARD File no. 622 (1349); Gr. no. 22; Bk. 17, p. 280 (18, 254)
Plat: Surveyed for Richard Berry, 300 A on waters of Turkey Creek, N side Davidsons Branch near William Watsons . . . James McAffees . . . 17 Feb 1766 William Dickson [Surv.] Frans. Ross & John Ross, C.B. Iss. 25 Sept 1766

BISHOP, EDMUND File no. 1379 (652); Gr. no. 52; Bk. 18, p. 260 (17, 286)
Plat: Surveyed for Edmund Bishop, 200 A on middle fork of Turkey Creek, including his own Improvement adj. John Millers line . . . 12 Apr 1766. William Dickson, Sur. John Miller, Druria Glover, C.B. Iss. 25 Sept 1766

BISHOP, JOHN File no. 1554 (833); Gr. no. 364; Bk. 18, p. 355 (17, 388)
Plat: Surveyed for John Bushop [sic], 200 A on Turkey Creek above James Browns plantation . . . 12 Apr 1766 William Dickson, Sur. James Brown, Isaac Brown, C.B. Iss. 25 Apr 1767

BISHOP, ROBERT File no. 1472 (744); Gr. no. 315; Bk. 18, p. 309 (17, 337)
Plat: Surveyed for Robert Bushop [sic], 200 A on both sides

Packolet about a mile above Skull Shoal . . . 2 Sept 1767 William Dickson, Sur. Alexr. Kill Patrick, James Mackbee, C.B. Iss. 26 Sept 1766

BISHOP, WILLIAM GLOVER File no. 1279 (553); Gr. no. 109; Bk. 18, p. 191 (17, 210)
Plat: Surveyed for William Glover Bishop, 100 A including forks of the Easternmost branch of Turkey Creek . . . 30 Aug 1765 William Dickson, Surv. Edmund Bishop, John Rolland, C.B. Iss. 30 Oct 1765

BISHOP, WILLIAM GLOVER File no. 1280 (554); Gr. no. 110; Bk. 18, p. 191 (17, 210)
Plat: Surveyed for William Glover Bishop, 150 A on a branch of Turkey Creek including his own improvement . . . 30 Augt 1765 William Dickson, Sur. Edmund Bishop, John Rolland, C.B. Iss. 30 Oct 1765

BLACK, GOWIN File no. 2368; Gr. no. 128; Bk. 23, p. 207
Plat: Jan. 14, 1767, Surveyed for Gowen Glack, 200 A on both sides Clarks fork of Bullocks Creek . . . Wilsons line . . . Mclewees line . . . Zach Bullock, Surv. James Wilson, Wm Mackelwe, C.B. Iss. 28 Apr 1768

BLACK, JOHN File no. 044
Plat: Surveyed for John Black,, 565 A on S side Allisons Creek including his improvement adj. John Flemmings . . . June 23d 1768 Peter Johnston [Surv.] Abraham Mill[er?], John Foster, C.B.

BLACK, JOSEPH File no. 1945; Gr. no. 297; Bk. 23, p. 12
Plat: 24 Mar 1766, Surveyed for Joseph Black, 200 A on both sides Clarks fork of Bullocks Creek . . . W Sims, Sur. Mathew Black, Robert Black, C.B. Iss. 25 Apr 1767

BLACK, MATTHEW File no. 696 (1434); Gr. no. 167; Bk. 17, p. 305 (18, 277)
Plat: Aug 29, 1765, Surveyed for Matthew Black, 100 A on both sides Clarks fork of Bullocks Creek . . . W Sims, Sur. Thomas Harrison, Robt. Black, C.B. Iss. 26 Sept 1766

BLACK, ROBERT File no. 1305 (578); Gr. no. 308; Bk. 18, p. 227 (17, 250)
Plat: August 27, 1765, Survey'd for Robert Black, 250 A on Clarks fork Bullocks Creek . . . P William Sims, Sur. Joseph Black, William Wilson, C.B. Iss. 30 Oct 1765

BLACK, THOMAS File no. 508 (1234); Gr. no. 63; Bk. 17, p. 201 (18, 183)
Plat: 2 July 1765, Surveyed for Thomas Black, 200 A on wa-

ters of Stoney fork of Fishing Creek between William Hannas & the Great Road ... William Dickson, Sur. James Hanna & William Hanna, C.B. Iss. 28 Oct 1765

BLACKWOOD, JAMES File no. 2456; Gr. no. 326; Bk. 23, p. 249
Plat: Surveyed for James Blackwood, 250 A on S side Lawsons Fork of Packelot adj. John Rottan, adj. Rottans corner near his house ... Dec 2, 1767 Peter Johnston, Sur. Iss. 29 Apr 1768. Samuel Knox, John Knox, C.C.

BLYTH, JAMES File no. 046; Entry no. 715
Warrant: Unto James Blyth, 400 A on S side Best [/] Creek adj. Robert Grays 18 Apr 1767 Wm Tryon
Plat: Survey'd for James Blyth, 400 A on S fork Packelet adj. John Crawfords ... 16 Jan 1768 Wm Sharp [surv.], Chas. Moore & Wm Sharp, C.B.

BOGGAN, WILLIAM File no. 2016; Gr. no. 441; Bk. 23, p. 37
Plat: March 20, 1766, Surveyed for William Boggan, 200 A on W branch of Bullocks Creek ... Loves line ... Zach Bullock [surv.] Adam Burchfield, Isaac Johnston, C.B. Iss. 27 Apr 1767

BOUNDS, GEORGE File no. 048; Entry no. 264
Warrant: Unto George Bounds, 150 A ... In fishing Creek adj. ____ Davison 6 Apr 1765 Wm Tryon
Plat: Surveyed for George bounds, 150 A on a branch of S fork Fishing Creek including his improvement ... 31 Aug 1765, William Dickson, Sur. John Rolton, John Dennis, C.B.

BRANDON, JNO. File no. 1679 (958); Gr. no. 216; Bk. 18, p. 383 (17, 421)
Plat: Surveyed for John Brandon, 200 A on waters of Turkey Creek on head of Tius branch on both sides Waggon Road including Wm Hillhouses Great Cowpen ... 27 July 1765 William Dickson, Surv. John Brandon, John Smith, C.B. Iss. 25 Apr 1767

BRANDON, JOHN File no. 957 (1678); Gr. no. 215; Bk. 17, p. 420 (18, 383)
Plat: 26 July 1765, Surveyed for John Brandon, 200 A on waters of Turkey Creek, including his Imprvt. on both sides Waggon Road ... William Dickson, Sur. John McKnitt Alexander, William Sharp, C.B. Iss. 25 Apr 1767

BRATTON, THOMAS File no. 1964; Gr. no. 316; Bk. 23, p. 11
Plat: April 22, 1766, Surveyed for Thomas Bratton, 200 A on S fork Fishing Creek, including his improvement ... McLanes ... Robert Brattons line ... Crafts line ... W Sims, Surv. David Bulton, Robt Bratton, C.B. Iss. 25 Apr 1767

BRIDGES, JAMES File no. 2252; Gr. no. 411; Bk. 23, p. 157
Plat: Surveyed for James Bridges, 375 A on both sides Thicketty Creek including the mouth of Mincums Creek ... between Haunas Balmes & John Howards lines ... 4 July 1767 Wm Dickson, Surv. Charles Robeson, Micajah Collins, C.B. Iss. 26 Oct 1767

BRIDGES, JAMES File no. 2024; Gr. no. 449; Bk. 23, p. 38
Plat: March 21, 1766, Surveyed for James Bridges, 150 A on middle fork of Bullocks Creek of Thicketty Creek ... Zach Bullock, Surv. Patrick Moore, William Twitty, C.B. Iss. 27 Apr 1767

BROWN, ALEXANDER File no. 2508; Gr. no. 474; Bk. 23, p. 294
Plat: Surveyed for Alexander Brown, 200 A on both sides S fork Fishing Creek between lines of George Craig, Henry Culp, William Miller, Joseph Boyd, David Lewis ... 11 Mar 1768 Wm Dickson, Sur. Iss. 29 Apr 1768. William Henry & James Henry, C.C.

BROWN, GABRIEL File no. 1242 (518); Gr. no. 71; Bk. 18, p. 184 (17, 202)
Plat: Surveyed for Gabriel Brown, Junior, Son of John Brown, 200 A on both sides Thicketty, a Branch of Broad River ... adj. Richard Miller, James McPeters, a small island ... 12 Mar 1765 William Dickson, Sur. Jabob Brown, John Johnston, C.B. Iss. 28 Oct 1765

BROWN, JAMES File no. 1552 (831); Gr. no. 61; Bk. 18, p. 354 (17, 387)
Plat: Surveyed for James Brown, 200 A on E side Turkey Creek on the Waggon Road between David Stephensons & his own lines ... Thomas Browns line ... 11 Apr 1766 William Dickson, Sur. John Bushop, Isaac Brown, C.B. Iss. 25 Apr 1767

BROWNLOW, JOHN File no. 2462; Gr. no. 401; Bk. 23, p. 282
Plat: Surveyed for John Brownlow, 320 A on S fork Fishing Creek adj. John Prices land ... Browns land ... Aug 19, 1767 ... Peter Johnston, Sur. Richd Ball, Banjn. Rainey, C.B. Iss. Apr 1768

BROWNLOW, JOHN & THOMAS RAINEY File no. 2051; Gr. no. 571; Bk. 23, p. 61
Plat: Surveyed for Thomas Rainy & John Brownlow, 130 A on waters of Fishing Creek adj. Thomas Betty & Peter Kuykendall ... 22 Dec 1766 Peter Johnston, Sur. Benjn. Philips, Thomas Rainey, C.B. Iss. 27 Apr 1767

BROWNLOW, JOHN & THOMAS RAINEY File no. 2050; Gr. no. 570; Bk. 23, p. 61
Plat: Surveyed for Thomas Rainey and John Brownlow on waters of fishing Creek, 370 A, adj. James Moor & Samuel Raineys land . . . 7 Mar 1767 Peter Johnston, Sur. John Conner, Saml Rainey, C.B. Iss. 27 Apr 1767

BRYSON, JAMES File no. 722 (1450); Gr. no. 291; Bk. 17, p. 332 (18, 304)
Plat: [n.d.], Surveyed for Samuel Bryson, 300 A upon Turkey Creek, near William Watson . . . By Jno. McK. Alexander, Sur. Samuel Davison, Wm Bean, C.C. Iss. 26 Sept 1766

BULLION, THOMAS File no. 052
Plat: Surveyed for Thomas Bullion 200 A on So side fairforest on both sides Lick Branch about a mile Below Millers waggon Road, adj. Giles Tillets land . . . 31 Dec 1767 Wm Sharp, Sur. Jas. Cook & Jas. Cook, C.B.

BULLOCK, SAMUEL HENDLEY File no. 051 [name appears on index card as SAMUEL HENDLEY BULLOCK]
Plat: Surveyed for Lenard Hendley Bullock, March 6, 1768, 400 A on both sides Tygar River . . . P Zach Bullock William Clark, Joab Mitchell, C.B.

BULLOCK, ZACHARIAH File no. 746 (1474); Gr. no. 391; Bk. 17, p. 354 (18, 324)
Plat: 13 May 1766, Surveyed for Zachariah Bullock, 540 A on both sides Jumping Run adj. Mcleweans Corner . . . Drapers line . . . Chrisr Colemans line . . . Zac Bullock, Sur. Thomas Draper, Randolph Haynes, C.B. Iss. 26 Sept 1766

BULLOCK, ZACHARIAH File no. 1476 (748); Gr. no. 394; Bk. 18, p. 324 (17, 355)
Plat: 5 May 1766, Surveyed for Zachariah Bullock 615 A on Ridge between Fair forest & Packlet adj. Thomas Mitchells, Mcleweans corner . . . P William Sims, Sur. Timothy Toney, Robert Easley, C.B. Iss. 26 Sept 1766

BULLOCK, ZACHARIAH File no. 2020; Gr. no. 445; Bk. 23, p. 37
Plat: 9 Feb 1767, Surveyed for Zacheriah Bullock, 400 A on Jumping Run, waters of Packlet . . . Simons line . . . Zacheriah Bullocks corner . . . P William Sims, Sur. John Hail, Dan Bush, C.B. Iss. 27 Apr 1767

BULLOCK, ZACHARIAH File no. 2021; Gr. no. 446; Bk. 23, p. 38
Plat: 18 Feb 1767, Surveyed for Zacheriah Bullock, 640 A

on waters of fairforest adj. his own line . . . P William Sims, Sur. John Hail, Daniel Bush, C.B. Iss. 27 Apr 1767

BULLOCK, ZACHARIAH File no. 2011; Gr. no. 437; Bk. 23, p. 36
Plat: Feb. 9, 1767, Surveyed for Zachariah Bullock, 580 A on Ridge between Turkey & Fishing Creek . . . Wm Sims, Sur. Robert Swan, James Darwin, C.B. Iss. 25 Apr 1767

BULLOCK, ZACHARIAH File no. 2026; Gr. no. 451; Bk. 23, p. 39
Plat: 13 Jan 1767, Surveyed for Zacheriah Bullock 300 A on Gillkeys Creek a fork of Thicketty . . . James [?] Youngs corner . . . P Zach Bullock, Sur. John Russel, John Clark, C.B. Iss. 27 Apr 1767

BULLOCK, ZACHARIAH File no. 2380; Gr. no. 140; Bk. 23, p. 209
Plat: Feb. 8th 1768, Surveyed for Zachariah Bullock, 300 A on the North fork of Packlet . . . Charles McNights corner . . . Pr Zach Bullock [surv.] Jas. Howard, John Potts, C.B. Iss. 28 Apr 1768

BULLOCK, ZACHARIAH File no. 2363; Gr. no. 114; Bk. 23, p. 205
Plat: June 16, 1767, Survey'd for Zachariah Bullock, 300 A on Main Thicketty Creek adj. Johnsons line . . . Zach Bullock Andrew Jones, John Johnson, C.B. Iss. 28 Apr 1768

BULLOCK, ZACHARIAH & JOHN FONDREN File no. 2364; Gr. no. 115; Bk. 23, p. 205
300 A on S fork Fishing Creek adj. William Dickson, Henry, Robert Carr . . . 28 Apr 1768 Wm Tryon

BURNS, WILLIAM File no. 1426 (698); Gr. no. 169; Bk. 18, p. 278 (17, 306)
Plat: 27 Aug 1765, Surveyed for William Burns, 150 A on middle fork of Bullocks Creek . . . Russells line . . . P W Sims, Surv. Tho Williams, Wm Burns, C.B. Iss. 26 Sept 1766

BYARS, DAVID File no. 2475; Gr. no. 414; Bk. 23, p. 285
Plat: 2 Feb 1767, Surveyed for David Byars, 150 A on heads of Turkey Creek . . . Zach Bulloch, Sur. Joseph Hardin, Matthew Porter, C.B. Iss. 29 Apr 1768

CAMPBELL, ANDREW File no. 1439 (711); Gr. no. 280; Bk. 18, p. 302 (17, 330)
Plat: Surveyed for Andrew Campbell 200 A on both sides Loves Creek adj. Pauls Land . . . Jno McK. Alexander, Sur. [n.d.] Jno McKinney, Wm Smith, C.C. Iss. 26 Sept 1766

CAMPBELL, ANDREW File no. 059
Plat: Surveyed for Andrew Campbell, 150 A on waters of Allisons Creek adj. his own land . . . Robert Adams . . . 19 Dec 1767 . . . Peter Johnston [surv.] James Campbell & James linton [?], C.B.

CAMPBELL, JAMES File no. 2422; Gran.e no. 285; Bk. 23, p. 239
Plat: Surveyed for James Campbell 58 A on waters of Allisons Creek adj. Alexander & Armstrong & his own line . . . By Jno. Mck. Alexander Sept 9, 1767 Andrew Campbell & Thomas Neysmith, C.B. Iss. 25 Apr 1768

CAMPBELL, JAMES File no. 313 (1045); Gr. no. 226; Bk. 17, p. 123 (18, 111)
Plat: [n.d.], Surveyed for James Campbell, 350 A on a branch of Allisons Creek adj. his own & John Thomas . . . By Francis Beaty, D Surv. Joseph Bradner, Daniel Pritchard, C.B. Iss. 16 Nov 1764

CARR, JOHN File no. 1232 (506); Gr. no. 61; Bk. 18, p. 183 (17, 200)
150 A on waters of Allisons Creek on E side of land he bought of James Harris . . . 28 Oct 1765 Wm Tryon

CARROL, JAMES File no. 2550; Gr. no. 558; Bk. 23, p. 310
Plat: Survey'd for James Carroll, 200 A on a branch of Tygar River called the Middle Creek above David Davis's . . . 9 Jan 1768 By Wm Sharp, Surv. David Davis, Jos Jones, C.B. Iss. 29 Apr 1768

CARROL, JOSEPH File no. 1350 (623); Gr. no. 23; Bk. 18, p. 254 (17, 280)
Plat: Surveyed for Joseph Carrol, 220 A on forks of Allisons Creek adj. John Barr, Wm Mackilmurry, John Venebel & his own land . . . 18 May 1766 William Dickson, Sur. Wm Mackilmurrey, Joseph Carrol, jr., C.B. Iss. 25 Sept 1766

CASE, THOMAS File no. 2262; Gr. no. 458; Bk. 23, p. 167
Plat: Survey'd for Thomas Case, 400 A on both sides fair forrest Creek . . . adj. Robert Dugans uper line . . . 12 Dec 1766 Wm Dickson, Survr. Thos Case & Jno Williamson, C.B. Iss. 26 Oct 1767

CASTON, JOHN & WILLIAM SIMS File no. 1986; Gr. no. 410; Bk. 23, p. 31
Plat: June 3, 1766, Surveyed for William Sims & John Caston 345 A on branches of Bullocks Creek at Loves corner . . . Robersons line . . . McAdos line . . . Wm Sims [surv] Adam Burchfield, William Boggan, C.B. Iss. 25 Apr 1767

CHAMBERS, JOHN File no. 070; Entry no. 660
Warrant: Unto John Chambers 100 A on both sides Rich Bottom Fork of Bullocks Creek including his Cabin . . . 23 Sept 1766 Wm Tryon
Two identical plats: Survey'd for John Chambers 100 A on both sides Rich Bottom Fork of Bullocks Creek including his own improvement [n.d.] [No surv given] . . . adj. Andrew Countryman. Robt Swann, Jno Countryman, C.B.

CLARK, BETSY File no. 1478; Gr. no. 396; Bk. 18, p. 325
Plat: May the 23, 1766, Surveyed for Betsey Clarke, 400 A on the North Fork of Packlet . . . Robert Tates corner . . . P Zach Bullock Alexander Kil Patrick, James Howard, C. Bearers. Iss. 26 Sept 1766

CLARK, HENRY File no. 2219; Gr. no. 374; Bk. 23, p. 151
Plat: Feb. the 21st, 1766, Surveyed for Henry Clark, 180 A on W side Broad River . . . Loves Corner . . . P W Sims, Survr. Wm Marchbanks, Nathl Clark, Ch: Bearers Iss. 26 Oct 1767

CLARK, ICHABOD File no. 1516 (795); Gr. no. 469; Bk. 18, p. 340 (17, 371)
Plat: 24th Feb 1766, Surveyed for Ichabod Clark, 200 A on West side of Broad River and joins the mouth of Thicketty Creek . . . P William Sims, Surv. William Marchbanks & Nathl Clark, Ch. Bearers. Iss. 27 Sept 1766

CLARK, JOHN File no. 651 (1378); Gr. no. 51; Bk. 17, p. 286 (18, 260)
Plat: Surveyed for John Clark, 400 A on S fork Packalet, below Beaverdam branch including the Rich Land Bottom . . . Hutchinsons corner . . . 31 Mar 1766 . . . William Dickson, Survr. William Dickson, James Howard, C.B. Iss. 25 Sept 1766

CLARK, JOSEPH File no. 828 (1549); Gr. no. 57; Bk. 17, p. 387 (18, 354)
Plat: 8 Feb 1766, Surveyed for Joseph Clark, 150 A on S side Allisons Creek, William Dickson, Sur. Robert Adams, James Adams, C.B.

CLARK, REYDIAS File no. 2379; Gr. no. 139; Bk. 23, p. 209
Plat: Feb 12, 1767, Survey'd for Reydias Clark, 200 A on S side Broad . . . Iccabod Clarks line . . . Henry Clarks line . . . William Loves corner . . . Zach Bullock, Sur. Ichebod Clark, Henry Clark, C.B. Iss. 28 Apr 1768

CLARK, THOMAS File no. 450 (1178); Gr. no. 70; Bk. 17, p. 161 (18, 146)

Plat [n.d.], Surveyed for Thomas Clark, 214 A on No branch of Allisons Creek, adj. Barrs land . . . George Alexander, Sur. Thomas Clark, Robt Harris, C.B. Iss. 6 Apr 1765

CLAYTON, WILLIAM File no. 2014; Gr. no. 439; Bk. 23, p. 36
Plat: Surveyed for William Clayton, 400 A on both sides Buckhorn fork of Bullocks Creek . . . Dicksons line . . . Wm Sims, Sur. Robert Swann, Saml Swan, C.B. Iss. 25 Apr 1767

CLEMENTS, ABRAHAM File no. 852 (1573); Gr. no. 84; Bk. 17, p. 392 (18, 359)
Plat: Surveyed for Abraham Clements, 150 A on the No fork of Packolet including the place he now lives on . . . 2d Apr 1766 William Dickson, Survr. James Howard, James Cozart, C.B. Iss. 25 Apr 1767

COLEMAN, CHRISTOPHER File no. 2378; Gr. no. 138; Bk. 23, p. 209
Plat: 8 June 1767, Survey'd for Christopher Coleman, 200 A on Mill Creek . . . Zachariah Bullocks . . . Randolph Hames line . . . sd. Colemans line . . . Zach Bullock [surv.] Thomas Draper, Randolph Hames, C.B. Iss. 28 Apr 1768

COLEMAN, CHRISTOPHER File no. 2229; Gr. no. 384; Bk. 23, p. 152
Plat: 15 Dec 1766, Surveyed for Christopher Coleman 200 A on Mill Creek of Packelot adj. Robert Coleman, Thomas Draper . . . Bullock . . . Zacha Bullock [surv.] Randolph Hames, Abner Coleman, C.B. Iss. 26 Oct 1767

COLEMAN, ROBERT File no. 2491; Gr. no. 438; Bk. 23, p. 288
Plat: Jan. 1, 1766, Surveyed for Robert Coleman, 600 A on both sides Mill Creek . . . Zac Bullock, Surv. [No CB] Iss. 29 Apr 1768

COLLINS, JAMES File no. 601; Gr. no. 351; Bk. 17, p. 259
Plat: August 13th 1765, Survey'd for James Collins 200 A on the East side of Broad River, including an Island . . . crossing McEntires Creek . . . Williams Sims, Sur. Samuel Richardson, Philip Henson, C.B. Iss. 30 Oct 1765

COLLINS, THOMAS File no. 076
Plat: Survey'd for Thomas Collins, 124 A on N fork Tygar adj. John Miller, Alexander Vernon, Francis Dodds, Thom McKlehennys . . . 24 May 1769 Peter Johnston, Sur. Alexr Vernon, John Collins, C.B.

COLLINS, THOMAS File no. 2205; Gr. no. 359; Bk. 23, p. 147
Plat: Survey'd for Thomas Collins 200 A on middle fork of

Tygar River adj. his own & Blacks land . . . 23 May 1767 Peter Johnston, Sur. Alex Vernor, John Collins, CB Iss. 26 Oct 1767

COLLINS, THOMAS File no. 2272; Gr. no. 51; Bk. 23, p. 179
Plat: Surveyed for Thomas Collins, 300 A on N side middle fork of Tyger River by Indian path at David Parks corner . . . 6 Mar 1766 Wm Dickson, Sur. Thomas Penney, Francis Dodds, CB Iss. 26 Oct 1767

COLLINS, THOMAS File no. 2188; Gr. no. 247; Bk. 23, p. 175
Plat: Survey'd for Thomas Collins, 200 A on So side N fork Tyger adj. Francis Wilson, Francis Doods's [sic] & Richard Sadlers line . . . 9 Dec 1766 Wm Dickson, Sur. Francis Dods, Thos Penny, CB Iss. 26 Oct 1767

CONNER, JOHN File no. 860 (1581); Gr. no. 97; Bk. 17, p. 394 (18, 361)
Plat: Surveyed for John Conner 100 A on waters of S fork fishing Creek, on hog hole Branch . . . waggon Road . . . 10 May 1766 . . . William Dickson, Sur. Edward Croft, Daniel Croft, CB Iss. 25 Apr 1767

COUNTRYMAN, ANDREW File no. 2298; Gr. no. 44; Bk. 23, p. 192
Plat: Feb 8, 1767, Surveyed for Andrew Countryman, 150 A on both sides Bullocks Creek including his Impvt . . . Robt Swanns line . . . [No CB] [No Surv.] Iss. 28 Apr 1768

CRAIN, CHARLES File no. 2180; Gr. no. 239; Bk. 23, p. 124
Plat: Surveyed for Charles Crain, 200 A on S side Broad on Hughs little Creek including his improvement . . . 31 Dec 1766 Wm Dickson, Sur. Saml Torbet, Richd Edwards, CB Iss. 26 Oct 1767

CRAWFORD, JNO. File no. 1346 (160); Gr. no. 19; Bk. 18, p. 253 (17, 279)
Plat: [n.d.], Surveyed for John Crawford, 300 A on both sides So fork Packolett . . . William Dickson, Sur. Anthony Hutchins, Joseph White, C.B. Iss. 25 Sept 1766

CRAWFORD, JOHN File no. 1342 (615); Gr. no. 15; Bk. 18, p. 253 (17, 279)
Plat: Surveyed for John Crawford, 150 A on S fork Packolett below the Cherokee path [n.d.] William Dickson, Sur. Anthony Hutchins, Joseph White, CB Iss. 25 Sept 1766

CRAVANS, ROBERT File no. 2251; Gr. no. 438; Bk. 23, p. 163
Plat: Jan. 17, 1767, Surveyed for Robert Cravens, 150 A on Clarks fork of Bullocks Creek . . . adj. Robert Patterson Line

. . . Zach Bullock, Sur. James Petterson, Newberry Stockton, CB Iss. 26 Oct 1767

CROFTS, DANIEL File no. 412 (1140); Gr. no. 31; Bk. 17, p. 154 (18, 139)
Plat: [n.d.], Surveyed for Daniel Crofts, 247 A between S & N forks of Fishing Creek, between Isaac Taylors & Widow Kuykendalls . . . Francis Beaty, Sur. John Moore, John Davies, CB Iss. 6 Apr 1765

CROFT, EDWARD File no. 741 (1469); Gr. no. 312; Bk. 17, p. 336 (18, 308)
Plat: Surveyed for Edward Croft, 300 A on S fork Fishing Creek adj. Wm Jones, John Davis . . . [n.d.], William Dickson, Sur. John Conner, Daniel Crofts, CB Iss. 26 Sept 1766

CRAFTS, EDWARD File no. 1036; Gr. no. 109; Bk. 18, p. 90
Plat: Surveyed for Edward Crofts, 300 A on waters of fishing Creek on the Waggon Road from Peter Kuykendalls to Charles Town . . . North from Charles Beaty . . . 2 Sept 1763 Francis, Beaty, D. Sur. Thomas Rainey & James Moore, CB Iss. 9 Nov 1764

CROFTS, EDWARD File no. 304; Gr. no. 109; Bk. 17, p. 97
300 A on waters of Fishing Creek on the Waggon Road from Peter Kuykendalls to Charlestown, north of Charles Beatys . . . 9 Nov 1764 Arthur Dobbs

CULWELL, CURTIS File no. 566 (1292); Gr. no. 295; Bk. 17, p. 247 (18, 225)
Plat: July the 27th, 1765, Survey'd for Curtis Culwell, 150 A on both sides Bullocks Creek . . . adj. his own line . . . Laughlins line . . . P William Sims Curtis Culwell, John Jones, CB Iss. 30 Oct 1765

CULWELL, CURTIS File no. 2369; Gr. no. 129; Bk. 23, p. 207
Plat: Feb 1th [sic], 1768, Surveyed for Curtis Culwell, 200 A on both sides Bullocks Creek . . . Writes line . . . Culwells line . . . George Cowens line . . . P Zach. Bullock Robert Cowen, John Cowen, C.B. Iss. 28 Apr 1768

DAVIDSON, SAMUEL File no. 2047; Gr. no. 477; Bk. 23, p. 43
35 A on Bullocks Creek . . . Curtis Caldwells Line . . . Stephensons line . . . Moors . . . 27 Apr 1767 Wm Tryon

DAVIDSON, WILLIAM File no. 2087; Gr. no. 95; Bk. 23, p. 98
200 A on the Callabash branch of Allisons Creek adj. John Barr . . . Carrolls . . . 26 Oct 1767 Wm Tryon

DAVIS, DAVID File no. 2079; Gr. no. 49; Bk. 23, p. 90
200 A on both sides N fork Tyger adj. Jonathan Newmans
line . . . 26 Oct 1767 Wm Tryon

DAVIS, DAVID File no. 1380; Gr. no. 53; Bk. 18, p. 260 (17,
285)
200 A on S branch N fork Tygar above Robert Millers land
. . . 25 Sept 1766 Wm Tryon

DAVIS, JOHN File no. 656; Gr. no. 56; Bk. 17, p. 287
300 A on W side Broad River, N fork Browns Creek above
Hugh Nelson [Wilson?] 25 Sept 1766 Wm Tryon

DAVIS, JOHN File no. 1116 (385); Gr. no. 293; Bk. 18, p. 126
(17, 140)
300 A on S fork Fishing Creek . . . 1/4 mile above the Seludy
Road . . . 16 Nov 1764 Arthur Dobbs

DAVIES, WALTER File no. 1158 (430); Gr. no. 49; Bk. 18, p.
143 (17, 157)
370 A on Rockey Allisons Creek near William Patricks Land
and Allisons Creek 6 Apr 1765 Wm Tryon

DAVISON, SAMUEL File no. 1434 (706); Gr. no. 274; Bk. 18,
301 (17, 328)
300 A upon both sides Turkey Creek including the mill seat
. . . James Brysons corner . . . 26 Sept 1766 Wm Tryon

DENIS, JOHN File no. 846 (1567); Gr. no. 78; Bk. 17, p. 391 (18,
358)
200 A on head of S fork Fishing Creek . . . 25 Apr 1767 Wm
Tryon

DICKSON, ALEXANDER File no. 907 (1628); Gr. no.'152; Bk.
14, p. 407 (18, 372)
200 A on both sides Lawsons fork of Packolet including a
small improvement above James Alexanders . . . 25 Apr 1767
Wm Tryon

DICKSON, DAVID File no. 1245 (519); Gr. no. 74; Bk. 18, p.
185 (17, 203)
150 A on S side Crowders Creek on the head of the long
branch near James Alexanders . . . 28 Oct 1765 Wm Tryon

DICKSON, EDWARD File no. 112 (226); Gr. no. 99; Bk. 13, p.
436 (17, 11)
230 A on S side Broad about 2 miles below the mouth of Little Broad River above the Cherokee ford of Broad River . . .
23 Dec 1763 Arthur Dobbs

DICKSON, JOHN File no. 2165; Gr. no. 224; Bk. 23, p. 121
350 A on Enoree adj. John Odells including his own improvement 26 Oct 1767 Wm Tryon

DICKSON, JOSEPH File no. 1372 (645); Gr. no. 45; Bk. 18, p. 259 (17, 285)
200 A on Both sides Enoree River above John Hendersons . . . John Andersons upper survey . . . 25 Sept 1766 Wm Tryon

DICKSON, MICHAEL File no. 1209 (482); Gr. no. 136; Bk. 18, p. 156 (17, 172)
300 A between Catawba River and Broad River, both sides Rockey Creek at the ford of the Seluda Road, land that was Surveyed for John Fondren . . . 16 Apr 1765 Wm Tryon

DICKSON, MICHAEL File no. 1011 (279); Gr. no. 34; Bk. 18, p. 156 (17, 80)
Warrant: Unto Michael Dickson 300 A on Bullocks Creek Below William Dicksons 19 Oct 1762 Arthur Dobbs
Plat: Survey'd for Michael Dickson 300 A on a Branch of the Et side of Bullocks Creek . . . 6th Augt 1764 William Dickson, Sur. John Macklmory & Wm Macklmory, C.B. Iss. 2 Nov 1764

DICKSON, ROBERT File no. 1761; Gr. no. 131; Bk. 20, p. 511
Plat: Surveyed for Robert Dickson, 300 A on E side Cuttawba on a Branch of 12 Mile Creek above William Osbornes Survey . . . including Noble Osbornes Cabbin, formerly Surveyed for James & John Osborne . . . William Osbornes corner . . . Wm Dickson, [Sur.] John Osborn & John Osborn, C.B. Iss. 16 Dec 1769

DICKSON, ROBERT File no. 117 (4); Gr. no. 15; Bk. 15, p. 474 (13, 383)
300 A on E side Moors Creek, a branch of Broad River on N side Susys Branch 19 Apr 1763 Arthur Dobbs

DICKSON, ROBERT File no. 646 (1373); Gr. no. 46; Bk. 17, p. 285 (18, 259)
220 A on E side Turkey Creek, N side Susy Bowells Branch adj. his own & David Reeds . . . 25 Sept 1766 Wm Tryon

DICKSON, ROBERT File no. 961 (229); Gr. no. 216; Bk. 18, 21 (17, 28)
220 A between Cataba & Broad River on a branch of Allisons Creek . . . 24 Dec 1763 Arthur Dobbs

DICKSON, THOMAS File no. 2474; Gr. no. 413; Bk. 23, p. 285
226 A on branches of Allisons Creek . . . Wilsons Corner . . .
Venables corner . . . 29 Apr 1768 Wm Tryon

DICKSON, WILLIAM File no. 091
Plat: Surveyed for William Dickson 600 (640) A on S fork
Packolet including Hutchins Cabbin, surveyed for Hutchins
. . . 29 Mar 1766 Wm Dickson, Sur. John Clark & James
Howard, CB

DICKSON, WILLIAM File no. 47 (159); Gr. no. 110; Bk. 13, p.
391 (15, 484)
200 A between Crowders Creek and Catauba River on a
branch of Mill Creek adj. James Craigs & Robert Leepers lines
. . . 22 Apr 1763 [This grant is partly in NC and partly in SC]

DICKSON, WILLIAM File no. 2164; Gr. no. 223; Bk. 23, p. 121
200 A on S side Lawsons fork of Packolett above Jones Waggon Road . . . McMurdys . . . 26 Oct 1767 Wm Tryon

DICKSON, WILLIAM File no. 2163; Gr. no. 222; Bk. 23, p. 121
300 A on S side Pacolett on both sides Richland Creek about
a mile above John Dennis . . . 26 Oct 1767 Wm Tryon

DICKSON, WILLIAM File no. 2162; Gr. no. 221; Bk. 23, p. 120
300 A on head branch of Fair forrest Creek between Tyger
River and Packolett On E side John Princes . . . 26 Oct 1767
Wm Tryon

DICKSON, WILLIAM File no. 2161; Gr. no. 220; Bk. 23, p. 120
130 A on W side Catawba on Stoney fork of Fishing Creek
called Prices branch adj. Thomas Price, John Thomas and his
own lines . . . 26 Oct 1767 Wm Tryon

DICKSON, WILLIAM File no. 1007 (275); Gr. no. 30; Bk. 18, p.
76 (17, 79)
200 A on a branch of E side Bullocks Creek above Michael
Dicksons Survey . . . 2 Nov 1764 Arthur Dobbs

DICKSON, WILLIAM File no. 110 (224); Gr. no. 97; Bk. 13, p.
435 (17, 11)
400 A on a Rocky fork of Fishing Creek . . . by the Cobus or
James Kuykendalls corner . . . William Prices line . . . below
the Waggon Road . . . Andrew Lekys late survey . . . 23 Dec
1763 Arthur Dobbs

DICKSON, WILLIAM File no. 111 (225); Gr. no. 98; Bk. 13, p.
435 (17, 11)
300 A on both sides Rockey fork of Fishing Creek . . . Andrew Lekys corner . . . 23 Dec 1763 Arthur Dobbs

DICKSON, WILLIAM File no. 1352 (625); Gr. no. 25; Bk. 18, p. 255 (17, 281)
640 A on waters of fishing Creek & Turkey Creek ... between Wm Henrys, Edward Laceys, James McNabbs, Price, John Thomas, John Fondrens lines ... 25 Sept 1766 Wm Tryon

DICKSON, WILLIAM File no. 1353 (626); Gr. no. 26; Bk. 18, p. 255 (17, 281)
350 A on S side Stoney fork of Fishing Creek, between Edward Crofts & William Haggarties ... Hannas line ... 25 Sept 1766 Wm Tryon

DILL, JOHN File no. 1942; Bk. 23, p. 11
250 A adj. W side Broad River 25 Apr 1767 Wm Tryon

DOBBS, FRANCIS File no. 2270; Gr. no. 49; Bk. 23, p. 179
400 A on both sides of S fork Tygar River including a shoal and mill seat 26 Oct 1767 Wm Tryon

DOBB, FRANCIS File no. 2271; Gr. no. 50; Bk. 23, p. 179
200 A on N side Tygar above Francis Willsons Land 26 Oct 1767 Wm Tryon

DOBB [DODD?], FRANCIS File no. 2415; Gr. no. 214; Bk. 23, p. 224
200 A on N fork Tyger River adj. Francis Wilson, John Nesbitt & his own land ... 28 Apr 1768

DOSSON, BARTHOLOMEW File no. 2314; Gr. no. 60; Bk. 23, p. 195
190 A on SW side S fork Fishing Creek ... John Rottan, Alexander Bounds, John Dennis ... 28 Apr 1768 Wm Tryon

DOWD, RICHARD File no. 552 (1278); Gr. no. 108; Bk. 17, p. 210 (18, 191)
150 A on a branch of Stoney fork of Fishing Creek above Hugh McClellands land ... old Broad River Road ... 30 Oct 1765 Wm Tryon

DRAPER, THOMAS File no. 2015; Gr. no. 440; Bk. 23, p. 37
451 A on Mill Creek of Packlett River ... adj. Joab Mitchell, Charles Coleman ... 27 Apr 1767 Wm Tryon

DUNCAN, PATRICK File no. 2393; Gr. no. 191; Bk. 23, p. 219
150 A on Cedar fork, a N branch of Fishing Creek adj. his own land ... 28 Apr 1768 Wm Tryon

DUNCAN, WILLIAM File no. 2361; Gr. no. 112; Bk. 23, p. 204
300 A on Beaverdam Creek of Fairforest 28 Apr 1768 Wm Tryon

ELLIOT, JOHN File no. 666; Gr. no. 66; Bk. 17, p. 288
200 A on waters of Fishing Creek . . . Thomas Hawkings corner . . . 25 Sept 1766 Wm Tryon

ERWIN, JNO File no. 1445; Gr. no. 286; Bk. 18, p. 303
150 A on S bank Tyger River . . . adj. Robert Cowdens line . . . . 26 Sept 1766 Wm Tryon

EVANS, JABES File no. 096; Entry no. 756
Warrant: Unto Jabez Evans 150 A adj. his own land including a fishing place and adj. Francis Beatys Island . . . 18 Apr 1767 Wm Tryon

FALLS, WILLIAM File no. 1161 (433); Gr. no. 53; Bk. 18, p. 143 (17, 158)
640 A on Turkey fork of Baals Creek about a mile from John Bridges . . . 6 Apr 1765 Wm Tryon

FANNING, JAMES File no. 2237; Gr. no. 392; Bk. 23, p. 154
200 A on Thicketty . . . 26 Oct 1767 Wm Tryon

FANNING, JAMES, JR., & WILLIAM SIMS File no. 1965; Gr. no. 317; Bk. 23, p. 15
Plat: Feb 6, 1767, Surveyed for William Sims & James Fanning Junr 400 A on both sides Gilkeys Creek of Thicketty P Zach Bullock, Sur. Hugh Wilson, Abraham Fanning, CB Iss. 25 Apr 1767

FANNING, JAMES, JR., & WILLIAM SIMS File no. 1966; Gr. no. 318; Bk. 23, p. 15
Plat: Feb 6, 1766, Surveyed for William Sims & James Fanning Junr . . . 400 A on Gilkeys Creek of Thicketty . . . Jeffress line . . . their own line . . . Zach Bullock [Sur.] Abraham Fanning, Hugh Wilson, CB Iss. 25 Apr 1767

FANNING, JAMES, JR., & WILLIAM SIMS File no. 2003; Gr. no. 428; Bk. 23, p. 34
Plat: Feb 6, 1767, Surveyed for William Sims & James Fanning Junr 400 A on both sides Gilkeys Creek of Thicketty . . . Zach Bullock, Sur. Abraham Fanning, Hugh Wilson, CB Iss. 25 Apr 1767

FANNING, JAMES File no. 2238; Gr. no. 393; Bk. 23, p. 154
300 A on both sides Bullocks Creek . . . Loves Creek . . . 26 Oct 1767 Wm Tryon

FERGUSON, MOSES File no. 098; Entry no. 252
Warrant: Unto Moses Ferguson, 300 A on N fork Tyger below Robert Miller Junior's land . . . 24 Oct 1765 Wm Tryon
Plat: March 1, 1766, Surveyed for Moses Ferguson, land on

main South fork of Tyger above Barnets land . . . Zach Bullock [Sur.] Thomas Clark, Joseph Thomson, CB

FIFER, JOHN File no. 0101
Plat: Surveyed for John Fifer, 500 A on S fork Packolett River above Maiden Meadow . . . below Hutchins's corner . . . 29 Mar 1766 Wm Dickson, Sur. John Clark & James Howard, C.B.

FISHER, NICHOLAS File no. 1658; Gr. no. 184; Bk. 18, p. 378
200 A on both sides Buffelow Creek about a mile from the mouth . . . Robert Humphrey line . . . 25 Apr 1767 Wm Tryon

FLEMMING, JOHN File no. 0100
Plat: Surveyed for John fleming 290 A on waters of Allison Creek adj. John McKnit Alexander & John Buchanan . . . Dec 28, 1768 . . . Peter Johnston, Sur. John Hall, Wm McDowall, C.B.

FLOYD, MATTHEW File no. 5 (18); Gr. no. 16; Bk. 13, p. 383 (15, 474)
Plat: Surveyed for Matthew Floyd, 200 A on Et side Moores Creek, A Branch of Broad River above his home place . . . Thomas Morris' line . . . 21 Mar 1763 William Dickson, D.S. James Miles, David Dickson, Cha. Bear. Iss. 19 Apr 1763

FLOYD, MATHEW File no. 505 (1231); Gr. no. 60; Bk. 17, p. 200 (18, 182)
300 A on waters of Bullocks Creek . . . Moss Weights land . . . 28 Oct 1765 Wm Tryon

FORGUSON, MOSES File no. 793 (1515); Gr. no. 468; Bk. 17, p. 371 (18, 339)
640 A on main So fork of Tyger Creek [sic] . . . 27 Sept 1766 Wm Tryon

FONDREN, JOHN & JAMES HANNAH File no. 0106; Entry no. 901
Warrant: Unto John Fondren & James Hannah 400 A on S fork Fishing Creek, adj. Andrew McNab, Thomas Davis . . . Edward Lases . . . 18 Apr 1767 Wm Tryon
Plat: Surveyed for John Fondren & James Hannah 400 A on waters of S fork Fishing Creek . . . Andrew McNabbs, Davises, Thomas Raineys . . . Wm Dickson, Sur. 12 Augt 1767 [No CB]

FOSTER, ANDREW File no. 0109
Plat: Survey'd for Andrew Foster 100 A on the No side of Fair Forrest on Harris's Branch Including his Improvement

and Mill Seat . . . 24 Decr 1766 1766 Wm Dickson, Sur John Kelsey, John Foster, CB

FOSTER, ANDREW File no. 0108; Entry no. 777
Warrant: Unto Andrew Foster, 200 A on the North side of fereforest [sic] on harrises Creek Below James Mays Survey and above his house . . . 10 Apr 1767
Plat: Survey'd for Andrew Foster 200 A on No side of Fair Forrest on both sides of Harris's Creek Between his own and James Mayes's lines . . . 16 June 1767 Wm Dickson, Sur. John Foster & John Kelsey, C.C.

FULTON, SAMUEL File no. 2564; Gr. no. 580; Bk. 23, p. 315
319 A on Bullocks Creek . . . McAdowes corner . . . Riggs line . . . Thomas Prices line . . . Flintons corner . . . 29 Apr 1768 Wm Tryon

GARVIN, JOHN File no. 850 (1571); Gr. no. 82; Bk. 17, p. 392 (18, 358)
150 A on head waters of a branch of Turkey Creek . . . near his own line . . . 25 Apr 1767 Wm Tryon

GARVIN, JOHN File no. 851 (1572); Gr. no. 83; Bk. 17, p. 392 (18, 359)
147 A on waters of Turkey Creek adj. his own land . . . Cedar fork . . . 25 Apr 1767 Wm Tryon

GARDNER, JOHN File no. 2409; Gr. no. 208; Bk. 23, p. 222
130 A on E side Bullocks Creek adj. John Stephensons and Andrew Dunbars land . . . including the improvement he lives on . . . 28 Apr 1768 Wm Tryon

GIBBS, JOHN File no. 0114
Plat: Dec 8, 1766, Surveyed for John Gibbs, 300 A on Duggins' Branch of Fairforest . . . Duggins corner . . . P Zach Bullock [sur.] Giles Tillet, Zach Gibbs, CB

GIBBS, ZACH'R File no. 0115
Plat: Dec 9, 1768, Surveyed for Zachariah Gibbs, 400 A on both sides Fairforrest Creek . . . Duggans lines . . . Zach Bullock [surv] James Tillet, John Gibbs, CB

GIBSON, GEORGE File no. 2562; Gr. no. 578; Bk. 23, p. 314
190 A on both sides bullocks Creek . . . Riggs line . . . Gayan Moores line . . . Stinsons line . . . John Smiths corner . . . 29 Apr 1768 Wm Tryon

GILLELAND, ARCHIBALD File no. 1157 (429); Gr. no. 48; Bk. 18, p. 142 (17, 157)
300 A Mecklenburg, on a Hicory Branch that runs into Fair

Forest Joining William Plummers line . . . 6th April 1765 Wm Tryon

GILL, JOHN File no. 933 (1654); Gr. no. 180; Bk. 17, p. 413 (18, 377)

500 A upon Crafts branch of S fork Fishing Creek . . . Johnstons & Conners line . . . Samuel Porters line . . . 25 Apr 1767 Wm Tryon

GILLHAM, CHARLES File no. 934 (1655); Gr. no. 181; Bk. 17, p. 414 (18, 377)

250 A on Stycys branch of Bullocks Creek . . . Sticys line . . . Alexander corner . . . 25 Apr 1767 Wm Tryon

GILLHAM, CHARLES File no. 1463 (735); Gr. no. 304; Bk. 18, p. 306 (17, 334)

248 A on E side Bullocks Creek, both sides Bells Creek . . . Bells line . . . Gilbert Delaps [sic] line . . . 26 Sept 1766 Wm Tryon

GILLHAM, EZEKIEL File no. 1464 (736); Gr. no. 305; Bk. 18, p. 307 (17, 335)

100 A on Et side Bullocks Creek . . . N side of Charles Gilhams survey . . . 26 Sept 1766 Wm Tryon

GILLHAM, THOMAS File no. 2125; Gr. no. 176; Bk. 23, p. 112

100 A on Bells Creek, a branch of Bullocks Creek . . . sd Gillhams line . . . 26 Apr 1767 Wm Tryon

GILLHAM, THOMAS File no. 1270 (544); Gr. no. 100; Bk. 18, 189 (17, 208)

300 A on waters of Bullocks Creek, on a branch of Bells Creek . . . Wm Hartgroves line . . . Shearers line . . . Charles Styes line . . . 30 Oct 1765 Wm Tryon

GLOVER, WILLIAM SENR File no. 834 (1555); Gr. no. 65; Bk. 17, p. 388 (18, 355)

340 A on ET branch of Turkey Creek below William Glover Juniors land . . . 25 Apr 1767 Wm Tryon

GOWDELOCK, ADAM File no. 2043; Gr. no. 472; Bk. 23, p. 42

300 A on both sides Thicketty Creek . . . Steans line . . . 27 Apr 1767 Wm Tryon

GOWDYLOCK, ADAM File no. 0122

Warrant: Unto Adam Gowddylock, 300 A on a Branch of Broad River . . . 23 Sept 1766 Wm Tryon

Two identical plats: Jan. 2, 1767, Surveyed for Adam Goudylock, 300 A on Thicketty Creek adj. Joseph Jolley . . . Joseph Jolley & William Jolley, CB

GOWDYLOCK, ADAM File no. 0123
Plat: Jan 1, 1767, Surveyed for Adam Gowdylock, 200 A on both sides Reedy Branch of Thicketty Creek . . . Collins line . . . P Zach Bullock, Sur. Joseph Jolley & John Gowdylock, CB

GREGORY, ISAAC File no. 2189; Gr. no. 248; Bk. 23, p. 125
200 A on S side Broad, on S fork Browns Creek above the waggon road . . . 26 Oct 1767 Wm Tryon

GRINDELL, JOHN File no. 829 (1550); Gr. no. 58; Bk. 17, p. 387 (18, 354)
150 A on both sides Packolet River . . . between the Swift Shoal and Carrol Shoal . . . 25 Apr 1767 Wm Tryon

GRINDELL, JOHN File no. 898 (1619); Gr. no. 143; Bk. 17, p. 404 (18, 370)
250 A on both sides Packolet adj. James Heweths at Carrols Shoal . . . 25 Apr 1767 Wm Tryon

HAILE, JOHN File no. 2230; Gr. no. 385; Bk. 23, p. 153
Plat: 17 Feb 1767, Survey'd for John Hail 289 A on Mill Creek of packlet about 1 mile above fair forrest path . . . Thomas Drapers corner . . . Zac Bullock, Sur. William Coleman, Joab Mitchel, CB Iss. 26 Oct 1767

HALL, JOHN File no. 2391; Gr. no. 189; Bk. 23, p. 219
Plat: Surveyed for John Hall 200 A on both sides Rockey Allisons Creek . . . Walter Davis corner . . . James Stevensons corner . . . 10 Feb 1767 . . . Peter Johnston, Sur. James Stevenson, Willm Whaley, CB Iss. 28 Apr 1768

HAMMETT, JAMES File no. 2458; Gr. no. 396; Bk. 23, p. 282
Plat: Surveyed for James Hammet 250 A on N side Fair Forrest on Kelseys Branch including his Improvement . . . 19 Dec 1767 Wm Dickson, Sur. James Hammet, John Gibbs, CB Iss. 29 Apr 1768

HANNAH, JAMES File no. 1255 (529); Gr. no. 89; Bk. 18, p. 187 (17, 305)
Plat: Surveyed for James Hannah, 300 A on S side Fishing Creek adj. William Haggertys and James Youngs lines . . . 29 June 1765 William Dickson, Surv. William Hanna jr., Joseph Scott, CB Iss. 30 Oct 1765

HANNAH, JAMES File no. 1246 (520); Gr. no. 75; Bk. 18, 185 (17, 203)
Plat: Surveyed for James Hannah 300 A on head waters of a branch of Turkey Creek, adj. Land he bought of Ephraim

McClaine ... 1 July 1765 William Dickson, Sur. James McNabb, Edward Lacey, CB Iss. 28 Oct 1765

HANNA, JAMES File no. 2169; Gr. no. 228; Bk. 23, p. 122
Warrant: Unto James Hanna, 300 A on head Branches of fishing Creek adj. Richard Bolde ... pattented land, formerly entered by John Wade ... 18 Apr 1767 Wm Tryon

Plat: Surveyed for James Hannah 146 A on S fork Fishing Creek on So side Waggon Road formerly surveyed for John Wade ... 12 Augt 1767 William Dickson, Sur. Charles Robeson, David Robeson, CB Iss. 26 Oct 1767

HANNA, JAMES File no. 1371 (644); Gr. no. 44; Bk. 18, p. 258 (17, 284)
Plat: Surveyed for James Hanna, 150 A on waters of S fork Fishing Creek, adj. land he bought of Ephraim McClain ... John Wades corner ... Benjamin Philips corner ... Samuel Raineys ... Balls lines ... 3 May 1766 William Dickson, Sur. John Wallace, David Roberson, CB Iss. 25 Sept 1766

HANNA, WILLIAM File no. 484 (1211); Gr. no. 138; Bk. 17, p. 172 (18, 157)
Plat: 20 Augt 1763, Surveyed for William Hannah, Senr, 340 A on S side Allisons Creek adj. William Davidson, John MacIlMurrays [sic] ... P William Dickson, D sur. John MacIlMurray, Joseph Hardin, CB Iss. 16 Apr 1765

HANNAH, WM File no. 1215 (488); Gr. no. 174; Bk. 18, p. 164 (17, 180)
Plat: [n.d.], Surveyed for William Hannah, 200 A on Stoney fork fishing Creek, adj. Thomas McClellands ... Francis Beaty, D Sur. John Harding, William Hannah, CB Iss. 16 Apr 1765

HANNAH, WILLIAM, JR. File no. 0135
Plat: Surveyed for William Hannah Jun., 180 A adj. Wm Hannah, Senr., Wm Dickson, Edward Croft, Thomas Black ... 8 Jan 1768 Wm Dickson, Sur. Robert Robinson, James Mahon, CB

HARDEN, JOHN File no. 857 (1578); Gr. no. 94, Bk. 17, p. 393 (18, 360)
Plat: Surveyed for John Harden 205 A on both sides Main Fishing Creek Joining and Between James Hannas and James Youngs Lines ... Cobres [?] Kuykendalls corner ... Lekyr [?] corner ... Hardens own land ... James Armstrongs corner ... 28 Apr 1766, William Dickson, Sur. John Wallace & Joseph Boggs, CB Iss. 25 Apr 1767

HARDIN, JOSEPH File no. 2413; Gr. no. 212; Bk. 23, p. 223
Plat: Survey'd for Joseph Hardin 200 A on Kings Creek about a mile above John Hardens . . . Jumping branch . . . August 3d 1767., Peter Johnston, Surv. William Lusk, John Mcklemurrey, CB Iss. 28 Apr 1768

HARDEN, JOSEPH File no. 893 (1614); Grk. no. 133; Bk. 17, p. 403 (18, 369)
Plat: Survey'd for Joseph Hardin, 300 A on waters of Kings Creek, on the So fork of Jumping Branch including the Glades below Whittecars Mountain . . . Jo. Greens path . . . 24 Feby 1767, Wm Dickson, Sur. John Hardin, & John Mackilmurry, C.B. Iss. Apr 25, 1767

HARDEN, JOSEPH File no. 1479 (751); Gr. no. 397; Bk. 18, p. 326 (17, 355)
Plat: June the 10th, 1766, Survey for Joseph Harden 84 A on Waters of Fishing Creek . . . Robert Gabb's corner . . . James Watsons Corner . . . P Zach Bullock Sur. [No CB], Iss. 26 Sept 1766

HARPER, ALEXANDER File no. 810 (1531); Gr. no. 10; Bk. 17, p. 377 (18, 345)
Plat: Apr 1765, Surveyed for Alexander Harper, 150 A upon Susan Bowls Branch, Turkey Creek adj. John Kellys line . . . Jno McK Alexander, Sur. Francis Prince, David Reed, C.C. Iss. 22 Apr 1767

HARPER, JOHN File no. 2454; Gr. no. 324; Bk. 23, p. 246
Plat: Surveyed for Robert Harper 200 A on waters of Turkey Creek adj. Kelleys, Gyse & his own land . . . 7 Dec 1767 Peter Johnston, Sur. David Stevenson, Alexr Harper, CB Iss. 29 Apr 1768

HARPER, ROBERT File no. 1497 (775); Gr. no. 440; Bk. 18, p. 334 (17, 365)
Plat: Surveyed for ROBERT HARPER, 200 A on waters of Turkey Creek on N side Morris Mill Branch . . . 28 Aug 1765 William Dickson, Sur. James Hamilton, Garrot Morris, CB Iss. 26 Sept 1766

HARRIS, ROBERT File no. 0138
Plat: Survey'd for Robert Harris 500 A on both sides of Harris's Creek, waters of fair-forrest Including the fork and James Harris's old survey . . . James Mayes corner . . . Bullocks Corner . . . Geo. Parks line . . . 29th Decr 1767 By Wm Sharp, Survr. James Mayes & Geo. Parks, C: Bear.

HARRIS, ROBERT File no. 2082; Gr. no. 52; Bk. 23, p. 91
Plat: Survey'd for Robert Harris 250 A on waters of Harris Creek falling into fair forrest Joining Parks & Bullocks lines . . . John Parks Corner . . . George parks line . . . 29th May 1767 By Wm Sharp, Survr. George Parks & John Sharp, Ch: Bear. Iss. 26 Oct 1767

HARRISON, NATHANIEL File no. 2216; Gr. no. 371; Bk. 23, p. 150
Plat: 28 Aug 1765, Surveyed for Nathaniel Harrison 140 A on both sides Clarks fork of Bullocks Creek . . . Blacks line . . . W Sims, Sur. Thos Harrisson, Robert Black, CB Iss. 26 Oct 1767

HATHLEY, EWING File no. 600 (1327); Gr. no. 350; Bk. 17, p. 259 (18, 234)
Plat: Aug 14, 1765, Surveyed for Ewing Hathley, 200 A adj. E side Broad . . . Pr. William Sims, S.M.C. Ewings [sic] Hathley, George Hathley, CB Iss. 30 Oct 1765

HATHLEY, GEORGE File no. 1291 (565); Gr. no. 294; Bk. 18, p. 225 (17, 247)
Plat: Surveyed for George Hathley, 100 A adj. E side Broad River . . . P William Sims, S.M.C. Ewing Hathley & John Shelton, CB 14 Aug 1765 Iss. 30 Oct 1765

HAWKINS, THOMAS File no. 1311 (584); Gr. no. 316; Bk. 18, p. 229 (17, 252)
Plat: Surveyed for Thomas Hawkins, 200 A on waters of Fishing Creek adj. Dickies line . . . Mr. Palmers line . . . Blaney Mills line . . . 20 Sept 1765 William Dickson, Sur. Martin Armstrong, John Grindall, CB Iss. 30 Oct 1765

HEARTNESS, JOHN File no. 1674 (953); Gr. no. 211; Bk. 18, p. 382 (17, 419)
Plat: Surveyed for John Hartness, 200 A on E side Bullocks Creek on Smith branch . . . 8 Apr 1766, William Dickson, Sur. Barnabas Henly, John Smith, CB Iss. 25 Apr 1767

HEARTNESS, JOHN File no. 1651 (930); Gr. no. 177; Bk. 18, p. 377 (17, 413)
Plat: Surveyed for John Heartness 200 A on Bullocks Creek including his own improvement . . . adj. Riggs, John Smith, Armstrong, Handley [n.d.], By Jno. McK. Alexander, Sur. John Gardner, James Tod, CB. Iss. 25 Apr 1767

HENDERSON, RICHARD File no. 2246; Gr. no. 401; Bk. 23, p. 155
Plat: Survey'd for Richard Henderson, 600 A on Both sides

No fork of Packlett . . . Margaret Campbells Line . . . John Wilsons Corner . . . Augt 15th 1767, P Zach Bullock. Jonathan Chisshim & William Monrupty, CB Iss. 26 Oct 1767

HENDERSON, ROBERT File no. 2449; Gr. no. 318; Bk. 23, p. 245
Plat: Survey'd for Robt Henderson 300 A on S fork Packelet on both sides Cubb Creek . . . 12 Jan 1768 Wm Sharp, Sur. Chas Moore, Wm Sharpe, CB Iss. 29 Apr 1768

HENDERSON, ROBERT File no. 1740; Gr. no. 272; Bk. 20, p. 466
Plat: Surveyed for Robt Henderson, 300 A on both sides Lawson fork of Packelet, adj. JOHNATHAN NEWMAN . . . 5 Jan 1768 . . . WM SHARP Sur. Joseph Jones & David Davis, CB. Iss. 4 May 1769

HENDERSON, ROBERT File no. 2438; Gr. no. 305; Bk. 23, p. 243
Plat: Survey'd for Robert Henderson, 300 A on N side Tyger on both sides the Dutchmans Creek . . . adj. Andrew Simysons line . . . 31 Dec 1767 . . . By Wm Sharp, Surv. Chas Moore, Robt Miller, CB Iss. 29 Apr 1768

HENLEY, BARNABAS, File no. 2054; Gr. no. 586; Bk. 23, p. 65
Plat: Barnabas Henley, 200 A on Et side Bullocks Creek on Nathan branch . . . Wm Adoos corner . . . John Hartness' line . . . 8 Apr 1766 William Dickson, Sur. John Smith, John Riggs, CB Iss. 27 Apr 1767

HENRY, JAMES File no. 932 (1653); Gr. no. 179; Bk. 17, p. 413 (18, 377)
Plat: Surveyed for James Henry, 100 A on the Ridge Between Fishing Creek & Rocky Creek both sides Henry Run . . . Jno Mck. Alexander, Dur. Alexander Brown, Will Sample, CB [no date] Iss. 25 Apr 1767

HENRY, THOMAS File no. 250 (982); Gr. no. 11; Bk. 17, p. 53 (18, 50)
Plat: [nd], Surveyed for Thomas Henry, 600 A on Cherokee Creek about 2 miles from Cherrokee foard of Broad River including Joseph Clements Improvements . . . By Francis Beaty John Neill & Benja. Shaw, CB Iss. 21 Apr 1764

HENRY, WILLIAM File no. 1127 (396); Gr. no. 13; Bk. 18, p. 136 (17, 151)
Plat: Surveyed for Wm Henry 336 A on Reedy branch of Allison Creek, on S side of the Little Mountain including his

own Improvment adj. Barrs land . . . By Francis Beaty, D Surv. [nd] David Watson, Thomas Clark, CB. Iss. 6 Apr 1765

HENRY, WILLIAM File no. 2402 (2124); Gr. no. 200; Bk. 23, 221 (23, 112)
Plat: Surveyed for William Henry 488 A on S fork Fishing Creek adj. John Ker, Oliver Wallace . . . 23 Dec 1767 Peter Johnston, Sur. George McQuowns, James Wallace, CB Iss. 28 Apr 1768

HENRY, WILLIAM File no. 1535 (814); Gr. no. 14; Bk. 18, p. 346 (17, 378)
Plat: Oct 1765, Surveyed for William Henry 190 A between S & N fork Fishing Creek . . . Samuel McCance's [?] line . . . Saml Neelys line . . . Hugh Whitesides line . . . William Neelys line . . . Elliott's line . . . Jno McK. Alexander, Sur. Alexr Brown, Saml Neely, C.C. Iss. 22 Apr 1767

HICKS, RICHARD JUNR File no. 2377; Gr. no. 137; Bk. 23, p. 209
Plat: Feb 6, 1768, Surveyed for Richard Hix, Junr, 187 A on S side Broad . . . James Fannings . . . Robert Spooner Baleys line . . . Zach Bullock, Sur. Robert Spooner Bailey, Jno Foster, CB Iss. 28 Apr 1768

HICKS, RICHARD File no. 2378; Gr. no. 136; Bk. 23, p. 209
Plat: Feb 6, 1767, Surveyed for Richard Hicks, 180 A on Broad River, N side . . . mouth of Dry Creek . . . Zac Bullock, Surv. Christr. Hicks, John Suggs, CB Iss. 28 Apr 1768

HILLHOUSE, JNO File no. 1362 (635); Gr. no. 35; Bk. 18, p. 257 (17, 183)
Plat: Surveyed for John Hillhouse, 180 A on W side Turkey Creek on Hillis' Spring Branch . . . adj. Reydairius Clarks line . . . William Hillhouse . . . 9 Apr 1766 William Dickson, Sur. William Hillhouse, John Riggs, CB Iss. 25 Sept 1766

HILLHOUSE, WILLIAM File no. 1361 (634); Gr. no. 34; Bk. 18, p. 256 (17, 282)
Plat: Surveyed for WILLIAM HILLHOUSE, 200 A on W side Turkey Creek between John Brandson and James Walkers . . . 9 Apr 1766 . . . William Dickson, Surv. John Hillhouse, John Riggs, C.B. Iss. 25 Sept 1766

HOLLINSWORTH, ABRAHAM File no. 237 (969); Gr. no. 47; Bk. 17, p. 40 (18, 35)
Plat: Surveyed for Abraham Hollingsworth, 145 A on S side Broad River, on both sides Cane Creek below his own land . . . 11 Aug 1763 William Dickson, Surv. William Hollingsworth, Robert Willson, CB Iss. 15 Feb 1764

HOOPER, THOMAS File no. 2053; Gr. no. 585; Bk. 23, p. 65
Plat: Surveyed for Thomas Hooper, 150 A on N side and in the Islands of Broad River . . . Ninety Nine Islands . . . 2 Augt 1765 . . . William Dickson, Surv. Thomas Hooper, Manin Gore, CB Iss. 27 Apr 1767

HOOPER, THOMAS File no. 1396 (669); Gr. no. 69; Bk. 18, 263 (17, p. 289)
Plat: Surveyed for Thomas Hooper, 160 A on W side Broad River including part of an Island . . . mouth of Enos Hoopers Creek . . . 22 Augt 1765 William Dickson, Surv. Thomas Hooper, Mannin Gore, CB Iss. 25 Sept 1766

HOWARD, JAMES File no. 2153; Gr. no. 212; Bk. 23, p. 119
Plat: Surveyed for James Howard, 250 A on the No fork of Packolet Joining and Between the lines of Elisabeth Clark and Alexander Kill Patrik including some beaverdams on a small Creek . . . 10th June 1767 Wm Dickson, Surv. John Moore & Jo. Dickson, C Bear Iss. 26 Oct 1767

HOWARD, JAMES File no. 0167
Plat: Surveyed for James Hutchins 400 A on both sides of the No fork of Seluda above the main forks including the foard of the Cherokee Path . . . 28 March 1766 William Dickson, Survr. John Clark and James Howard, Cha. Bear

HOWARD, PETER File no. 2360; Gr. no. 111; Bk. 23, p. 204
Plat: March 15, 1766, Surveyed for Peter Howard, 200 A on Island Creek [No Surveyor given] Patrick Moore, Peter Howard, CB Iss. 28 Apr 1768

HUGHS, RICHARD File no. 871 (1592); Gr. no. 108; Bk. 17, p. 397 (18, 363)
Plat: 31 Dec 1766, Surveyed for Richard Hughs, 150 A on W side Broad River about 1/2 mile above Loves Waggon Foard including his own Imprvt . . . Wm Dickson, Survr. Charles Crain, Joseph Polston, CB Iss. 25 Apr 1767

HUGHS, RICHARD File no. 2150; Gr. no. 208; Bk. 23, p. 118
Plat: Surveyed for Richard Hughs, 100 A on W side Broad River above his own land . . . on the River bank . . . 18 June 1767 Wm Dickson, Sur. Jo Dickson Wm Winters, CB Iss. 26 Oct 1767

HUTCHINS, JAMES File no. 0180
Plat: Surveyed for James Hutchins, 640 A on both sides 640 A below Joseph Whites . . . William Dickson Surv. [nd] Anthony Hutchins, Joseph White, CB

HUTCHINS, JAMES File no. 0181
Plat: Surveyed for James Hutchins, 640 A on both sides S fork Packolet . . . John Crawford . . . [nd] . . . William Dickson, Sur. Anthony Hutchins, Joseph White, CB

HUTCHINS, JAMES File no. 0182
Plat: Surveyed for James Hutchins 300 A on middle fork of Tyger River below the Glass Mountain about 2 or 3 miles below the Cherokee Path . . . 29 Mar 1766 William Dickson, Surv. 29 Mar 1766 John Clark, James Howard, CB

HUTCHINS, JAMES File no. 0183
Plat: Surveyed for James Hutchins, 300 A on middle fork Tyger River . . . Indian graves . . . about 2 miles below the Cherokee path . . . 29 Mar 1766 William Dickson, Surv.

HUTCHINS, JAMES File no. 0184
Plat: Surveyed for James Hutchins, 640 A on N fork Seluda 3 or 4 miles above the Cherokee path . . . 28 Mar 1766 William Dickson, Surv. John Clark, James Howard, CB

HUTCHINS, JAMES File no. 0185
Plat: Surveyed for James Hutchins, 400 A on S fork Pacolet called Pretty Meadow near 2 miles above Batchlor Hall . . . 31 Mar 1766 William Dickson, Surv. [same CB]

HUTCHINS, JAMES File no. 0186
Plat: Surveyed for James Hutchins 200 A on N fork Seluda 28 Mar 1766 William Dickson, Surv. [Same CB]

HUTCHINS, JAMES File no. 0187
Plat: Surveyed for James Hutchins 500 A on waters of Broad River above the Maiden Meadow above Mr. Lyon's land . . . 29 Mar 1766 William Dickson, Surv. [Same CB]

HUTCHINS, JAMES File no. 0188
Plat: Surveyed for James Hutchins, 400 A on middle Tyger River, about a mile below the Cherokee path . . . 29 Mar 1766 William Dickson, Surv. [Same CB]

HUTCHINS, JAMES File no. 0189
Plat: Surveyed for James Hutchins 500 A on N fork Seluda about 2 miles above the Cherokee path . . . 28 Mar 1766 William Dickson, Surv [Same CB]

HUTCHINS, JAMES File no. 0190
Plat: Surveyed for James Hutchins, 640 A on S fork Packolett, a place called Batchelors Hall . . . 29 Mar 1766 William Dickson, Surv. [Same CB]

HUTCHINS, JAMES File no. 0191
Plat: Surveyed for James Hutchins, 200 A on N fork Packolett [nd] William Dickson Surv. Anthony Hutchins, Joseph White, CB

HUTCHINS, JAMES File no. 0192
Plat: Surveyed for James Hutchins, 300 A on N branch middle fork Tyger . . . 29 Mar 1766 William Dickson; John Clark, James Howard, CB

HUTCHINS, JAMES File no. 0193
Plat: Surveyed for James Hutchins 300 A on S side S fork Packolett on Cub Creek . . . 1 Apr 1766 William Dickson, Surv. John Clark, James Howard, CB

HUTCHINS, JAMES File no. 0194
Plat: Surveyed for James Hutchins, 300 A on No fork of Packolet a little below the Mountain . . . above the mouth of Skiaika's branch [probably meant for Skyuka] . . . below the old Indian Townhouse . . . 1 Apr 1766 William Dickson, Surv Anthony Hutchins, Joseph White, CB

IRWIN, JOHN File no. 717; Gr. no. 286; Bk. 17, p. 331
Plat: [nd], Surveyed for John Irwin, 150 A on S side Tyger in Robt Cowdens line . . . by Jno McK. Alexander, Sur Iss. 26 Sept 1766 Robert Cowdon & Moses Wily, C.C.

IRWIN, ROBERT File no. 1313 (586); Gr. no. 318; Bk. 18, p. 229 (17, 252)
Plat: Surveyed for Robert Irwin, 300 A on both sides fair Forrest Creek including the mouth of McClures branch adj. John Willson, James Means . . . 6 Sept 1765 William Dickson, Surv. James Mackilwean, James Means, CB Iss. 30 Oct 1765

IRWIN, ROBERT File no. 1538 (817); Gr. no. 17; Bk. 18, p. 346 (17, 379)
200 A on both sides a branch of fair forrest Creek near one mile Wt from George Storys . . . 23 Apr 1767 Wm Tryon

IRWIN, ROBERT File no. 2073; Gr. no. 42; Bk. 23, p. 89
200 A adj. S side Tyger River about 2 miles above John Irwins patent . . . 26 Oct 1767 Wm Tryon

IRWIN, WILLIAM & NATHANIEL File no. 1643 (922); Gr. no. 168; Bk. 18, p. 375 (17, 410)
200 A on waters of Turkey Creek between Loves & Burlesons fork . . . Thomas Garvins corner . . . Loves land . . . 25 Apr 1767 Wm Tryon

JAMESON, JAMES File no. 2497; Gr. no. 462; Bk. 23, p. 291
100 A on E side Broad adj. William Willson including his Improvement at the head of a Hollow . . . 29 Apr 1768

JAMESON, JAMES File no. 1241 (515); Gr. no. 70; Bk. 18, p. 184 (17, 202)
200 A on waters of Bullocks Creek both sides of the road above Charles Stye land . . . John Brandons line . . . 28 Oct 1765 Wm Tryon

JARROT, JOHN File no. 2563; Gr. no. 579; Bk. 23, p. 315
194 A on Broad River . . . Daniel Richardsons corner on Bullocks Creek . . . including an Island . . . 29 Apr 1768 Wm Tryon

JEFFERSON, NATHANIEL File no. 1310; Gr. no. 228; Bk. 18, p. 228
300 A on both sides Thicketty Creek . . . 30 Oct 1765

JEFFERSON, NATHANIEL File no. 583; Gr. no. 315; Bk. 17, p. 251
300 A on both sides Thicketty Creek including the mouth of Gilkeys Creek and adj. James Fanning & Joseph Jolly . . . 30 Oct 1765 Wm Tryon

JOHNSON, PETER File no. 0206
Plat: Oct 20, 1768, Surveyed for Peter Johnston, 300 A on both sides Fair Forest Creek . . . Zac Bullock, Sur. Thomas Case & John Portman, Junr., CB

JOHNSTON, WILLIAM File no. 2115; Gr. no. 165; Bk. 23, p. 110
100 A on both sides Abbisons [sic] Creek . . . Willsons line . . . Parkers line . . . Barrens . . . 26 Oct 1767 Wm Tryon

JOHNSTON, WILLIAM File no. 2138; Gr. no. 190; Bk. 23, p. 115
100 A on W side Broad, both sides Gilkeys Creek . . . Gilkeys land . . . 26 Oct 1767 Wm Tryon

JOLLY, JOSEPH File no. 2031; Gr. no. 456; Bk. 23, p. 40
600 A on both sides Thicketty adj. Nathaniel Jeffers[on] . . . 27 Apr 1767 Wm Tryon

JONES, JOSEPH File no. 0208
Plat: Feb 26, 1768, Surveyed for Joseph Jones 200 A on N fork Tygar . . . McRee line . . . Zach Bullock Joseph Jones, Joseph Thompson, CB

JONES, JOSEPH File no. 2285; Gr. no. 195; Bk. 23, p. 181
200 A on both sides N fork Tygar river . . . 26 Oct 1767 Wm Tryon

JONES, MOSES File no. 0209
Warrant: Unto Moses Jones 200 A on both sides Thicketty Creek below Millars land 25 Sept 1766 Wm Tryon
Plat: Dec 31, 1767, Surveyed for Moses Jones 200 A on Thicketty Creek adj. John Millers land ... Zach Bullock [Surv.] James Bridges, William Richardson, CB

JORDAN, JOHN File no. 2249; Gr. no. 404; Bk. 23, p. 156
100 A on head of Allisons Creek adj. his old line ... James Willsons line ... Wm Henrys line ... 26 Oct 1767 Wm Tryon

KELLEY, JNO File no. 1055 (323); Gr. no. 236; Bk. 18, p. 113 (17, 126)
300 A on waters of Turkey Creek about half a mile SW of Wades old Store near Harper line ... 16 Nov 1764 Arthur Dobbs

KELLY, JOSEPH File no. 0216
Plat: Surveyed for Joseph Keller, 178 A on waters of N fork Tyger adj. Josh. Millers Mill Seat, David Davis ... July 7, 1766 Peter Johnston, Sur. Alexr McCorler [?], Joseph Thompson, CB

KERR, JOHN JR File no. 2291; Gr. no. 207; Bk. 23, p. 182
200 A on both sides middle fork of Tygar river nearly joining Jones land ... 26 Oct 1767 Wm Tryon

KERR, JOHN JR & ROBERT McNABB File no. 956 (1677); Gr. no. 214; Bk. 17, p. 420 (18, 382)
Warrant: Unto Robert McNab and John Ker, Jnr ... on both sides a small branch of S fork Fishing Creek adj. Samuel Guys line ... 27 Sept 1766 Wm Tryon
Plat: Surveyed for Robert McNab & John Ker Hunr ... 100 A ... Hugh Bratons line ... Adams line ... Thos Raineys line ... Leeckes corner ... John Moores line ... 6 Jan 1767 Peter Johnston, Sur. John Graham, Samuel Lacey, CB Iss. 25 Apr 1767

KER, PATRICK File no. 1724; Gr. no. 90; Bk. 20, p. 134
Plat: [nd], Surveyed for Patrick Kerr, 126 A on E side Catawba, Bum Branch of Long Creek ... adj. James Brown, John Allen, Sarah Hannah ... By Jno McK. Alexander ... John Allen, Robt Ker, C.C. Iss. 4 May 1769

KERR, ROBERT File no. 614 (1341); Bk. 17, p. 275
400 A on both sides S fork Fishing Creek ... Kuykendalls corner ... William Henrys ... McLeans line ... [resurveyed] 25 Sept 1754

KERR, ROBERT File no. 2116; Gr. no. 166; Bk. 23, p. 110
62 A on S fork Fishing Creek adj. his other survey, Widow Kuykendalls ... William Hennerys ... 26 Oct 1767 Wm Tryon

KILLPATRICK, ALEXANDER File no. 2154; Gr. no. 213; Bk. 23, p. 119
200 A on both sides of the No fork of Packolett adj. and between James Howard and Samuel Youngs lines ... 26 Oct 1767 ... Wm Tryon

KIMBRO, JOHN File no. 2538; Gr. no. 530; Bk. 23, p. 305
200 A on both sides Allisons Creek adj. Indian lands ... 29 Apr 1768 Wm Tryon

KNOX, DAVID File no. 0212
Plat: Surveyed for David Knox 300 A on waters of N fork Tyger adj. John Miller, John Brown ... dec 1, 1767 Peter Johnston, Sur Samuel Knox, Alexr Ree, CB

KNOX, JEAN File no. 2207; Gr. no. 361; Bk. 23, p. 148
300 A on middle fork of Tygar ... path from Joseph Jones to his old plantation ... Joseph Alexander ... 26 Oct 1767 Wm Tryon

KNOX, JOHN JR. File no. 2411; Gr. no. 210; Bk. 23, p. 223
300 A on waters of N fork Tygar river ... David Knox and John Browns land ... 28 Apr 1768 Wm Tryon

KNOX, SAMUEL File no. 2408; Gr. no. 207; Bk. 23, p. 222
200 A on waters of N fork of Tyger ... John Miller and David Knox ... 28 Apr 1768 Wm Tryon

KOLB, HARMAN File no. 1553 (832); Gr. no. 62; Bk. 18, p. 355 (17, 387)
Plat: Surveyed for Harman Kolb, 200 A on E side of Turkey Creek adj. Robert Dickson, Robert Adair, & James Stephensons line ... 9 Mar 1767 Wm Dickson, Sur Robert Adair, James Hamilton, CB Iss. 25 Apr 1767

KUYKENDAL, ABRAHAM File no. 50 (162); Gr. no. 130; Bk. 13, p. 393 (15, 486)
640 A on both sides Fishing Creek adj. his Brothers James and Peter Kuykendals and Andrew Woods line including his Improvement ... 22 Apr 1763 Arthur Dobbs

KUYKENDALL, PETER File no. 867 (1588); Gr. no. 104; Bk. 17, p. 396 (18, 362)
400 A on N side fishing Creek adj. Humphreys, Beatys, Millicans, & Armstrong ... 25 Apr 1767 Wm Tryon

KUYKENDALL, REBECCA File no. 1071 (339); Gr. no. 306; Bk. 18, p. 117 (17, 130)
300 A on waters of Fishing Creek adj. John Kuykendalls, Thomas Raineys. Edward Crofts . . . 16 Nov 1764 Arthur Dobbs

LACEY, EDWARD File no. 2500; Gr. no. 446; Bk. 23, p. 292
640 A on E side Broad River, waters of Turkey Creek on Susy Bowles branch, including the improvement he bought of Thomas Larney . . . Alexanders line . . . 29 Apr 1768 Wm Tryon

LACEY, EDWARD File no. 324 (1056); Gr. no. 237; Bk. 17, p. 126 (18, 113)
240 A on waters of S fork Fishing Creek on both sides the Waggon Road between Wm Adairs & Thomas Raineys lands . . . 16 Nov 1764 Arthur Dobbs

LACEY, EDWARD File no. 541 (1240); Gr. no. 69; Bk. 18, p. 184 (17, 202)
200 A on head waters of a branch of Turkey Creek near Robert Ewarts land 28 Oct 1765 Wm Tryon

LACEY, EDWARD File no. 1250 (524); Gr. no. 79; Bk. 18, p. 186 (17, 204)
300 A on waters of S fork Fishing Creek . . . above John Prices line . . . 28 Oct 1765 Wm Tryon

LACEY, EDWARD SENIOR File no. 2464; Gr. no. 403; Bk. 23, p. 283
300 A on waters of S fork Fishing Creek on head of flag branch . . . Mathias Ardises corner . . . Hugh Brattons line . . . Samuel Guys line . . . John Moores line . . . 29 Apr 1768 Wm Tryon

LACEY, SAMUEL & SAMUEL RAINEY File no. 2506; Gr. no. 472; Bk. 23, p. 293
400 A on S side S fork Fishing Creek on both sides of Loves fork . . . Benjamin Lewis & Nathaniel Alexanders corner . . . John Price . . . William Adairs line . . . 29 Apr 1768 Wm Tryon

LAFFERTY, PATRICK File no. 2310; Gr. no. 56; Bk. 23, p. 194
100 A on a branch of Broad River . . . 28 Apr 1768 Wm Tryon

LAUGHLAND, JOHN File no. 2293; Gr. no. 39; Bk. 23, p. 191
228 A on both sides Bullocks Creek 28 Apr 1768 Wm Tryon

LAYCOCK, JOHN File no. 1657 (936); Gr. no. 183; Bk. 18, p. 378 (17, 414)

200 A on E side of S fork Fishing Creek . . . Samuel Wherrys corner . . . 25 Apr 1767 Wm Tryon

LEEPER, ROBERT File no. 841 (1562); Gr. no. 72; Bk. 17, p. 390 (18, 357)
325 A on W side Cataba on Mill Creek . . . his own corner . . . William McCullohs line . . . 23 Apr 1767 Wm Tryon

LEWIS, PETER File no. 2231; Gr. no. 386; Bk. 23, p. 153
100 A on both sides Lawsons fork of Packolett above Jones road . . . 26 Oct 1767 Wm Tryon

LONDON, JOHN File no. 2555; Gr. no. 566; Bk. 23, p. 321
111 A on both sides Bullocks Creek . . . McAdos line . . . Bells corner . . . Loves line . . . 29 Apr 1768 Wm Tryon

LOVE, ALEXANDER File no. 890 (1611); Gr. no. 129; Bk. 17, p. 402 (18, 368)
216 A on waters of fishing Creek between his own, Ratchford & Scotts lines 25 Apr 1767 Wm Tryon

LOVE, ALEXANDER File no. 891 (1612); Gr. no. 130; Bk. 17, p. 402 (18, 368)
28 A on Dickies branch of Fishing Creek, adj. William Ratchford, James Millican 25 Apr 1767 Wm Tryon

LOVE, ALEXANDER File no. 2557; Gr. no. 568; Bk. 23, p. 312
32 A on head waters of Dickies branch of Fishing Creek adj. his own, James Millicans, Blany Mills, Michael Magarrotys being surplus land in lines of land he bought of Samuel Davison . . . 29 Apr 1768 Wm Tryon

LOVE, JOHN File no. 968 (236); Gr. no. 46; Bk. 18, p. 35 (17, 40)
130 A on E side Moores Creek otherwise called Turkey Creek, a branch of Broad River adj. his own land . . . Waggon Foard . . . Loves branch . . . 15 Feb 1764 Arthur Dobbs

LOVELETTY, MARSHALL File no. 2374; Gr. no. 134; Bk. 23, p. 208
200 A on Abbertons Creek . . . Thomas Loveletty corner . . . 28 Apr 1768 Wm Tryon

LUSK, ELIZABETH File no. 1546 (825); Gr. no. 54; Bk. 18, p. 353 (17, 386)
150 A on waters of fishing Creek on head of Long Branch . . . Robert Lusks lines . . . 25 Apr 1767 Wm Tryon

LUSK, JAMES File no. 2128; Gr. no. 179; Bk. 23, p. 113
70 A on W side fishing creek . . . Samuel Lusks line . . . James Muldoons line . . . 26 Oct 1767 Wm Tryon

LUSK, ROBERT File no. 940 (1661); Gr. no. 187; Bk. 17, p. 415 (18, 379)
200 A on both sides Thicketty Creek adj. John Steen . . . 25 Apr 1767 Wm Tryon

LUSK, ROBERT File no. 2429; Gr. no. 295; Bk. 23, p. 241
190 A on S side Thicketty Creek adj. his own, Goudelocks & Moores lines . . . 28 Apr 1768 Wm Tryon

LUSK, ROBERT File no. 1266 (540); Gr. no. 96; Bk. 18, p. 189 (17, 207)
250 A on a branch of Fishing Creek including the place he now lives on . . . 30 Oct 1765 Wm Tryon

McAFFEE, JAMES File no. 422 (1150); Gr. no. 41; Bk. 17, p. 156 (18, 141)
Warrant: Unto James McAffee Junr, 400 A on a branch of Turkey Creek . . . about 2 miles SW from Joseph Hardins . . . 21 Apr 1764 Arthur Dobbs
Plat: [nd], Surveyed for James McAffee Jurn, 296 A on E branch of Turkey Creek . . . Francis Beaty [Surv.], Joseph Harding, John McElmurry, CB Iss. 6 Apr 1765

McBRAYER, SAMUEL File no. 939 (1650); Gr. no. 176; Bk. 17, p. 412 (18, 376)
Warrant: Unto Samuel McBrayer, 200 A on W side Turkey Creek adj. Moors & Hillhous land including his own Improvement . . . 27 Sept 1766 Wm Tryon
Plat: Surveyed for Samuel McBrayer, 164 A on W side Turkey Creek including the Improvement he lives on . . . Moores, Hillhouses [nd] Jno Mck Alexander [surv.] John Riggs, John Durroh, CB Iss. 25 Apr 1767

McBRAYER, SAMUEL File no. 2498; Gr. no. 464; Bk. 23, p. 292
Warrant: Unto Samuel McBrier . . . 350 A on E side Bullocks Creek on Nathan Branch adj. Quails, Henley, Willsons lines . . . 23 Sept 1766 Wm Tryon
Plat: Surveyed for Samuel McBryer, 300 A on waters of Bullocks Creek, Nathans branch . . . Barnabas Henleys corner . . . Charles Quails line . . . Kerrs branch . . . Tius corner . . . 10 Mar 1767 William Dickson, Sur. John Riggs, William Hillhouse, CB Iss. 29 Apr 1768

McCANCE, ANDREW File no. 1249 (523); Gr. no. 78; Bk. 18, p. 185 (17, 204)
Warrant: Unto Andrew McCane, 250 A on fishing Creek adj. SAMUEL & THOMAS NEYLES [sic] . . . 6 Apr 1765 Wm Tryon
Plat: Surveyed for Andrew McCane, 350 A on Et side Fishing

Creek including his own Improvements . . . Thomas Neeleys . . . Samuel Neelys . . . 26 June 1765 William Dickson, [Surv.] Robt Neeley, Samuel Wherry, CB Iss. 28 Oct 1765

McCARTER, ALEX File no. 0237
Plat: Surveyed for Alexander McCarter, 300 A on S fork Tyger adj. Robert Carrs Feb 27, 1766, Zach Bullock, Surv. "Indians Land Order not Executed on Land"

McCARTER, ALEXANDER File no. 2455; Gr. no. 235; Bk. 23, p. 246
Warrant: Unto Alexander McCarter, 300 A on S branch N fork Little River between Robert Millers & David davis . . . 24 Oct 1765 Wm Tryon
Plat: Surveyed for Alexander McCarter, 150 A on S bank N fork Tyger above John Sharpe . . . 4 Jan 1768 Joseph Thompson, Joseph JONES CB By Wm Sharp, [Surv.] Iss. 29 Apr 1768

McCARTER, ALEXANDER File no. 2452; Gr. no. 322; Bk. 23, p. 246
Warrant: Unto Alexander McCarter, 150 A on S fork Little River adj. Robert Carr . . . 24 Oct 1765 Wm Tryon
Plat: Feb 28, 1766, Surveyed for Alexander McCarter on S fork Tyger River Z. Bullock, Thomas Clark, Hugh Barnet, CB Iss. 29 Apr 1768

McCARTER, ALEXANDER File no. 2451; Gr. no. 321; Bk. 23, p. 246
Warrant: Unto Alexander McCarter, 300 A on S fork Little River adj. Robert Car . . . 24 Oct 1765 Wm Tryon Iss. 29 Apr 1768

McCARTER, ALEXANDER File no. 2290; Gr. no. 206; Bk. 23, p. 182
Warrant: Unto Alexander McCarter, 150 A on S branch of N fork of Tygar above Joseph Jones mill seat place . . . 22 Sept 1766 Wm Tryon
Plat: Surveyed for Alexander McCarter, 150 A on N fork Tygar . . . 27 Nov 1766 By Wm Sharp, Sur. Elisha Thompson, John Ker, CB Iss. 26 Oct 1767

McCARTER, JOHN File no. 0238
Plat: Surveyd for John McCarter, 300 A on S side N fork Tygar adj. Mr. Alexanders . . . 9 Jan 1768 By Wm Sharp, Surv. James Reynolds, David Davis, CB

McCARTER, JOHN File no. 2453; Gr. no. 323; Bk. 23, p. 246
Warrant: Unto John McCarter, 300 A on S branch S fork Ti-

ger above John Kerrs Entry . . . 22 Sept 1766 Wm Tryon
Plat: Surveyed for John McCarter, 300 A on head branches
of N fork Tyger called Fergusons Creek . . . 4 Dec 1766 Peter
Johnston, Sur. Moses Ferguson, Jonathan Newman, CB Iss.
29 Apr 1768

McCARTER, MOSES File no. 0239
Plat: Surveyed for Moses McCarter, 300 A on Bullocks Creek
. . . Loves line Feb. 21, 17___ Wm Sims [Surv.]

McCARTER, MOSES File no. 697; Gr. no. 168; Bk. 17, p. 305
300 A on Bullocks Creek & the long Watery Branch . . . mac-
cadoes line . . . 26 Sept 1766 Wm Tryon

McCARTER, MOSES File no. 1733; Gr. no. 119; Bk. 20, p. 439
Plat: Surveyed for Moses McCarter, 250 A in Tryon Co. on
Susey Boles Branch of Turkey Creek including his improve-
ment . . . Seth Johnsons line . . . John McKnit Alexanders . . .
8 Dec 1768 Peter Johnston, Surv. Thomas Larney, Francis
Travis, CB Iss. 4 May 1769

McCLAINE, CHARLES File no. 486 (1213); Gr. no. 172; Bk. 17,
p. 179 (18, 164)
Plat: [nd], Surveyed for Charles Maclaine, 170 A on a branch
of fishing Creek adj. Joseph Hardings . . . Francis Beaty, D.S.
Joseph Harding, Thomas Clark, CB Iss. 19 Apr 1765

McCLAINE, EPHRAIM File no. 366 (1098); Gr. no. 275; Bk. 17,
p. 136 (18, 122)
Warrant: Unto Ephraim Maclain, 500 A on N fork Fishing
Creek adj. his own & McNabs lines . . . 20 Dec 1763 Arthur
Dobbs
Plat: [nd], Survey'd for Ephraim Maclaine, 500 A on N side S
fork Fishing Creek adj. his own & Andrew McNabbs . . . By
Francis Beaty Chas Beatey, Wm Dunlap, CB Iss. 16 Nov 1764

McCLEHAN, FINNEY File no. 0432
Plat: Surveyed for Finney McClenaham, 200 A on N side
Broad opp. a little Island, below James Moores Survey . . . 5
Apr 1766 William Dickson, Surv. Archd Mcdowell, Thomas
Hooper, CB

McCLELLAND, HUGH File no. 542 (1268); Gr. no. 98; Bk. 17, p.
288 (18, 189)
Warrant: Unto Hugh McClelland, 300 A on both sides stony
fork of Fishing Creek including his Improvement . . . 6 Apr
1765 Wm Tryon
Plat: Surveyed for Hugh McClelland, 300 A on Rockey fork
of Fishing Creek adj. Wm Smith, Thomas Neely, his & Sam-

uel Lusk lines . . . 19 June 1765 William Dickson, Surv.
Thomas McMurray, William Smith, CB Iss. 30 Oct 1765

McCLELLAND, ROBERT File no. 1559 (838); Gr. no. 69; Bk.
18, p. 356 (17, 389)
Warrant: Unto Robert McClelland 200 A on Fishing Creek
adj. Thomas McMurray & the Indians Line . . . 24 Oct 1765
Wm Tryon
Plat: Surveyed for Robert McClelland, 200 A adj. Indian Line
. . . Thomas McMurray . . . 24 Apr 1766 William Dickson,
Surv. Repentance Townsend, John Sellars, CB Iss. 25 Apr
1767

McCLELON, THOMAS File no. 1193 (465); Gr. no. 86; Bk. 18, p.
149 (17, 164)
Warrant: Unto Thomas McClellan, 200 A on Stoney fork of
fishing Creek, adj. William Hannas . . . 2 Nov 1764 Arthur
Dobbs
Plat: [nd], Surveyed for Thomas McClelon, 190 A on Stony
Fork of Fishing Creek adj. William Hannas . . . George Alexander, D.S. Robert McClellon, David McClellen, CB Iss. 6 Apr
1765

McCOOL, ADAM File no. 847 (1568); Gr. no. 79; Bk. 17, p. 391
(18, 358)
Warrant: Unto Adam McCoole, 150 A on E side Broad River,
adj. his own line where he lives . . . 24 Oct 1765 Wm Tryon
Plat: Surveyed for Adam McCoole, 120 A adj. N Side Broad
adj. his own plantation . . . 15 Mar 1766 William Dickson,
Sur. William Hughes, Solomon Elliot, CB Iss. 25 Apr 1767

McCORD, JAMES File no. 2058; Gr. no. 666; Bk. 23, p. 80
Plat: Surveyed for James McCord, 108 A on Allisons Creek
including the Improvement he now lives on . . . William Henrys line . . . David Watson . . . Wm Dicksons line . . . Jno McK
Alexander, Sur. [nd], Wm Read, Adam McCord, CB [Grant
reads 140 A] Iss. 16 Apr 1765

McCORD, JOHN File no. 0241; Entry no. 248
Warrant: Unto John McCord, 150 A on Allisons Creek adj.
Wm Henry, Dickson . . . 2 Nov 1764 Arthur Dobbs
Plat: Surveyed for James McCord, 140 A including his im-
provement . . . William Henries line . . . Dickson land . . .
David Watson . . . George Alexander, DS [nd]. William Read,
Adam McCord, CB

McCORMACK, JOHN File no. 840 (1561); Gr. no. 71; Bk. 17, p.
389 (18, 356)
Warrant: Unto John McCormack, 250 A on waters of Alli-

sons Creek, on Indian path above the little Mountain . . . including his own improvement . . . 24 Oct 1765 Wm Tryon
Plat: 5 Feb 1766, Surveyed for John McCormack, 250 A on the Indian path . . . little Mountain . . . adj. Wm McConnels . . . Robert Patrick . . . William Dickson, Surv. Thomas Patton, David Hall, CB Iss. 25 Apr 1767

McCRACKEN, JAMES File no. 0243; Entry no. 112
Plat: Surveyed for James McCracken, 300 A on S side Broad River on both sides S fork Packelet adj. Joseph Whites lower line . . . 10 Jan 1768 Wm Sharp, Surv. Chas Moore, Wm Sharp, CB

McCULLOH, ALEXANDER File no. 2201; Gr. no. 354; Bk. 23, p. 146
Warrant: Unto Alexander McCulloh, 300 A on middle fork Tyger adj. Richard McRee . . . 23 Sept 1766 Wm Tryon
Plat: Surveyed for Alexander McCulloch, 300 A on both sides Middle fork Tyger about 2 miles below Hutchin's Beaverdams . . . Daniel McRees line . . . 6 Dec 1766 Wm Dickson, Surv. David McRee, James Carruth, CB Iss. 26 Oct 1767

McCULLOCK, JOHN File no. 2471; Gr. no. 410; Bk. 23, p. 284
Warrant: Unto John McCulloh 200 A on S side Rockey Allisons Creek adj. Walter Davis Survey . . . 6 Apr 1765 Wm Tryon
Plat: Surveyed for John McCulloh 192 A on S side Allisons Creek adj. Robert Shaw, David Templeton, William Whaleys . . . Wm Dickson, Surv. [nd] James Stevenson, John Kimbroh, CB Iss. 29 Apr 1768

McCULLOCK, JOHN File no. 1633 (921); Gr. no. 157; Bk. 18, p. 373 (17, 418)
Warrant: Unto John McCulloh, 200 A on waters of Allisons Creek . . . 24 Oct 1765 Wm Tryon
Plat: Surveyed for John McCulloh in Allisons & Beaver dam Creek on a branch called Camp Run including James Armours Improvement . . . 23 Mar 1767 Peter Johnston, Surv. Andrew Armour, James Davis, CB Iss 25 Apr 1767

McCULLOCK, THOMAS File no. 1498 (776); Gr. no. 441; Bk. 18, p. 334 (17, 366)
Warrant: Unto Thomas McCulloh, 150 A on Fishing Creek adj. Neeley & Whites lines . . . 6 Apr 1765 Wm Tryon
Grant: 200 A on N side Fishing Creek adj. Phillip Walker, Hugh White, John Neeleys, & Indian line . . . 26 Sept 1766 Wm Tryon

McDOWELL, ROBERT File no. 518 (1244); Gr. no. 73; Bk. 17, p. 203 (18, 185)
160 A on waters of Allisons Creek below the Waggon Road including his Improvement . . . 28 Oct 1765 Wm Tryon

McDOWELL, WILLIAM File no. 0246
Plat: Surveyed for William McDowell, 233 A on waters of Allisons Creek including his improvement . . . John McCullohs line . . . 13 Mar 1767 Robt & James McDowall, CB Peter Johnston, Surv.

McDOWELL, WILLIAM File no. 2175; Gr. no. 234; Bk. 23, p. 123
Warrant: Unto William McDowell, 150 A on waters of Allisons Creek adj. Et side Robert McDowells land . . . 24 Oct 1765 Wm Tryon
Plat: Surveyed for William McDowel 150 A on waters of Allisons Creek adj. Robt McDowels line . . . 7 Feb 1766 Wm Dickson, Surv. John McCulloh, Robert McDowell, CB Iss 26 Oct 1767

McELLULLY, JOHN File no. 1795; Gr. no. 74; Bk. 20, p. 551
Plat: Surveyed for John McEllily, 200 A on waters of S side S fork Fishing Creek adj. Samuel Morrows land . . . By Jno McK. Alexander, Sur. 2 Dec 1769 William Miller, Hugh Neely, CB Iss. 9 Apr 1770

McGARRITY, MICHAEL File no. 2268; Gr. no. 252; Bk. 23, p. 178
Plat: Surveyed for Michel McGarrity 227 A on Ridge between Turkey & Fishing Creek . . . Loves line . . . Rosses line . . . Zach Bullock, Surv. 3 Feb 1767 William Ratchford, William Grimes [?], CB Iss. 26 Oct 1767

McILWEAN, JAMES File no. 2186; Gr. no. 245; Bk. 23, p. 125
300 A on fair forrest about 6 miles above Thomas Cases . . . 26 Oct 1767 Wm Tryon

MACKELWEAN, JAMES File no. 0249
Plat: Surveyed for James Mackilwean 300 A on Fair Forest about 6 miles above Thomas Cases . . . 12 Dec 1766 William Dickson, Surv. Thos Case, Alexr Rea, CB

McKINNEY, JOHN File no. 2433; Gr. no. 299; Bk. 23, p. 242
Warrant: Unto John McKinney 100 A adj. W side Broad & His own plantation 27 Sept 1766 Wm Tryon
Plat: Surveyed for John McKinney, 100 A on W side Broad adj. his own corner . . . 27 Nov 1768 Wm Sharp, Surv. Iss 28 Apr 1768 Saml Sharp & Philip Henson, C.C.

McKINNEY, JOHN File no. 719 (1447); Gr. no. 288; Bk. 17, p. 331 (18, 303)
Warrant: Unto John McKinney, 200 A on waters of Bullocks Creek ... head of Loves branch, including his own improvment ... 24 Oct 1765 Wm Tryon
Plat: [nd], Surveyed for John McKinney, 200 A on both sides Gawin [sic] Moores By Jno McK. Alexander, Surv. Henry Smith, Jacob Gardner, C.B.

McKINNEY, JOHN File no. 559 (1285); Gr. no. 257; Bk. 17, p. 249 (18, 218)
250 A on S side Broad opposite Mathew Floyds land ... at some Old Indian Camps 30 Oct 1765 Wm Tryon

McKLEGHENY, JOHN File no. 0251
Plat: Surveyed for John McKleheny, 200 A on waters of N fork Tyger on Brown Branch adj. John Prince 27 May 1767 Francis Dodds, John Mclehenny, CB

McKLEWEAN, JAMES File no. 2537; Gr. no. 529; Bk. 23, p. 305
200 A on waters of Fair Forrest on Mackleweans branch above his own Land 29 Apr 1768 Wm Tryon

McLEEWEE, WILLIAM File no. 0256; Entry no. 680
Warrant: Unto William Mclewee 100 A on both sides Clark fork of Bullocks Creek adj. his own upper line ... 23 Sept 1766 Wm Tryon
Two identical plats: Jan 14, 1767, Surveyed for William Mclewee 100 A on both sides Clark fork of Bullocks Creek ... Zach Bullock, Surv. Gowen Black, James Wilson, CB

McLEWEE, WILLIAM File no. 1329 (602); Gr. no. 352; Bk. 18, p. 235 (17, 259)
Warrant: Unto William Mclewee, 100 A on both sides Clark fork of Bullocks Creek adj. his own line ... 23 Sept 1766 Wm Tryon
Plat: Jan 14, 1767, Surveyed for William Mclewe 100 A on both sides Clarks fork of Bullocks Creek P Zach Bullock Gowen Black, James Wilson, CB

McMACHAN, CORNELIUS File no. 2371; Gr. no. 131; Bk. 23, p. 208
Plat: February 23, 1768, Surveyed for Cornelius McMachan, 350 A on the south fork of Raburns Creek ... on the Indian line ... P Zach. Bullock Joseph Kettle, John Copeland, CB Iss. 30 Oct 1765

McMACHEN, WILLIAM File no. 2194; Gr. no. 289; Bk. 23, p. 133

150 A on both sides N fork Tygar including the narrow passage and his own improvement . . . 26 Oct 1767 Wm Tryon

McMILLEN, JNO File no. 1649 (928); Gr. no. 175; Bk. 18, p. 376 (17, 412)
Warrant: Unto John McMillen, 100 A on both sides Abbisons Creek adj. his lower line . . . 27 Sept 176___
Plat: Surveyed for John McMullan 100 A on Bullocks Creek . . . Riggs, Stephenson, Smith, Heartness, Armstrongs lines . . . Jno McKnitt Alexander, Surv. Iss. 25 Apr 1767 John Heartness, John Smith, CB

McMILLEN, JOHN File no. 2200; Gr. no. 315; Bk. 23, p. 138
200 A on both sides Abbettons Creek, a West branch of Broad River, below Lovelettys land . . . 26 Oct 1767 Wm Tryon

McMILLEN, WILLIAM File no. 1429; Gr. no. 172; Bk. 18, p. 278
Warrant: Unto William McMullen, 100 A on W side Broad adj. his own line . . . 6 Apr 1765 Wm Tryon
Plat: Surveyed for William McMillen, 100 A on S side Broad River adj. his own line 29 July 1765 W Sims, Surv. John McMillan, Andrew McMillan, CB Iss. 26 Sept 1766

McMILLEN, WILLIAM File no. 701; Gr. no. 272; Bk. 17, p. 306
100 A on S side Broad River . . . 26 Sept 1766 Wm Tryon

McMULLIN, JOHN File no. 774 (1496); Gr. no. 439; Bk. 17, p. 365 (18, 334)
Warrant: Unto John McMillon, 200 A on watters of Turkey Creek west of Wades old Store house . . . 6 Apr 1765 Wm Tryon
Plat: Surveyed for John McMullen, 200 A on Turkey Creek, Susy Bowles Branch, adj. Robert Dickson, Robert Harper . . . 11 Apr 1766 William Dickson, Surv. Robert Adair, Edward Linton, CB. Iss. 26 Sept 1766

McMURDIE, ROBERT File no. 0258
Plat: Surveyed for Robert McMurdie, 300 A on S side Lawsons fork of Packolet, Jones Waggon Road . . . John Millers . . . 14 Dec 1766 William Dickson John Williamson, Elisha Williamson, CB

McMURRY, THOS File no. 0260
Plat: Surveyed for Thomas McMurray 150 A on S side Fishing Creek adj. Robert McClallonds . . . 22 Nov 1767 Peter Johnston, Surv. Wm Dickson, Wm McMurray, CB

McMURRY, THOMAS File no. 1187 (459); Gr. no. 80; Bk. 18, p. 148 (17, 163)

Warrant: Unto Thomas McMurry, 250 A on fishing Creek adj. Indian line about a mile above Hitchcocks path . . . 2 Nov 1764 Arthur Dobbs

Plat: [nd], Surd for Thomas Mcmury, 216 A on fishing Creek adj. Indian line . . . Alexander Lewis . . . George Alexander, Surv. [No CB] Iss. 6 Apr 1765

McNABB, JAMES File no. 1267 (541); Gr. no. 97; Bk. 18, p. 189 (17, 207)
250 A on head waters of Turkey & Fishing Creek . . . Thomas Prices . . . 30 Oct 1765 Wm Tryon

McNABB, JAMES File no. 809 (1530); Gr. no. 9; Bk. 17, p. 377 (18, 345)
200 A on waters of Broad River, on a branch of Turkey Creek adj. Balls, Harpers, Kelleys . . . Alexander Harpers corner . . . 22 Apr 1767 Wm Tryon

McREE, DAVID File no. 791 (1513); Gr. no. 466; Bk. 18, p. 339 (17, 371)
Warrant: Unto David McRee, 200 A on N branch Tyger adj. place where Joseph Jones lives . . . 24 Oct 1765 Wm Tryon
Plat: 3 Mar 1766, Surveyed for David McRee, 200 A on middle fork Tyger adj. John McRee . . . Zach Bullock, Surv. Hugh Barnet, James Carruth, CB Iss. 27 Sept 1766

McBEE, JAMES File no. 2554; Gr. no. 565; Bk. 23, p. 312
200 A on S side Packolet River . . . on the Reedy branch including an Improvement he bought of Charles Park . . . 29 Apr 1768 Wm Tryon

McREE, JOHN File no. 1511 (789); Gr. no. 464; Bk. 18, p. 339 (17, 370)
Warrant: Unto John McRee, 640 A on middle fork Tyger above Joseph Jones . . . 24 Oct 1765 Wm Tryon
Plat: 1 Mar 1766, Surveyed for John McRee, 640 A on middle fork Tyger . . . Zach Bullock, Surv. Joseph Thompson, Jacob Ormond, CB Iss. 27 Sept 1766

McREE, JOHN File no. 1512 (790); Gr. no. 465; Bk. 18, p. 339 (17, 371)
Warrant: Unto John McRee, 300 A on S branch middle fork Tyger . . . 24 Oct 1765 Wm Tryon
Plat: 3 Mar 1766, Surveyed for John McRee 200 A on a branch of Tyger River . . . Z. Bullock, Sur. James Carruth, Jacob Ormand, CB Iss. 27 Sept 1766

McREE, ROBERT File no. 2280; Gr. no. 116; Bk. 23, p. 181
Warrant: Unto Robert McRee 300 A on S branch of N fork

Tyger River adj. where Joseph Jones now lives and David Davis line . . . 22 Sept 1766 Wm Tryon

Plat: Surveyed for Robert McRee, 300 A on SW branch of N fork Tyger adj. David Davis . . . 2 Dec 1766 Peter Johnston, Surv. William Dickson, David McRee, D Bear. Iss. 26 Oct 1767

McWHORTER, ELENOR File no. 743 (1471); Gr. no. 314; Bk. 17, p. 377 (18, 308)

Plat: 3 Sept 1765, Surveyed for Elenor McWhorter, 300 A on both sides Packolett including her own improvement . . . [No Surv.] John Portman, George McWhorter, CB Iss. 26 Sept 1766

MACKILMURRY, JOHN File no. 277 (1009); Gr. no. 32; Bk. 17, p. 80 (18, 77)

Warrant: Unto John Mcilmurry, 250 A on branch of S side Allisons Creek adj. Joseph Hardins, including where he now lives . . . 19 Dec 1763 Arthur Dobbs

Plat: Surveyed for John MacIlmury, 245 A on So side Allisons Creek adj. Joseph Hardins . . . 20 Augt 1763 William Dickson, D Surv. Iss. 2 Nov 1763 William Hanna Senr & William Hanna junr., C.C.

MACILMURREY, JOHN File no. 868 (1589); Gr. no. 105; Bk. 17, p. 396 (18, 363)

Warrant: Unto John Mackilmury 300 A on waters of Allisons Creek adj. William Hanna . . . 24 Oct 1765 Wm Tryon

Plat: 13 Feb 1766, Surveyed for John Mackilmury, 300 A on S side Allisons Creek on Charles Moores branch, adj. William Hanna . . . Davisons . . . William Dickson, Surv. William Dickson, James Mac Affee, CB Iss. 26 Apr 1767

MACKELROY, JAMES File no. 0265

Plat: [nd], Surveyed for James Mackilroy, 350 A on both sides Lawsons fork of Packolet including a mill seat . . . Wm Dickson, Surv. Thomas Williamson, Thomas Case, CB

MAKAN, JAMES File no. 0263

Plat: Surveyed for James Makan [Mahan?] 200 A on Stoney fork of Fishing Creek adj. William Hannah, Jr. & Cups [sic] land . . . 10 Dec 1768 Peter Johnston, Surv. Daniel & James Brices, CB

MAFFOOT, JOHN File no. 952 (1673); Gr. no. 205; Bk. 17, p. 419 (18, 382)

Warrant: Unto John Mafoot 200 A on waters of Bullocks Creek near Allisons Creek & near David Watsons . . . 27 Sept 1766 Wm Tryon

Plat: Surveyed for John Maffoot 150 A on middle fork of Bullocks Creek, on path from David Wattsons to Wm Byers ... Wm Sharp, Surv. John & Gilbert Watson, CB 27 Dec 1766 Iss. 25 Apr 1767

MARCHBANKS, WILLIAM File no. 2236; Gr. no. 391; Bk. 23, p. 154
300 A on both sides a large branch of Thicketty Creek ... 26 Oct 1767 Wm Tryon

MARCHBANKS, WM & WM SIMS File no. 1995; Gr. no. 419; Bk. 23, p. 33
Plat: Feb. 7, 1766, Surveyed for William Sims & William Marchbanks, 400 A on Boaches branch of Thickety Creek ... Zacr Bullock, Surv. James Fanning, Hugh Wilson, CB Iss. 25 Apr 1767

MARRS, ROBERT File no. 2172; Gr. no. 231; Bk. 23, p. 122
260 A on South side of Enoree on a branch of Indian Creek called the Hunters fork joining and between Jacob Pennington, Jonans Carrols, Abraham Andersons, and Vandormans lines ... 26 Oct 1767 Wm Tryon Iss. 26 Oct 1767 [Warrant states "near Thomas Gordens"]

MARTIN, ALEXANDER File no. 941 (1662); Gr. no. 188; Bk. 17, p. 416 (18, 379)
Warrant: 200 A on both sides Peoples Creek 27 Sept 1766
Plat: Survey'd for Alexander Martain 200 A on the Wt side of main Broad on both sides Cherrokee Creek about 2 miles from the mouth ... 8 Nov 1766 By Wm Sharp, Surv. Samuel Richardson, James Collins, CB Iss. 25 Apr 1767

MARTAIN, ALEXANDER File no. 942 (1663); Gr. no. 189; Bk. 17, p. 417 (18, 376)
Warrant: 300 A on W side Main Broad upon both sides Cherokee Creek
Plat: Survey'd for Alexander Martain, 300 A on Wt side Main Broad River including the mouth of Cherrokee Creek ... Hugh Quinns corner ... 13th Dec 1766 By Wm Sharp, Surv. Isom Peoples, Thomas Clark, CB Iss. 25 Apr 1767

MASSEY, JOSEPH File no. 1510 (788); Gr. no. 463; Bk. 18, p. 339 (17, 370)
Warrant: Unto Joseph Massey, 500 A on S fork Little Broad, a branch of Tyger including the Middle Indian path ... 6 Apr 1765 Wm Tryon
Plat: Feb 27, 1766, Surveyed for Joseph Massey, 500 A on S fork Tyger ... P Zach Bullock Thomas Clark, Hugh Barnet, CB Iss. 27 Sept 1766

MATHIS, PHILLIMON File no. 0268; Entry no. 414
Warrant: Unto Phillimon Mathis 200 A on S fork of Bullocks Creek of Thicketty where Coles path leaves the Creek . . . 20 Oct 1767 Wm Tryon
Plat: Surveyed for Phillip Mathews [sic] 200 A on a large branch of Bullocks Creek of Thickety 16 Nov 1768 Zach Bullock [No CB]

MAYES, JAMES File no. 2185; Gr. no. 244; Bk. 23, p. 125
Plat: Survey'd for James Mayes 200 A on the N side of Fair Forrest on Harris's Branch above Andw. Fosters Survey . . . 29th Novr. 1766 Wm Dickson, Surv. Andrew Foster, Jno. Kelsey, C: Bear. Iss. 26 Oct 1767

MAYES, JAMES File no. 824 (1545); Gr. no. 53; Bk. 17, p. 386 (18, 353)
Warrant: Unto James Mayes, 200 A on waters of Fair Forrest on Beaverdam, Robert Harris . . . 24 Oct 1765 Wm Tryon
Plat: Survey'd for James Mayes, 200 A on N side of Fair Forrest on both sides Harris's Creek . . . Robert Harris's corner . . . George Parks line . . . 13 Mar 1766 James Mayes, William Mills, Cha. Bear. Iss. 25 Apr 1767

MEANES, JAMES File no. 1544; Gr. no. 523; Entry no. 260; Bk. 18, p. 353
Warrant: Unto James Means, 300 A on waters of Fair Forrest on Mitchell Branch adj. Mitchels line . . . 24 Oct 1765 Wm Tryon
Plat: Survey'd for James Means, 300 A on No side Fair Forrest on Mitchels Branch . . . near Mitchels line . . . 13 March 1766 William Dickson, Surv. James Meanes, Thomas Armstrong, Cha. Bear. Iss. 25 Apr 1767

MEANES, JAMES File no. 823; Gr. no. 52; Bk. 17, p. 386
300 A on N side Fair Forrest on Mitchells branch . . . Mitchells line . . . 25 Apr 1767
[This grant appears to be the same as the preceding, although the grant numbers are different.]

MILLER, JAMES File no. 0276
Plat: Surveyed for James Miller 250 A on So fork Tyger River adj. his own line . . . 12 Sepr 1768 Wm Sharp, Surv. [No CB]

MILLER, JAMES File no. 0277
Plat: Surveyed for James Miller, 100 A on S side Middle fork Tygar adj. Robt Millers . . . 7 Jan 1768 Wm Sharp, Surv.

MILLER, JAMES File no. 0279
Warrant: Unto James Millar, 300 A on N fork Tyger above Francis Wilsons, on the wagon road from Joseph Jones to Alexander Varners . . . Robert Millers land . . . 18 Apr 1767 Wm Tryon
Plat: Survey'd for James Miller, 180 A on S side N fork Tygar on Jemmeys Creek, adj. Vernons, Penneys, & Leeches . . . 7 Jan 1768 Wm Sharp, Surv. Thos Collins, Alexander Ray, CB

MILLER, JAMES File no. 2289; Gr. no. 204; Bk. 23, p. 182
Warrant: Unto James Miller 200 A on N side main fork of Tygar on both sides the Waggon Road leading from Robert Millers to Charles town . . . 27 Sept 1766 Wm Tryon
Plat: [nd], Surveyd for James Miller 200 A on both sides ye S fork Tygar on both sides the Waggon road from Robert Millers to Charles Town . . . By William Sharp, Sur. John Nichols, John Miller, CB Iss. 26 Oct 1767

MILLER, JOHN File no. 0280
Warrant: Unto John Miller, 200 A on Turkey Creek, including Burlesons improvement . . . 22 Sept 1766 Wm Tryon
Plat: Surveyed for John Miller, 200 A on a branch of Turkey Creek including Burlesons old improvement . . . 26 Nov 1766 Peter Johnston, James & George Rosss [sic], CB

MILLER, JOHN File no. 2273; Gr. no. 73; Bk. 23, p. 179
Warrant: Unto John Miller, 200 A on a branch of Tyger River . . . 29 Oct 1765 Wm Tryon
Plat: Surveyed for John Miller, 200 A on N side N fork Tyger adj. Joseph Jones plantation . . . Jonathan Newmans line . . . 6 Mar 1766 William Dickson, Surv. Joseph Jones, Alexander Ray, CB Iss. 26 Oct 1767

MILLER, JOHN File no. 0281
Plat: Surveyed for John Miller, 100 A on a branch of Turkey Creek, being the place where Sagriff now lives . . . 25 Aug 1767 Peter Johnston, Surv. Hugh Sagriff, William Wood, CB

MILLER, JOHN File no. 921 (1642); Gr. no. 166; Bk. 17, p. 410 (18, 374)
Warrant: Unto John Miller 600 A on the dividing ridge between Turkey Creek and Fishing Creek . . . both sides of the ditch Waggon Road . . . Loves line . . . Jos. Harding . . . 22 Sept 1766 Wm Tryon
Plat: 24 Dec 1766, Surveyed for John Miller 600 A on dividing ridge between Turkey Creek and Fishing Creek . . . both sides of the ditch waggon road . . . Loves line . . . Alex Hard-

ings line ... Elliots line ... Peter Johnston Surv. John Ross, James Martin, CB Iss. 25 Apr 1767

MILLER, JOHN File no. 729 (1457); Gr. no. 298; Bk. 18, p. 305 (17, 333)

Plat: Surveyed for John Miller, 200 A on So side Lawsons fork of Packolet near Jones Waggon Road ... 5 Mar 1766 William Dickson, Surv. Francis Ross, James Ross, CB. Iss. 26 Sept 1767

MILLER, JOHN File no. 878 (1599); Gr. no. 117; Bk. 18, p. 365 (17, 399)

Warrant: Unto John Miller, 200 A upon S side Lawsons Creek adj. his own line ... 29 Sept 1766 Wm Tryon

Plat: Surveyed for John Millar, 200 A on S side Lawsons Forch [sic] of Packolate adj. his own & Robert McMurrys line ... 14 Dec 1766 Wm Dickson, Surv. John Williamson, Elisha Williamson, CB

MILLER, JOHN File no. 2276; Gr. no. 90; Bk. 23, p. 180

Warrant: Unto John Miller, 100 A on N side N fork of Tyger River on Wards branch abt. a mile above Wards land & near or Joining Robert Millers land ... on both sides of the waggon Road ... 22 Sept 1766 Wm Tryon

Plat: Surveyed for John Miller 100 A on N side N fork Tyger on Wards Branch adj. Charles Moore ... 17 Dec 1766 Wm Dickson, Surv. Nathaniel Miller, Martin Oates [Cates?], CB Iss. 26 Oct 1767

MILLER, JOHN File no. 1563 (842); Gr. no. 74; Bk. 18, p. 357 (17, 390)

Plat: Surveyed for John Miller, 150 A on middle fork of Turkey Creek called Burlisons fork ... 19 Feb 1766 William Dickson, Surv. Frances Ross, John Moore, CB Iss. 25 Apr 1767

MILLICAN, JAMES File no. 1312 (585); Gr. no. 317; Bk. 18, p. 229 (17, 252)

Warrant: Unto James Millican, 100 A on middle fork of Fishing Creek, adj. his own land ... 6 Apr 1765 Wm Tryon

Plat: 20 Sept 1765, Surveyed for James Millican 100 A on middle fork Fishing Creek, between Dickies, Davis, Bleny Mills ... William Dickson, Surv. Thomas Hawkins, Abraham Kuykendall, CB Iss. 30 Oct 1765

MILES, JAMES File no. 853 (1574); Gr. no. 86; Bk. 17, p. 392 (18, 359)

125 A on both sides N fork Susy Bowles's branch ... im-

provement made by THOMAS STEPHENSON ... adj. Robert Dickson ... 25 Apr 1767 Wm Tryon

MINTER, WILLIAM File no. 900 (1621); Gr. no. 145; Bk. 17, p. 405 (18, 370)
Warrant: Unto William Minter, 200 A on E side Turkey Creek adj. his own & James Miles plantation ... 23 Sept 1766 Wm Tryon
Plat: Surveyed for William Minter, 120 A on E side Turkey Creek adj. Mathew Floyd, James Miles ... 1 Jan 1767 Wm Dickson, Surv. Iss. 25 Apr 1767

MITCHELL, JOAB File no. 2264; Gr. no. 495; Bk. 23, p. 174
Warrant: Unto Joab Mitchell 500 A on Packlett River including James Wilsons improvement ... 27 Sept 1766 Wm Tryon
Plat: 3 June 1767, Survey'd for Joab Mitchell, 446 A on So side Packolet in James Wilsons line ... Colemans line ... Drapers corner ... Zach Bullock, Surv. [No CB] Iss. 26 Oct 1767

MITCHELL, JOAB File no. 2263; Gr. no. 494; Bk. 23, p. 174
Warrant: Unto Joab Mitchell, 200 A on both sides Packlett adj. his other entry ... 27 Sept 1766 Wm Tryon
Plat: Surveyed for Joab Mitchell, 178 A on both sides Packlet ... Hughes line ... Beckhams ... 2 June 1767 ... Zach Bullock, Surv. John Beckham, John Hail, CB Iss. 26 Oct 1767

MITCHELL, JOAB File no. 2044; Gr. no. 473; Bk. 23, p. 41
Warrant: Unto Joab Mitchell, 300 A on Hughes line ... down Packlet River adj. John Elliots line ... 23 Sept 1766 Wm Tryon
Plat: [nd], Surveyed for Joab Mitchell, 300 A on both sides Packlet ... hugheys [sic] line ... Ellits line ... Zach Bullock, Surv. David Hodges, Charles Blackwel, CB Iss. 27 Apr 1767

MITCHELL, JOB File no. 2045; Gr. no. 474; Bk. 23, p. 42
Warrant: Unto Joab Mitchell 300 A on Grindals upper line ... both sides Packlet ... 23 Sept 1766 Wm Tryon
Plat: Surveyed for Joab Mitchell, 300 A on both sides Packlet above Sharrols Shoals ... Grindals line ... Beckhams line ... 20 Feb 1767 ... Zach Bullock, Surv. Chas Roberson, John Beckham, CB Iss. 27 Apr 1767

MITCHELL, JOSEPH File no. 2142; Gr. no. 194; Bk. 23, p. 115
100 A on a branch of N side S fork fishing Creek ... between Brown & Millars land ... 26 Oct 1767 Wm Tryon

MITCHELL, THOMAS File no. 2370; Gr. no. 130; Entry no. 615; Bk. 23, p. 208

Plat: Feb. 8th 1768, Survey'd Thomas Mitchel 100 A on the North Side of Broad River Including his Improvement. P Zach Bullock Mattw Patterson, John Patterson, Cha. Bearers. Entered 20 Oct 1767 Iss. 28 Apr 1768

MOFFAT, JOHN File no. 859 (1580); Gr. no. 96; Bk. 17, p. 394 (18, 360)
Warrant: Unto John Moffet, 200 A adj. to Robert Shaw on Ridge between Rocky Allisons & Big Allisons Creek ... 25 Oct 1765 Wm Tryon
Plat: Surveyed for John Moffat, 200 A on Rockey Allisons Creek, adj. Robert Shaw, John Henry ... 7 Feb 1767 Peter Johnston, Surv. Samuel Watson, Willm Whaley, CB Iss. 25 Apr 1767

MONTFORT, JOSEPH File no. 2561; Gr. no. 577; Bk. 23, p. 314
500 A on N fork Packolet and adj. his own corner ... 29 Apr 1768 Wm Tryon

MONTFORT, JOSEPH File no. 1288; Gr. no. 288; Bk. 18, p. 224
600 A on both sides N fork Pacalet ... 30 Oct 1765 Wm Tryon

MONTFORT, JOSEPH File no. 562; Gr. no. 290; Bk. 17, p. 246
Warrant: Unto Joseph Montfort, 600 A on Catawba or Broad River ... 6 Apr 1765 Wm Tryon
Plat: 6 Sept 1765, Surveyed for Joseph Montfort 600 A on both sides N fork Packlet above Campbells line ... Peter Howard & Alexr Kilpatrick, CB William Sims, Surv. Iss. 30 Oct 1765

MONTFORT, JOSEPH File no. 605; Gr. no. 353; Bk. 17, p. 260
600 A on both sides main N fork Pacalett above Campbells Land ... 30 Oct 1765 Wm Tryon

MOORE, CHARLES File no. 2228; Gr. no. 202; Bk. 23, p. 182
100 A on N fork Tyger ... Robert Millers line ... 26 Oct 1767 Wm Tryon

MOORE, CHARLES File no. 2078; Gr. no. 48; Bk. 23, p. 90
300 A on both sides Tyger River generally known as Lawsons Creek ... Hugh Lawsons line ... 26 Apr 1767 Wm Tryon

MOORE, GEORGE File no. 1947; Gr. no. 299; Bk. 23, p. 12
Warrant: Unto George Moore, 300 A on lower side Packlet River, adj. Fannings upper line ... 24 Oct 1765 Wm Tryon
Plat: March 8, 1766, Surveyed for George Moore 270 A on S side Packlett adj. James Fannings line ... W Sims, Surv. James Fanning, Abraham Fanning, CB Iss. 25 Apr 1767

MOORE, HUGH File no. 2019; Gr. no. 444; Bk. 23, p. 37
Warrant: Unto Hugh Moore, 400 A on a large bank of Thicketty Creek including a mill place & some Indian Camps . . . 25 Oct 1765 Wm Tryon
Plat: Surveyed for Hugh Moore, 200 A on Bullocks Creek of Thicketty Creek . . . near the falls . . . 19 Mar 1766 Zach Bullock, Surv. William Twittey, Patrick Moore, CB Iss. 25 Apr 1767

MOORE, HUGH File no. 2022; Gr. no. 76; Bk. 18, p. 185
Plat: May 3, 1766, Surveyed for Hugh Moore 400 A on both sides Thicketty Creek . . . Zach Bullock, Surv. Peter Howard, John Porteman, CB Iss. 27 Apr 1767

MOORE, JAMES File no. 73 (186); Gr. no. 78; Bk. 13, p. 425 (17, 4)
Warrant: Unto James Moore, 200 A on S fork fishing Creek adj. Charles Beatys & ____ Kuykendalls . . . 16 Apr 1765 Arthur Dobbs
Plat: Surveyed for James Moore 226 A on S fork Fishing Cre Creek adj. Charles Beatys . . . By Francis Beaty, D Sur. Thos Rainey, Wm Adair, CB Iss. 21 Dec 1763

MOORE, JAMES File no. 1236 (510); Gr. no. 65; Bk. 18, p. 183 (17, 201)
Warrant: Unto James Moore, on waters of S fork Fishing Creek on the Waxaw Road adj. Walkers, Taylors below the Gum log foard . . . 8 Apr 1765 Wm Tryon
Plat: 27 June 1765, Surveyed for James Moore 300 A on waters of S fork Fishing Creek on Crab Tree Branch Wm Taylors line . . . Waggon Road . . . William Dickson, Surv. Ben. Philips, Jonathan Price, CB Iss. 28 Oct 1765

MOORE, JOHN File no. 854 (1575); Gr. no. 87; Bk. 17, p. 393 (18, 359)
300 A on waters of S fork Fishing Creek adj. Edward Lacey, James Moore on both sides Waggon Road 25 Apr 1767 Wm Tryon

MOORE, JOHN File no. 1576; Gr. no. 88; Bk. 18, p. 359
150 A on dry branch leading into the Gum log adj. his own & Rebeccah Cockendals 25 Apr 1767 Wm Tryon

MOORE, MOSES File no. 386 (1117); Gr. no. 294; Bk. 17, p. 140 (18, 126)
50 A on waters of Indian Creek adj. his own & Reynolds land . . . 16 Nov 1764 Arthur Dobbs

MOORE, PATRICK File no. 2029; Gr. no. 454; Bk. 23, p. 39
Plat: March the 15th 1766, Surveyed for Patrick Moore . . .
400 A on both sides the No fork of Packlet . . . P Zach Bullock, Sur. Peter Howard, John Porteman, CB
Warrant: Unto Patrick Moore, on a N branch of Packlet . . .
below the Cherokee path . . . 24 Oct 1765 Wm Tryon Iss. 27
Apr 1767

MORRIS, ROBERT File no. 1604; Gr. no. 122; Bk. 18, p. 366
Warrant: Unto Robert Morris, 200 A on So fork Fishing
Creek adj. Edward Crofts & Robert Browns lines . . . 22 Sept
1766 Wm Tryon
Plat: Surveyed for Robert Morris, 200 A on N branch of So
fork Fishing Creek, adj. Robert Brown, John Davis . . . 16
Jan 1767 William Dickson, Sur. William Smith, George Trumbo, CB Iss. 25 Apr 1767

MORRIS, THOMAS File no. 910 (1631); Gr. no. 155; Bk. 17, p.
407 (18, 372)
95 A on E side Turkey Creek on Morris Mill Branch . . . his
own corner . . . 25 Apr 1767 Wm Tryon

MULDOON, JAMES File no. 1276; Gr. no. 106; Bk. 18, p. 190
Plat: Surveyed for James Muldoon 100 A on Main branch of
Fishing Creek between his own & Hugh Whites lines . . . 20
June 1765 William Dickson, Surv. Richd Dowd, Saml Porter,
CB Iss. 30 Oct 1765

MURPHEY, JAMES File no. 0293
Plat: Surveyed for James Murphey, 150 A on S fork Fishing
Creek, adj. land he now lives on, adj. William Addairs . . . 8
June 1768 Peter Johnston, Surv. John Price, William Adair,
CB

MUSKETTY, JAMES File no. 1623; Gr. no. 147; Bk. 18, p. 371
100 A on waters of Turkey Creek adj. S.E. corner of John
Moore . . . Thomas Rainey . . . John Garvin . . . 25 Apr 1767
Wm Tryon

MUSKETTY [-LLY?], JAMES File no. 1622 (901); Gr. no. 146;
Bk. 17, p. 405 (18, 370)
Warrant: Unto James Muskelly, 100 A on waters of Turkey
Creek adj. land he bought of John Moore towards McNabbs
. . . 22 Sept 1766 Wm Tryon
Plat: Surveyed for James Miskelly, 100 A on Turkey Creek,
McNabbs branch below McNabbs, below his other survey . . .
6 Jan 1767 Wm Dickson, Surv. John Garvin & Thomas Garvin, C.C. Iss. 25 Apr 1767

NESBET, SAMUEL File no. 0296; Entry no. 404
Warrant: Unto Samuel Neisbet, 200 A on Main fork of Tygar River adj. his own, Joseph Jones, David Davis, Robert Millar . . . 26 Apr 1768 Wm Tryon
Plat: Surveyed for Samuel Neisbet, 200 A in Tryon County on N fork Tyger including the improvement he lives on 9 Feb 1769 Peter Johnston, Surv. Thomas Penny, James Neisbet, CB

NEEL, DAVID File no. 1001 (269); Gr. no. 29; Bk. 18, p. 68 (17, 72)
Plat: [nd], Surveyed for David Neill, 400 A on N side Crowders Creek adj. Robert Leeper . . . Francis Beaty, Sur. John Carrell, Thos Johnson, CB Iss. 21 Apr 1764

NEELEY, WILLIAM File no. 2277; Gr. no. 91; Bk. 23, p. 180
Plat: Survey'd for William Neely 200 A on S side N fork Tygar River adj. Charles Moores . . . 17 Dec 1766 Wm Dickson, Surv. John Miller, Martin Oates [Cates?], C.B. Iss. 26 Oct 1767

NEISBET, JAMES File no. 1760; Gr. no. 123; Bk. 20, p. 510
Plat: Surveyed for James Niesbet 160 A on N side Middle fork of Tyger River adj. Black, Collins, & Pennys land . . . 20 May 176___ Peter Johnston, Surv. Daniel Brice, Samuel Brice, CB Iss. 16 Dec 1769

NEILL, THOMAS File no. 252 (984); Gr. no. 13; Bk. 17, p. 53 (18, 30)
Plat: Surveyed for Thomas Neill, 170 A on W side Catawba adj. Neill's old place [nd] By Francis Beaty, D Surv. [Plat shows Jno. Catheys] . . . Thomas Johnson, David Neill, CB Iss. 21 Apr 1764

NISBET, JOHN File no. 1366 (639); Gr. no. 39; Bk. 18, p. 257 (17, 283)
Plat: Surveyed for John Neisbett, 300 A on N side N fork Tyger in forks of Willsons Mill Creek, 24 Feb 1766, William Dickson, Surv. Francis Prince, Nathanl Miller, CB Iss. 25 Sept 1766

NEISBETT, SAMUEL File no. 895 (1616); Gr. no. 136; Bk. 17, p. 403 (18, 369)
Plat: Surveyed for Samuel Nesbett 200 A on both sides S branch N fork Tyger adj. David Davis, Robert Millar . . . 18 Mar 1766 Wm Dickson, Surv. Joseph Jones, Thomas Penny, CB Iss. 25 Apr 1767

NEISBETT, SAMUEL File no. 2283; Gr. no. 141; Bk. 23, p. 181
Plat: Surveyed for Samuel Niesbett, 150 A on both sides S
fork Tyger . . . Francis Dods corner . . . 10 Dec 1766 Wm
Dickson, Sur. Thomas Penny, Saml Brice, CB Iss. 26 Oct
1767

NEWMAN, JONATHAN File no. 1375 (648); Gr. no. 48; Bk. 18,
p. 259 (17, 285)
Plat: Survey'd for Jonathan Newman, 300 A on N fork Tyger
River above Joseph Jones . . . 3 Mar 1766 William Dickson,
Sur. Joseph Jones, Thomas Penney, CB Iss. 25 Sept 1766

NEYSMITH, THOMAS File no. 1719; Gr. no. 85; Bk. 20, p. 433
Plat: Surveyed for Thomas Neysmith, 100 A upon a Branch
of Allisons Creek . . . adj. James Campbell . . . 9 Sept 1767
Jno McK. Alexander. James & Andrew Campbell, CB Iss. 4
May 1769

NICHOLS, JOHN File no. 2149; Gr. no. 207; Bk. 23, p. 118
Plat: Survey'd for John Nichols 150 A on No fork Tyger River above Robert Millers . . . including a Mill Seat . . . 18 Dec
1766 Wm Dickson, Surv. James Miller, Nathl Miller, CB Iss.
26 Oct 1767

NUCKOLS, JOHN File no. 2375; Gr. no. 135; Bk. 23, p. 205
Plat: Aug 8, 1767, Surveyed for John Nuckols, 400 A on
both sides Thickety . . . Stephen Jones line . . . David Robersons line . . . Zach Bullock Joab Mitchell, Stephen Jones, CB
Iss. 28 Apr 1768

ORR, JOHN File no. 2151; Gr. no. 210; Bk. 23, p. 118
Plat: Surveyed for John Orr, 160 A on S branch of N Fork
Tyger adj. Alexander Vernon, John Miller, James Miller . . .
William Dickson, Surv. 13 June 1767 Alexr Vernon, James
Miller, CB Iss. 26 Oct 1767

OSBORN, ALEXANDER File no. 1105 (373); Gr. no. 282; Bk.
18, p. 124 (17, 138)
Plat: Surveyed for Collo. Alexander Osburn 530 A adj. W
Side of Cataubo River, including the mouth of Crowders
Creek and between Catheys land and said river . . . Thomas
Niells's line . . . By Francis Beaty, D Surv [nd] Robert Finley,
Matthew Bigger, CB Iss. 16 Nov 1764

PAGAN, ALEXANDER File no. 525 (1251); Gr. no. 80; Bk. 17,
p. 204 (18, 186)
Plat: 25 June 1765, Surveyed for Alexander Pagan, 200 A on
N side S fork Fishing Creek below George Glovers . . . William Dickson, Surv. Robt Lusk, Samuel Porter, Cha Bear Iss.
28 Oct 1765

PALMER, ROBERT File no. 616 (1343); Gr. no. 16; Bk. 17, p. 279 (18, 369)
Plat: 7 Apr 1766, Surveyed for Robert Palmer, Esquire, 300 A on N side Broad River on Gayan Moores Creek, adj. Gayan Moores line . . . William Dickson, Surv. David Robison, Julius Webb, CB Iss. 25 Sept 1766

PARK, JOSEPH File no. 896 (1617); Gr. no. 137; Bk. 17, p. 404 (18, 369)
Plat: Surveyed for Joseph Parks, 200 A on S side Fereforest, both sides McClures branch & both sides of the Waggon Road . . . 29 Nov 1766 Wm Dickson, Surv. James Mackilwean, George Park, CB Iss. 25 Apr 1767

PATTERSON, ROBERT File no. 2220; Gr. no. 375; Bk. 23, p. 151
Plat: Surveyed for Robert Patterson Junr, 150 A on both sides Clarks fork of Bullocks Creek . . . W Sims, Surv. Wm Cravens, Thos Petterson, CB Iss. 26 Oct 1767

PATTERSON, ROBERT File no. 821 (1542); Gr. no. 21; Bk. 17, p. 380 (18, 347)
Plat: 22 Mar 1766, Surveyed for Robert Patterson, 200 A on Clarks fork of Bullocks Creek adj. Robert Blacks . . . Wm Sims, Surv. Mathew Black, Robert Cravins, CB Iss. 22 Apr 1767

PATTERSON, THOMAS File no. 820 (1541); Gr. no. 20; Bk. 17, p. 380 (18, 347)
60 A on both sides Clarks fork of Bullocks Creek adj. Robert Blacks, Harrisons . . . 22 Apr 1767 Wm Tryon

PATTON, JOHN File no. 796 (1517); Gr. no. 470; Bk. 17, p. 371 (18, 340)
Plat: 19 May 1766, Surveyed for John Patton, 200 A on S side Allisons Creek adj. John Kerr, John Taggerts . . . William Dickson, Surv. John Kerr, Adam McCord, CB Iss. 27 Sept 1766

PATRICKS, WILLIAM File no. 28 (141); Gr. no. 39; Bk. 13, p. 388 (15, 480)
Plat: [nd], Surveyed for WILLIAM Patrick 300 A on Allisons Creek . . . By Francis Beaty, D Surv. Robert Patrick, Robert Patrick Junr, CB Iss. 19 Apr 1763

PATRICK, WILLIAM File no. 439 (1167); Gr. no. 59; Bk. 17, p. 159 (18, 144)
Plat: [nd], Surveyed for William Patrick 270 A on S side Allisons Creek, including an Indian path . . . Francis Beaty, D. Surv. Robert Leeper, Dd. Neill, CB Iss. 6 Apr 1765

PATRICK, WILLIAM File no. 916 (1637); Gr. no. 161; Bk. 17, p. 409 (18, 373)
Plat: Feb 1767, Surveyed for William Patrick, 300 A on waters of Crouders and Allisons Creeks, adj. Henderson, McCullohs, James Moor . . . Peter Johnston, Surv. Robert Patrick, John Chittam, CB Iss. 25 Apr 1767

PATRICK, WILLIAM File no. 362 (1094); Gr. no. 271; Bk. 17, p. 136 (18, p. 122)
Plat: 20 Mar 176____, Surveyed for Wm Patrick, 400 A on waters of Allisons Creek adj. George Renicks old survey . . . Andrew Allisons old line . . . Joseph Davies' corner . . . Francis Beaty, DS James Campbell, Hugh Beatey, CB Iss. 16 Nov 1764

PENETON, BENEJAH File no. 2208; Gr. no. 362; Bk. 23, p. 148
Plat: Surveyed for Benijah Pennenton, 300 A on waters of Rockey Allisons Creek . . . Rusks & his own line . . . 4 Feb 1767 Peter Johnston, Surv. Archd Barron, Benijah Penninton, CB Iss. 26 Oct 1767

PENINGTON, BENAJAH File no. 418 (1146); Gr. no. 37; Bk. 17, p. 55 (18, 141)
Plat: 24 Mar 1764, Surveyed for Benajah Pennington 187 A on a branch of Allisons Creek . . . George Alexander, D Sur. Ceagy Penington, Abraham Kuykendall, CB Iss. 6 Apr 1765

PENNINGTON, MICAJAH File no. 1182 (454); Gr. no. 73; Bk. 18, p. 147 (17, 162)
Plat: [nd], Survd. for Micajah Penington, 152 A on a branch of Fishing Creek including his improvement on N side John Humphreys land . . . George Alexander, DS Benejah Pennington, Martain Armstrong, CB Iss. 6 Apr 1765

PENNY, THOMAS File no. 2269; Gr. no. 48; Bk. 23, p. 178
Plat: Survey [sic] for Thomas Penny 300 A on middle fork of Tyger River . . . Zac Bullock, Surv. James Ross, Alexander Ray, CB Iss. 26 Oct 1767

PENNY, THOMAS File no. 2282; Gr. no. 140; Bk. 23, p. 181
Plat: Surveyed for Thomas Penny 200 A on North and middle fork of Tyger on Jammes branch about a mile above Alexander Verners . . . 9 Dec 1766 Wm Dickson, Surv. John Black, Alexr Vernon, CB Iss. 26 Oct 1767

PEOPLES, ISOM File no. 2436; Gr. no. 302; Bk. 23, p. 242
Warrant: Unto John Purson [sic] 300 A on Sadle fork of Silver Creek . . . above Canada . . . cabin begun by sd. Purson . . . 25 Sept 1766 Wm Tryon

Plat: Surveyed for Isom Peoples 150 A on W side Broad River including mouth of Peoples Creek . . . 2 June 1767 By Wm Sharp, Sur. Iss. 29 Apr 1766 Thomas Clark & Henry Hamilton, C.C.

PHILLIPS, BENJAMIN File no. 1585 (864); Gr. no. 101; Bk. 18, p. 361 (17, 395)
Plat: Surveyed for Benjamin Phillips 400 A on main fishing creek adj. John Harden, William Dickson, James Young, James Hanna . . . 27 Apr 1766 Wm Dickson, Surv. James Hanna, Bartholomw. Dosson, CB Iss. 25 Apr 1767

PHILLIPS, STEVEN File no. 2212; Gr. no. 367; Bk. 23, p. 149
Plat: 23 Aug 1766, Surveyed for Stephen Phillip 100 A on both sides a large fork of Kings Creek . . . W. Sims, Sur. Thomas Linn, John Linn, CB Iss. 26 Oct 1767

PORTER, DAVID File no. 2041; Gr. no. 469; Bk. 23, p. 41
Plat: Jan 23, 1766, Surveyed for David Porter, 180 A on Turkey Creek . . . Byars line . . . Zac Bullock, Surv. James Porter, William Byars, CB Iss. 25 Apr 1767

PORTER, MATTHEW File no. 0314
Plat: May 20, 1767, Surveyed for Matthew Porter, 300 A on Turkey Creek adj. David Byars . . . P Zach Bullock Joseph Harding, James McAfee, CB

PORTER, SAMUEL File no. 865 (1586); Gr. no. 102; Bk. 17, p. 395 (18, 362)
Plat: Surveyed for Samuel Porter, 300 A on So side of So fork of Fishing Creek . . . Richard Carrols by the Saludy Rode . . . George Glovers . . . 16 Jany 1767 William Dickson, Survr. Saml Porter, Saml Lusk, CB Iss. 25 Apr 1767

PORTER, SAMUEL File no. 659 (1389); Gr. no. 59; Bk. 17, p. 287 (18, 261)
Plat: Surveyed for Samuel Porter, 200 A on both sides Fishing Creek above Mary Smiths . . . by the Indian line . . . 26 June 1765. P William Dickson, Survr. Robert Neely, Robert Lusk, CB Iss. 25 Sept 1766

PORTMAN, JOHN File no. 538 (1264); Gr. no. 93; Bk. 17, p. 207 (18, 188)
Plat: Surveyed for John Portman 200 A on both sides of Packolett River including his own Improvemts. 3d Septr. 1765 William Dickson, Survr. James Byers, John Moore, Cha. Bear. Iss. 30 Oct 1765

PORTMAN, JOHN File no. 2225; Gr. no. 380; Bk. 23, p. 152
Plat: March 15, 1766, Surveyed for John Portman, 200 A on Island Creek . . . [No Sur., No CB] Iss. 26 Oct 1767

PORTMAN, JOHN JR. File no. 2038; Gr. no. 463; Bk. 23, p. 41
Plat: Surveyed for John Portman Junr 200 A on both sides Pacolet River ... Widow McWhorters Corner ... P Za Bullock [nd] [No CB] Iss. 27 Apr 1767

POTTS, JOHN File no. 1970; Gr. no. 322; Bk. 23, p. 15
Plat: March 22, 1766, Surveyed for John Potts, 250 A on both sides Clarks fork of Bullocks Creek ... W Sims ... Robert Cravens, Newbery Stockton, CB Iss. 25 Apr 1767

POTTS, JONATHAN File no. 1982; Gr. no. 334; Bk. 23, p. 17
Plat: March 25, 1766, Surveyed for Jonathan Potts, 300 A on both sides Clarks fork of Bullocks Creek ... W Sims- Julius Webb, Newberry Stockton, CB Iss. 25 Apr 1767

PRICE, JOHN File no. 1557 (836); Gr. no. 67; Bk. 18, p. 355 (17, 388)
Plat: Surveyed for John Price 270 A on So fork Fishing Creek adj. Jones, Kuykendall, & his own line ... Wm Jones corner ... 9 May 1766 William Dickson, Surv. John Conner, Edward Croft, CB Iss. 25 Apr 1767

PRINCE, JOHN File no. 2518; Gr. no. 507; Bk. 23, p. 301
Plat: Surveyed for John Prince 300 A on the No Fork of Tyger on the Waters of Willsons Mill Creek and on Jones's Waggon Road joining above his other survey ... 11 Decr 1766 William Dickson, Surv. Francis Dodds, Sauny Ray, Cha. Bear. Iss. 29 Apr 1768

PRINCE, JOHN File no. 2519; Gr. no. 508; Bk. 23, p. 301
Plat: Survey'd for John Prince 640 A on No side of the No Fork of Tyger River on the Waters of Willsons Mill Creek, adj. Francis Wilsons Corner, John Nisbetts corner ... 11 Dec 1766 Wm Dickson, Surv. Thomas Case, Francis Prince, Cha. Bear. Iss. 29 Apr 1768
[Spartanburg SC Deed Book B, pp. 103-105: Mary, widow of John Prince, Robert Prince & wf Jane ... Robt, son of John Prince]

PRITCHARD, DANIEL File no. 247 (977); Gr. no. 6; Bk. 17, p. 52 (18, 49)
Plat: [nd], Surveyed for Daniel Pritchard, 300 A on 'Both sides Allisons Creek adj. John McCullohs line ... Pr Francis Beaty, D Surv. James Campbell, Saml Humphry, CB Iss. 21 Apr 1764

QUARLES, MOSES File no. 1337; Bk. 18, p. 242-3
Plat: Aug 24, 1765, Surveyed for Moses Quarles, 200 A on both sides Kings Creek ... Bells line ... P William Sims, S.M.C. Wilkerson turner, Joseph Neal, CB Iss. 30 Oct 1765

QUINN, HUGH File no. 2009; Gr. no. 435; Bk. 23, p. 35
Plat: Feb the 23 1766, Surveyed for Hugh Quinn, 200 A on East sid of Broad River . . . P Zach Bullock, Sur. Samuel Richardson, James Collens, Cb Iss. 25 Apr 1767

QUINN, HUGH File no. 2202; Gr. no. 356; Bk. 23, p. 147
Plat: August 18th, 1767, Surveyed for Hugh Quinn, 400 A on the South side of Broad River including Isam Wamocks improvement . . . Beatys corner . . . P Zach Bullock, Sur. John Gousel, James Collens, CB Iss. 26 Oct 1767

RAINEY, BENJAMIN File no. 835 (1556); Gr. no. 66; Bk. 17, p. 388 (18, 355)
Plat: 25 Apr 1766, Surveyed for Benjamin Rainey 350 A on S side Main fishing Creek . . . William Hannas line . . . James Hannas line . . . James Young line . . . Alexander Lewis . . . Thomas McMurray line . . . William Dickson, Sur. John Anderson, Benjn Phillips, CB Iss. 25 Apr 1767

RAINEY, THOMAS File no. 325 (1057); Gr. no. 238; Bk. 17, p. 126 (18, 113)
Plat: April ye 28, 1764, Survd. for Thomas Rainey on ye West side Cataba on ye So fork Fishing Creek, adj. David Lewis [?] . . . By George Alexander Samuel Rainey, Edward Croft, CB [194 A] Iss. 16 Nov 1764

RAINEY, THOMAS File no. 2203; Gr. no. 357; Bk. 23, p. 147
Plat: Surveyed for Thomas Rany 75 A on Rockey Fork of Fishing Creek . . . William Hannahs line . . . 20 Aug 1767 Peter Johnston, Surv. [No CB]. Iss. 26 Oct 1767

RAINEY, THOMAS File no. 674 (1401); Gr. no. 74; Bk. 17, p. 290 (18, 263)
Plat: Surveyed for Thomas Rainey, 140 A between Robert Ewarts land & Ephraim McClains land he bought of William Moore, on a branch of Turkey Creek . . . 13 May 1766 Ben. Rainey, Sam Rainey, CB Iss. 25 Sept 1766

RAINEY, THOMAS File no. 32 (1053); Gr. no. 234; Bk. 17, p. 125 (18, 113)
Plat: Surveyed for Thomas Rainey 280 A on middle branches of S fork Fishing Creek . . . including his own house . . . Francis Beaty, D Surv. [nd], John Moore, Joseph Duncan, CB Iss. 16 Nov 1764

RAINEY, THOMAS File no. 251 (983); Gr. no. 12; Bk. 17, p. 53 (18, 50)
Plat: Surveyed for Thomas Rainey 400 A on middle branch of S fork fishing Creek adj. McNabb . . . By Francis Beaty, D Surv. Joseph Duncan, John Strand, CB Iss. 21 Apr 1764

RAINEY, THOMAS File no. 350 (1082); Gr. no. 258; Bk. 17, p. 132 (18, 119)
Plat: [nd], Surveyed for Thomas Rainey, 300 A on middle branch of S fork Fishing Creek adj. where he now lives . . . Francis Beaty, D Surv. John Moore, Joseph Duncan, CB Iss. 16 Nov 1764

RAINEY, THOMAS & BENJAMIN File no. 2407; Gr. no. 206; Bk. 23, p. 222
Plat: Surveyed for Thomas & Benjamin Rainey 500 A on middle ground between Sandy River and a small dry fork of fishing Creek known as the Englishman branch 6 Jan 1766 Peter Johnston, Sur. Iss. 28 Apr 1768 Thomas Larney & John Dennis, C.C.

RAINEY, THOMAS & BENJAMIN File no. 2085; Gr. no. 92; Bk. 23, p. 97
Plat: Surveyed for Thomas and Benjamin Rainey 190 A on waters of Turkey Creek adj. James McNabs line . . . 26 Dec 1766 Peter Johnston, Surv. Benjn & Thomas Rainey, CB Iss. 26 Oct 1767

RAINEY, THOMAS & BENJAMIN PHILLIPS File no. 2086; Gr. no. 93; Bk. 23, p. 98
Plat: Surveyed for Thomas Raney and Benjamin Phillips 600 A on No fork Fishing Creek at James Wallace . . . Sadlers line . . . John Thomas's line . . . 22 Dec 1767 Peter Johnston, Surv. Samuel Lacey, John Mahan, CB Iss. 26 Oct 1767

RAYE, ALEXANDER File no. 2232; Gr. no. 387; Bk. 23, p. 153
Plat: Dec 8, 1766, Surveyed for Alexr Ray 150 A on both sides North Fork Tiger River . . . John Millers line . . . Zacha Bullock. Joseph Jones, William Sharp, CB Iss. 26 Oct 1767

READ, ABRAHAM File no. 2210; Gr. no. 365; Bk. 23, p. 149
Plat: 17 Feb 1767, Surveyed for Abram Read, 200 A on both sides Bullocks Creek including his own Improvement . . . William Sims, Surv. Abram Reed, Eliza. Gambel, CB Iss. 26 Oct 1767
[A female chain bearer is quite unusual — BHH]

REED, DAVID File no. 818 (1539); Gr. no. 18; Bk. 17, p. 379 (18, 347)
Plat: 10 Apr 1766, Surveyed for David Reed, 100 A on E side turkey Creek on Susy Bowles branch . . . William Dickson, Surv. Wm Minter, John Miles, CB Iss. 22 Apr 1767

RENNICK, MARY File no. 2171; Gr. no. 23; Bk. 23, p. 122
Plat: Surveyed for Mary Rennick, 150 A on waters of Fishing

Creek . . . Andrew Woods line . . . Robert Allisons corner . . . Thomas Prices land . . . Robert Leepers line . . . 22 July 1767 Wm Dickson, Surv. James Young, Mathew Armstrong, CB Iss. 26 Oct 1767

RENICK, GEORGE File no. 94 (208); Gr. no. 46; Bk. 13, p. 429 (17, 7)
Plat: [nd], Survey'd for George Renick, 200 A on Wt side N fork Fishing Creek . . . adj. a tract formerly his own (now John Davies's) . . . By Francis Beaty, James Armstrong, Geo: Renick, CB Iss. 21 Dec 1763

RICHARDSON, SAMUEL File no. 2437; Gr. nò. 304; Bk. 23, p. 243
Plat: Survey'd for Saml Richardson, 120 A on E side Broad River on Beaverdam Creek adj. James Chambers & Patrick Lapherties . . . 20 Dec 1767 Wm Sharp, Surv. John McKinney, James Campbell, CB Iss. 29 Apr 1768

RICHMOND, JOHN File no. 2356; Gr. no. 107; Bk. 23, p. 203
Plat: 14 May 1767, Surveyed for John Richmond on N fork Fishing Creek . . . Peter Kuykendalls . . . James Rushes corner . . . Burnes' line . . . Catawbo Indian Line . . . P William Sims, Surv. John Fondren, Martin Armstrong, CB Iss. 28 Apr 1768

RIGGS, JOHN File no. 1595 (874); Gr. no. 111; Bk. 18, p. 364 (17, 398)
Plat: Surveyed for John Riggs 300 A on both sides Bullocks Creek adj. John Hartness, Wm Mcaddos, Gayn [sic] Moores, & Fultons line . . . 9 Apr 1766 Wm Dickson, Surv. John Hillhouse, James Hillhouse, CB Iss. 25 Apr 1767

ROSS, WILLIAM File no. 2250; Gr. no. 409; Bk. 23, p. 157
Plat: Surveyed for William Ross, 400 A on E side Broad, branch of Turkey Creek . . . Alexander Loves corner . . . Michael Megarritys line . . . Wm Dickson, Surv. 6 June 1767 George Ross, Jo. Dickson, CB Iss. 26 Oct 1767

RISKS, JAMES File no. 305 (1037); Gr. no. 110; Bk. 17, p. 97 (18, 90)
Plat: [nd], Surveyed for James Risk, 300 A on a branch of fishing Creek on the great Road from John Armstrongs to Peter Kuykendals, including William Moores improvement . . . Francis Beaty, D Surv. Samuel Watson, Moses Forster, CB Iss. 9 Nov 1764

ROBESON, DAVID File no. 2167; Gr. no. 226; Bk. 23, p. 121
Plat: Surveyed for David Robeson, 400 A on N side Broad River, waters of Turkey Creek . . . both sides of waggon Road including Wades old Store house . . . John Kellys . . . John

Wades line . . . John Rottons line . . . James hannah's line . . . 3 July 1767 . . . Wm Dickson, Surv. John Rotton, Alexander Harper, CB Iss. 26 Oct 1767

ROBINSON, ARCHIBALD File no. 732; Gr. no. 301; Bk. 17, p. 334
Plat: Surveyed for Archibald Robeson, 100 A on waters of Bullocks Creek between Shearers, Bells, & Alexanders line . . . Zachariah Bells, John McKnitt Alexander . . . 16 Sept 1765 William Dickson, Surv. Archd Robeson, Thomas Collins, CB Iss. 26 Sept 1766

ROBINSON, JAMES File no. 903 (1624); Gr. no. 148; Bk. 17, p. 405 (18, 371)
Plat: Surveyed for James Robinson, 100 A on a branch of Fishing Creek, called Burns branch . . . William Neelys line . . . 9 Jan 1767 Wm Dickson, Surv. James Smith, George Smith, CB Iss. 25 Apr 1767

ROBINSON, SAMUEL File no. 954 (1675); Gr. no. 212; Bk. 17, p. 419 (18, 382)
Plat: 14 Sept 1765, Surveyed for Samuel Robeson, 200 A on Et side Broad River, on Loves Creek, a branch of Bullocks Creek . . . William Dickson, Surv. Archd Robeson, William Bell, CB Iss. 25 Apr 1767

ROBINSON, ARCHIBALD File no. 737 (1465); Gr. no. 306; Bk. 17, p. 335 (18, 307)
Plat: 13 Sept 1765, Surveyed for Archabald Roberson, 200 A on both sides Gilkeys Creek . . . P William Sims, S.M.C. William Marchbanks, James Fanning, CB Iss. 26 Sept 1766

ROBINSON, ARCHIBALD File no. 1460 (732); Gr. no. 301; Bk. 18, p. 306 (17, 334)
100 A on waters of Bullocks Creek adj. Shearers, Bells, & Alexanders . . . 26 Sept 1766 Wm Tryon

ROSS, FRANCIS File no. 908 (1629); Gr. no. 153; Bk. 17, p. 407 (18, 372)
Plat: 25 July 1766, Surveyed for Francis Ross, 200 A on head of Burrelson [sic] branch . . . Zach Bullock John Miller, William Ross, CB Iss. 25 Apr 1767

ROSS, FRANCIS File no. 1566 (845); Gr. no. 77; Bk. 18, p. 357 (17, 391)
Plat: Surveyed for Frances Ross, 200 A on main branch of Turkey Creek above James Walkers survey . . . 18 Feb 1766 William Dickson, Surv. William Champ, John Couch, CB Iss. 25 Apr 1767

ROSS, GEORGE File no. 621 (1348); Gr. no. 21; Bk. 17, p. 280 (18, 254)
Plat: 19 Feb 1766, Surveyed for George Ross 200 A on waters of dry fork of Turkey Creek . . . path that leads from Bullocks Creek to Pattons mill called old Indian path . . . William Dickson, Surv. John Ross, James Ross, CB Iss. 25 Sept 1766

ROSS, JOHN File no. 0348
Warrant: Unto John Ross 150 A on waters of Tirkey [sic] Creek adj. William Graham and Allexander hardens land . . . 26 Apr 1768 Wm Tryon
Plat: Surveyed for John Ross 130 A on waters of Turkey Creek between Willm Graham & Alexr Hardins . . . 24 Dec 1767 John Miller, James Martin, CB Peter Johnston, Surv.

ROSS, JOHN File no. 2414; Gr. no. 213; Bk. 23, p. 223
Plat: Surveyed for John Ross, 100 A on both sides Turkey Creek adj. Brysons and his own land . . . Peter Johnston, Surv. [nd] James Ross, George Hogg, Junr, CB Iss. 28, Apr 1768

ROSS, JOHN File no. 2112; Gr. no. 121; Bk. 23, p. 102
Plat: Surveyed for John Ross, 195 A on a branch of Turkey Creek adj. William Graham, his own, William Ross 25 Augt 1767 Peter Johnston, Surv. Nicholas Smith, George Ross, CB Iss. 26 Oct 1767

ROTTAN, JOHN File no. 2396; Gr. no. 194; Bk. 23, p. 220
Plat: Surveyed for John Rottan, 300 A on S fork Lawsons fork of Pacalot including his Improvement . . . 26 May 1767 Peter Johnston, Surv. Iss. 28 Apr 1768 John Earle & Henry Gabrill, C.C.

SADLER, MARY File no. 0353
Plat: Surveyed for Mary Sadler 100 A on waters of N fork Tyger adj. James Neisbet, Danl Brice, Alexander McCarters . . . 31 May 1768 Peter Johnston, Surv. Alexr Vernon, John Leetch, CB

SADLER, RICHARD File no. 2281; Gr. no. 139; Bk. 23, p. 181
Plat: Surveyed for Richard Sadler 400 A on So side No fork Tyger on both sides Jameys branch . . . Francis Willsons corner . . . near Alexander Vernors house . . . 9 Dec 1766 . . . Wm Dickson, Surv. Thomas Penney, Alexander Vernor, CB Iss. 26 Oct 1767

SARTIN, JOHN File no. 2244; Gr. no. 399; Bk. 23, p. 155
Plat: 16 Aug 1767, Surveyed for John Sartain, 200 A on s fork Packlet above John Clerks Zach Bullock [surv], Joab Mitchel, James Finley, CB Iss. 26 Oct 1767

SCOTT, JAMES File no. 2005; Gr. no. 430; Bk. 23, p. 35
Plat: Feb 4, 1767, Surveyed for James Scott, 200 A on both sides a branch of Bullocks Creek, southward of Robert Pettersons . . . Wm Sims, Surv. Robt Black, Joseph Black, CB Iss. 25 Apr 1767

SCOTT, THOMAS File no. 315 (1047); Gr. no. 228; Bk. 17, p. 124 (18, 112)
Plat: 3 Sept 1763, Surveyed for Thomas Scott, 325 A on waters of Fishing Creek above William Watsons, including his own Improvement . . . McClure branch . . . Francis Beaty, D Surv. Wm Watson, John Carrell, CB Iss. 16 Nov 1764

SELLER, JOHN File no. 837 (1558); Gr. no. 68; Bk. 17, p. 389 (18, 356)
Plat: 24 Apr 1766, Surveyed for John Sellder on main branch of Fishing Creek . . . Robert McClellands . . . 200 A . . . William Dickson, Surv. Robert McClelland, William Lea, CB Iss. 25 Apr 1767

SHARP, JOHN File no. 2070; Gr. no. 39; Bk. 23, p. 88
Plat: Surveyed for John Sharp, 400 A on west side broad both sides Horses Creek . . . 6 June 1767 Wm Sharp, Surv. Phillip & Nicholas Henson, CB Iss. 26 Oct 1767

SHARP, JOHN File no. 2069; Gr. no. 45; Bk. 23, p. 86
Plat: Surveyed for John Sharp, 200 A on both sides So branch of N fork Tyger River . . . below Robert Millers land . . . near the Waggon Road . . . 22 May 1767 Wm Sharp, Surv. Wm McMacken, James Miller, CB Iss. 26 Oct 1767

SHARP, WILLIAM File no. 0368
Plat: Surveyed for William Sharp, 200 A on S fork Broad River about 1 1/2 miles above Fifers land . . . 7 Sept 1768 Wm Sharp Wm Henson, Wm Robbins, CB

SHARP, WILLIAM File no. 549 (1275); Gr. no. 105; Bk. 17, p. 209 (18, 190)
Plat: 17 June 1765, Surveyed for William Sharp, 200 A on waters of Bullocks Creek, head of Stinson branch . . . William Dickson, D Surv. John Stillhouse, John Riggs, CB Iss. 30 Oct. 1765

SHARP, WILLIAM File no. 2071; Gr. no. 40; Bk. 23, p. 88
Plat: Surveyed for William Sharp 300 A on W side Broad on both sides Suck Creek . . . 6 June 1767 Wm Sharp, Surv. Phillip & Nicholas Henson, CB Iss. 26 Oct 1767

SHARP, WILLIAM File no. 2075; Gr. no. 44; Bk. 23, p. 89
Plat: Surveyed for William Sharp 400 A on both sides S fork

Tyger River, about 3 miles from Joseph Jones ... 23 May 1767 Wm Sharp, Surv. Joseph Jones, John Sharp, CB Iss. 26 Oct 1767

SIMONSON, MAGNUS File no. 238 (970); Gr. no. 48; Bk. 17, p. 40 (18, 35)
Plat: Surveyed for Magnus Simonson, 100 A on S side Broad River on lower Fishdam Creek including his Improvement ... 12 Augt 1763 P William Dickson, D Surv. George Underwood, Magnus Simonson, CB Iss. 15 Feb 1764

SIMMONS, JOHN & THOMAS File no. 2245; Gr. no. 400; Bk. 23, p. 155
Plat: 16 Aug 1767, Surveyed for John & Thomas Timmons, 400 A on S Packlet called Jacks branch ... Zach Bullock John McGrew, Alexr Killpatrick, CB Iss. 26 Oct 1767

SIMPSON, ARTHUR File no. 2515; Gr. no. 481; Bk. 23, p. 295
Plat: Surveyed for Arthur Simpson, 200 A on s side Fair Forrest on both sides Waggon Road adj. Joseph Parks line ... 4 Mar 1768 Wm Dickson, Surv. Samuel Cloney, George Story, CB Iss. 29 Apr 1768

SIMPSON, HUGH File no. 816 (1537); Gr. no. 16; Bk. 17, p. 379 (18, 346)
Plat: Surveyed for Hugh Simpson, 138 A on Turkey Creek, including the improvement he now lives on ... near Dicksons line ... Mr. Kolbs corner ... Riggs line ... Campbells ...'. Floyds line ... Jno McK. Alexander _____ Oct 1765 Jas Culp, Robt Lusk, CB Iss. 22 Apr 1767

SIMPSON, SAMUEL File no. 911 (1632); Gr. no. 156; Bk. 17, p. 407 (18, 372)
Plat: 9 Sept 1765, Surveyed for Samuel Simpson, 400 A on N side Fair Forrest on Harris branch adj. Robert Harris line ... William Dickson, Surv. James Mayes, William Mills, CB Iss. 25 Apr 1767

SIMS, WILLIAM File no. 1946; Gr. no. 298; Bk. 23, p. 12
Plat: 1 May 1766, Surveyed for William Sims, 400 A on Ridge between Packlet & Thicketty creeks ... on both sides Johnses path ... Zach Bullock, Surv. William Marchbanks, Adam Burchfield, CB Iss. 25 Apr 1767

SMITH, HENRY File no. 1602 (881); Gr. no. 120; Bk. 18, p. 366 (17, 400)
Plat: Surveyed for Henry Smith 150 A on Et side Broad River by the Island, Gayan Moores corner ... Howards branch ... 23 Aug 1765 William Dickson, Surv. Wm McMullon, William Crow, CB Iss. 25 Apr 1767

SMITH, HENRY File no. 1283 (557); Gr. no. 113; Bk. 18, p. 392
(17, 211)
Plat: Surveyed for Henry Smith 100 A adj. E side Broad
above William Loves, including Improvement bought of
Michael Taylor . . . 23 Augt 1765 William Dickson, Surv. William McMullen, William Crow, CB Iss. 30 Oct 1765

SMITH, ISAAC File no. 861 (1582); Gr. no. 98; Bk. 17, p. 394
(18, 361)
Plat: Surveyed for Isaac Smith 250 A on both sides Fishing
Creek adj. Philip Walker & John Latta . . . 9 Jan 1767 Wm
Dickson, Surv. James Smith, George Smith, CB Iss. 25 Apr
1767

SMITH, JAMES File no. 862 (1583); Gr. no. 99; Bk. 17, p. 395
(18, 361)
Plat: 8 Jan 1767, Surveyed for James Smith 83 A on N side
Fishing Creek, adj. John Smith, Mary Smith . . . Wm Dickson,
Surv. John Smith, George Smith, CB Iss. 25 Apr 1767

SMITH, JAMES File no. 2248; Gr. no. 403; Bk. 23, p. 155
Plat: 31 Jan 1767, Surveyed for James Smith, 300 A on
Buckhorn fork of Bullocks Creek . . . adj. Dicksons line . . .
John McNet Alexanders line . . . Za Bullock, [Surv.], William
Watson, James Watson, CB Iss. 25 Apr 1767

SMITH, JAMES File no. 2505; Gr. no. 471; Bk. 23, p. 293
Plat: Surveyed for James Smith, 200 A on W side Cuttawba
on N side Fishing Creek on both sides Kaney Run . . . both
sides Waggon Road . . . William Neeleys line . . . 16 Jan 1767
Wm Dickson, Surv. William Smith, George Smith, CB Iss. 29
Apr 1768

SMITH, JOHN File no. 0376
Plat: Surveyed for John Smith, 200 A on W side Cuttaubo on
N side Fishing Creek on Smiths branch called Stillhouse
branch . . . Mary Smiths line . . . 9 Jan 1767 William Dickson,
Surv. James Smith, Isaac Smith, CB

SMITH, JOHN File no. 1659 (938); Gr. no. 185; Bk. 18, p. 378
(17, 415)
Plat: Surveyed for John Smith, 200 A on Bullocks Creek adj.
John Heartness, Stephenson . . . Jno McK. Alexander, Surv.
John Heartness, Joseph Watson, CB Iss. 25 Apr 1767

SMITH, MARY File no. 100 (214); Gr. no. 52; Bk. 13, p. 430 (17,
8)
Plat: Surveyed for Mary Smith, Widow, 300 A on N side
Fishing Creek including the Improvements of her late hus-

band, William Smith, Decd . . . 29 Augr 1763 . . . Francis
Beaty, D.S. Isaac Smith, George Smith, CB Iss. 21 Dec 1763

SMITH, REBECCA File no. 917 (1638); Gr. no. 162; Bk. 17, p. 409 (18, 374)
Plat: Surveyed for Rebecca Smith, 200 A on a head branch of Rockey Allisons Creek adj. Benijah Pennington including her own improvement . . . 12 Feb 1767 Peter Johnston, Surv. Thomas Scott, John Young, CB Iss. 25 Apr 1767

SMITH, SAMUEL File no. 2113; Gr. no. 162; Bk. 23, p. 109
Plat: 9 Feb 1767, Surveyed for Saml Smith 390 A on S side Packlet . . . George Moors . . . Zach Bullock, [surv.] John Wideman, Phillip Wideman, CB Iss. 26 Oct 1767

SMITH, WILLIAM File no. 905 (1626); Gr. no. 150; Bk. 17, p. 406 (18, 371)
Plat: Surveyed for William Smith, 250 A on S side Fishing Creek adj. William Davis, Philip Walkers . . . near John Dunhams Improvement . . . 10 Jan 1767 Wm Dickson, Surv. James Smith, John Smith, CB Iss. 25 Apr 1767

SMITH, WILLIAM File no. 1351 (624); Gr. no. 24; Bk. 18, p. 254 (17, 280)
Plat: Surveyed for William Smith 260 A on both sides Fishing Creek adj. Samuel Porters corner on the Indian line . . . McClelland line . . . Mary Smith line . . . 30 Apr 1766 William Dickson, Surv. Thomas McMurray, Hugh McClelland, CB Iss. 25 Sept 1766

SPENCER, SAMUEL File no. 2034; Gr. no. 459; Bk. 23, p. 40
Plat: March 18, 1767, Surveyed for Samuel Spencer 300 A on S fork Packlet . . . Zack Bullock, Surv. Jas. Howard, Alexr Kilpatrick, CB Iss. 27 Apr 1767

STEEN, JOHN File no. 2235; Gr. no. 390; Bk. 23, p. 153
Plat: June 6, 1767, Survey'd for John Steen, 200 A on both sides Thicketty Creek adj. his other survey . . . Zach Bullock James Steen, Timothy Calaham, CB Iss. 26 Oct 1767

STEEN, JOHN File no. 2239; Gr. no. 394; Bk. 23, p. 154
Plat: Aug 1, 1767, Surveyed for John Steen 200 A on Thicketty Creek adj. his So survey . . . Zach Bullock, Surv. Timothy Calaham, James Lain, CB Iss. 26 Oct 1767

STEEN, JOHN File no. 2240; Gr. no. 395; Bk. 23, p. 154
Plat: Surveyed for John Steen, 200 A on Thicketty Creek, adj. Cornelius Oneal, Henry Ditemore . . . June 6, 1767 . . . Zach Bullock, Surv. James Steen, Timothy Calaham, CB Iss. 26 Oct 1767

STEEN, JOHN File no. 2241; Gr. no. 396; Bk. 23, p. 154; Entry no. 989
Plat: Aug 1, 1767, Surveyed for John Steen, 250 A on Thicketty Creek adj. his other survey . . . Zach Bullock, Surv. Timothy Callaham, James Lain, CB Iss. 26 Oct 1767

STEEN, JOHN File no. 2148; Gr. no. 206; Bk. 23, p. 118
Plat: Survey'd for John Steen, 100 A on W side Broad River above Edward McNeals land including one improvement made by John Harper . . . 22 June 1767 . . . Wm Dickson, Surv. John Steen, Nathl Jefferson, CB Iss. 26 Oct 1767

STEVENSON, JAMES File no. 2423; Gr. no. 286; Bk. 23, p. 239
Plat: Surveyed for James Stevenson, 175 A on waters of Turkey Creek adj. Alexander, Adair & Kolbs line . . . Nov 29 1767 Jno Mck. Alexander, Surv. James Hamilton, William Sample, CB Iss. 28 Apr 1768

STEPHENSON, JNO File no. 1360 (633); Gr. no. 33; Bk. 18, p. 256 (17, 282)
Plat: Surveyed for John Stephenson, 100 A on Et side Bullocks Creek adj. his own line . . . 8 Apr 1766 William Dickson, Surv. Barnabas Henley, John Hartness, CB Iss. 25 Sept 1766

STEVENSON, JAMES File no. 2397; Gr. no. 195; Bk. 23, p. 220
Plat: Surveyed for James Stevenson 200 A on both sides Rocky Allisons Creek . . . John Halls corner . . . Walter Davis line . . . Feb 10, 1767 Peter Johnston, Surv. John Hall, William Whaley, CB Iss. 28 Apr 1768

STOREY, GEORGE File no. 906 (1627); Gr. no. 151; Bk. 17, p. 406 (18, 371)
Plat: Surveyed for George Story 200 A on the waters of the No side of Fair Forrest on Kelseys Branch 12 March 1766 William Dickson, Surv. Giles Stillet [sic], Anthoney Story, Cha. Bear. Iss. 25 Apr 1767

SWANN, ROBERT File no. 1416 (688); Gr. no. 159; Bk. 18, p. 276 (17, 304)
Plat: March 26, 1766, Surveyed for Robert Swann, 150 A on Bullocks Creek P William Sims, John Countryman, Thos Harrisson, CB Iss. 26 Sept 1766

SWANN, ROBERT File no. 1999; Gr. no. 423; Bk. 23, p. 34
Plat: 26 Mar 1766, Surveyed for Robert Swann 200 A on waters of Watsons Creek & the Rock Bottom fork . . . above Narrow Knob . . . Dicksons line . . . William Sims, Sam Swann, CB Iss. 25 Apr 1767

SWANN, ROBERT File no. 2012; Gr. no. 438; Bk. 23, p. 36
Plat: March 26, 1767, Surveyed for Robert Swann, 200 A on branches of David Watsons Fork of Bullocks Creek, near Wrights line ... Rosses line ... Wm Sims, Surv. [No CB] Iss. 25 Apr 1767

SWANN, ROBERT File no. 2325; Gr. no. 74; Bk. 23, p. 197
Plat: Apr 29, 1768, Surveyed for Robert Swann, 240 A on a branch of Bullocks Creek adj. John Laughlands Survey ... P William Sims Robert Swann, John Laughland, CB Iss. 28 Apr 1768

SWANN, ROBERT File no. 2326; Gr. no. 75; Entry no. 658; Bk. 23, p. 198
Warrant: Unto Robert Swann 150 A on a branch of Bullocks Creek about a mile above Williams' Survey ... 23 Sept 1766 Wm Tryon
Plat: April 29, 1768, Surveyed for Robert Swann, 150 A on both sides Watsons fork of Bullocks Creek. Pr William Sims. Sam: Swann, Andrew Peterson, CB Iss. 28 Apr 1768

TAGGART, JNO. File no. 1196 (468); Gr. no. 89; Bk. 18, p. 149 (17, 176)
Plat: [nd], Surveyed for John Taggart, 170 A on S side Allisons Creek adj. John Patton, Joseph Clarke ... Jno McKnitt Alexander, D Surv. John Patton, John Armstrong, CB Iss. 6 Apr 1765

TEMPLE, MAJOR File no. 2184; Gr. no. 243; Bk. 23, p. 124
Plat: Surveyed for Major Temple. 150 A on a branch of Allisons Creek a little above William McDowels near the Waggon Road ... 8 Feb 1766 William Dickson, Surv. John Young Senr., John Young Junr., CB Iss. 26 Oct 1767

THACKSTON, JAMES File no. 0396
Plat: Surveyed for James Thackston, 200 A on So branch of Lawson fork of Packelot, about 4 miles above Joseph Jones and above his Buffaloe waggon ford adj. Furgusons, Lowrys corner 5 Dec 1766, Peter Johnston, Surv. Jonathan Newman, Moses Ferguson, CB

THOMPSON, ARCHIBALD File no. 2392; Gr. no. 190; Bk. 23, p. 219
Plat: Surveyed for Archibald Thomson, 150 A on waters of Allisons Creek ... Joseph Clarks corner ... John Keers corner ... Feb 20, 1767 Peter Johnston, Surv. Iss. 28 Apr 1768 [No CB]

THOMPSON, ELISHA File no. 2450; Gr. no. 319; Bk. 23, p. 245
Plat: Survey'd for Elisha Thompson, 400 A on middle fork Tyger adj. Thomas Pennys upper line . . . 6 Jany 1768 By Wm Sharp, Surv. Joseph Thompson, Joseph Jones, CB Iss. 29 Apr 1768

THOMPSON, ELISHA File no. 2435; Gr. no. 301; Bk. 23, p. 242
Plat: Surveyed for Elisha Thompson, 200 A on N branch Tyger River adj. David Davis . . . By Wm Sharp, Surv. 9 Jan 1768, Joseph Jones, David Davis, CB Iss. 29 Apr 1768

THOMPSON, JOHN File no. 512 (1338); Gr. no. 67; Bk. 17, p. 202 (18, 184)
Plat: Surveyed for John Thomson, 400 A on Callabash branch of Allisons Creek, adj. Henry Johnston . . . 23 July 1765 William Dickson, Surv. James Adams, James Thomson, CB Iss. 28 Oct 1765

THOMPSON, JAMES File no. 1216 (489); Gr. no. 175; Bk. 18, p. 164 (17, 180)
Plat: [nd], Surveyed for James Thompson, 300 A on Callibash Branch of Allisons Creek adj. Capt. Robert Adams, Henry Johnsons . . . Francis Beaty, D Surv. Robert Adams, James Adams, CB Iss. 16 Apr 1765

THOMPSON, JOSEPH File no. 2286; Gr. no. 196; Bk. 23, p. 182
Plat: Surveyed for Joseph Thompson, 300 A on middle fork Tyger adj. Elisha Thompsons late survey . . . 28 Nov 1766 By Wm Sharp, Surv. John Ker, James Nichols, CB Iss. 26 Oct 1767

THOMPSON, WILLIAM File no. 2386; Gr. no. 141; Bk. 23, p. 310
Plat: Aug 29, 1767, Surveyed for William Thompson, 300 A on Mackelroys Creek of Fairforrest . . . Zacka Bullock, Saml Hamby, Ezekel Guffey, CB Iss. 28 Apr 1768

THOMSON, JNO. File no. 1238; Gr. no. 67; Bk. 18, p. 184
Plat: 23 July 1765, Surveyed for John Thomson, 400 A on Callabash Branch of Allisons Creek . . . Henry Johnstons corner . . . William Dickson, Surv. James Adams, James Thomson, CB Iss. 28 Oct 1765

TILLET, GILES File no. 2030; Gr. no. 455; Bk. 23, p. 39
Plat: 7 Mar 1767, Surveyed for Giles Tillet 640 A on fair forrest Zach Bullock, Surv. Jas Tillet, Jno Gibbs, CB Iss. 27 Apr 1767

TILLETT, JAMES File no. 0394
Plat: Oct 18, 1768, Surveyed for James Tillett, 200 A on S

side Fair Forrest adj. Tates, Tillets old line . . . Zach Bullock, Surv. Hancock Smith, James Gibbs, CB

TILLET, JAMES File no. 2037; Gr. no. 462; Bk. 23, p. 41
Plat: March 7, 1767, Surveyed for James Fillet on Tates Branch . . . Tate line . . . Zach Bullock John Gibbs Jur., Giles Tillet, CB Iss. 27 Apr 1767

TORBET, SAMUEL File no. 2190; Gr. no. 249; Bk. 23, p. 125
Plat: Survey'd for Samuel Torbert, 100 A on So side Broad River above Richard Hughes's including his improvement in the Bent of the River including a small Island . . . 31 Decr 1766 Wm Dickson, Survr. Chas Crain, Richd Addis, CB Iss. 26 Oct 1767

TRIVISH, FRANCIS File no. 849; Gr. no. 81; Bk. 17, p. 392
Plat: Surveyed for Francis Trivish, 65 A on both sides fishing creek between William Watson & Patrick Duncan . . . 11 Feb 1767 Peter Johnston, Surv. William watson, James Duncan, CB Iss. 25 Apr 1767

TWITTY, WILLIAM File no. 2033; Gr. no. 458; Bk. 23, p. 40
Plat: May 19, 1766, Surveyed for William Twitty, 200 A on Ridge Between Thicketty & Packlet . . . Za Bullock, Surv. Hugh Moore, Patrick Moore, CB Iss. 27 Apr 1767

VANCE, DAVID File no. 920 (1641); Gr. no. 165; Bk. 17, p. 410 (18, 374)
Plat: 26 Dec 1766, Surveyed for David Vance, 100 A on a branch of Turkey Creek, Peter Johnston, Surv. John Garvin, James Wilson, CB Iss. 25 Apr 1767

VERNON, ALEXANDER File no. 2187; Bk. 23, p. 125
Plat: Surveyed for Alexander Vernon 300 A on So branch of N fork Tyger River below Robert Millers . . . adj. John Millers . . . 10 Dec 1766 Willm. Dickson, Surv. Alexr Rea, Francis Dods, CB Iss. 26 Oct 1767

VINEYARD, ISHMAEL File no. 2373; Gr. no. 133; Bk. 23, p. 208
Plat: 3 Feb 1767, Surveyed for Ishmael Vinard, 200 A on a branch of Turkey Creek . . . John Kemerhams line . . . Za Bullock, Surv. David Byars, David Porter, CB Iss. 28 Apr 1768

WADE, JOHN File no. 483 (1210); Gr. no. 137; Bk. 17, p. 172 (18, 156)
Plat: Surveyed for John Wade, 300 A on waters of Turkey Creek including his improvement called Wades old Store . . .

19 Augt 1764 ... P William Dickson, Surv. Wm Dickson, Matthew Floyd, CB Iss. 16 Apr 1765

WADE, JOHN File no. 1286 (560); Gr. no. 259; Bk. 18, p. 319 (17, 240)
Plat: Surveyed for John Wade, 300 A on N side Broad, W side Bullocks Creek, Loves Branch including an improvement he bought of Matthew Floyd ... 19 Augt 1764 William Dickson, Surv. John McKinney, Timothy Calohan, CB Iss. 30 Oct 1765

WALKER, JAMES File no. 2473; Gr. no. 412; Bk. 23, p. 285
Plat: Surveyed for James Walker, 150 A on main branch of Turkey Creek, including the place he now lives ... 18 Feb 1766 William Dickson, Surv. William Champ, John Couch, CB Iss. 29 Apr 1768

WATSON, DAVID File no. 326 (1058); Gr. no. 239; Bk. 17, p. 126 (18, 114)
Plat: [nd], Surveyed for David Watson, 200 A on Head Waters of middle branch of Bullocks Creek on Great Road, near James Wilsons ... Francis Beaty, D Surv. John Watson, William Watson, CB Iss. 16 Nov 1764

WATSON, JAMES File no. 870 (1591); Gr. no. 107; Bk. 17, p. 397 (18, 363)
Plat: Surveyed for James Watson, 150 A ... No side of fishing Creek and on both sides of Mclures branch ... between a survey of his own and John Kers and Thomas Scotts ... Febry 14th 1767, Peter Johnston, Surv. James Duncan, Thomas Scott, Ch. Bear. Iss. 25 Apr 1767

WATSON, JAMES File no. 1233; Gr. no. 63; Bk. 18, p. 163
Plat: 13 July 1765, Surveyed for James Watson on waters of Allisons Creek, adj. Samuel Watson ... Simerals line ... 200 A ... William Dickson, Surv. William Watson, James Rush, CB Iss. 28 Oct 1765

WATSON, JAMES File no. 507; Gr. no. 62; Bk. 17, p. 201
200 A on waters of Allisons Creek ... Samuel Watsons corner ... 28 Oct 1765 Wy Tryon

WATSON, JAMES File no. 0404; Entry no. 781
Warrant: Unto James Watson, 100 A on waters of Bullocks Creek, near Williams open line [torn ...]
Plat: Feb 7, 1767, Surveyed for James Watson 87 A on N fork Bullocks Creek ... Williams line ... P William Sims Jas Watson, Frans. Adams, CB

WATSON, JAMES File no. 0405; Entry no. 687
Warrant: Unto James Watson, 150 A adj. DAVID WATSON
... lines of Land sd. Watson lives on ... 23 Sept 1766 Wm
Tryon

WATSON, SAMUEL File no. 863 (1584); Gr. no. 100; Bk. 17, p.
395 (18, 361)
Plat: Surveyed for Samuel Watson, 400 A on waters of
Rocky Allisons Creek, adj. his new survey, Summeral & the
Indian Line ... 19 Feb 1767 Peter Johnston, Surv. William
Reed, Archibald Barron, CB Iss. 25 Apr 1767

WATSON, SAMUEL File no. 1138 (410); Gr. no. 23; Bk. 18, p.
139 (17, 154)
Plat: [nd], Surveyed for Samuel Watson, 400 A on Rocky
Allisons Creek, below Simorals, adj. land where he now liv-
eth ... Francis Beaty, D Surv. Moses Forster, Robert Shaw,
CB Iss. 6 Apr 1765

WATSON, SAMUEL File no. 2394; Gr. no. 192; Bk. 23, p. 219
Plat: Surveyed for Samuel Watson, 250 A on Rockey Allisons
creek adj. Simonton, Simmeral & his own land, part of Archibald Barons Improvement ... Feb 13, 1767 Peter Johnston,
Surv. Benijah Pennington, Alexr Barron, CB Iss. 28 Apr 1768

WATSON, SAMUEL File no. 407; Gr. no. 23; Bk. 17, p. 153
400 A on Rocky Allisons Creek below Simerals land ... Watsons other Survey ... 6 _____ "Error Not Issued."

WATSON, SAMUEL File no. 1137 (409); Gr. no. 14; Bk. 18, p.
139 (17, 154)
Plat: [nd], Surveyed for Samuel Watson, 360 A on Rockey
Allisons Creek, adj. Simeralls ... Siminton ... Francis Beaty,
D Surv. Moses Forster, John McCulloh, CB Iss. 6 Apr 1765

WATSON, WILLIAM File no. 0406
Plat: Surveyed for William Watson, 550 A on both sides Fishing creek adj. his own & Gillaspies, Thomas Scotts line ... 19
Mar 1766 William Dickson, Surv. John Wilson, William Henry, CB

WATSON, WILLIAM File no. 1560 (839); Gr. no. 70; Bk. 18, p.
356 (17, 389)
340 A on waters of fishing creek adj. his own & Gillespys 25
Apr 1767 Wm Tryon

WATSON, WILLIAM File no. 1260 (534); Gr. no. 89; Bk. 18, p.
187 (17, 206)
Plat: Surveyed for William Watson, 400 A on main fork of

Turkey Creek adj. George Davison and Richard Berrys . . . 21 Sept 1765 William Dickson, Surv. Thomas Scott, John Wilson, CB Iss. 30 Oct 1765

WATSON, WILLIAM File no. 71 (184); Gr. no. 16; Bk. 13, p. 425 (17, 4)
Plat: Surveyed for Wm Watson, 236 A on N fork fishing Creek adj. his own lands . . . [nd] Francis Beaty, S.D. William Moore, John Neill, CB Iss. 21 Dec 1763

WEIR, GEORGE File no. 2511; Gr. no. 477; Bk. 23, p. 295
Plat: Surveyed for George Weir, 150 A on both sides N fork Sandy River about 3 miles above the Suck . . . 12 Mar 1768 Wm Dickson, Surv. Simon Cameron, John Walker, CB Iss. 29 Apr 1768

WHALEY, WILLIAM File no. 1757; Gr. no. 462; Bk. 20, p. 488
285 A on Rockey Allisons Creek adj. Samuel Wattson, Robert Shaw, Symenton, Simmirlas & Indian Lands and Major Temples and John Hall . . . 6 May 1769 Wm Tryon

WHERRY, SAMUEL File no. 904 (1625); Gr. no. 150; Bk. 17, p. 406 (18, 371)
Plat: Surveyed for Samuel Wherry 250 A on S side Fishing Creek both sides Watsons branch on McClenchans olde Rode . . . adj. George Smith 9 Jan 1767 Wm Dickson, Surv. James Smith, George Smith, CB Iss. 25 Apr 1767

WHERRY, SAMUEL File no. 1277 (551); Gr. no. 107; Bk. 18, p. 191 (17, 209)
Plat: Surveyed for Samuel Wherry, 200 A on waters of So fork Fishing Creek on Stamp branch above Seluda Road . . . 25 June 1765, William Dickson, Surv. Robt Lusk, Samuel Porter, CB Iss. 30 Oct 1765

WHITE, HUGH File no. 1394 (667); Gr. no. 67; Bk. 18, p. 262 (17, 289)
Plat: Surveyed for Hugh White, 350 A on both sides Fishing Creek including the house and mill . . . Phillip Walkers line . . . John Neeleys line . . . James Mulddons line . . . 30 Apr 1766 William Dickson, Surv. Saml Wherry, William Campbell, CB Iss. 25 Sept 1766

WHITE, JOSEPH File no. 2242; Gr. no. 397; Bk. 23, p. 155
Plat: Survey'd for Joseph White 200 A on No fork of Packlet . . . Margaret Campbell's line . . . Augt 14 1767 . . . Zach Bullock, Joab Mitchell, John McGrew, CB Iss. 26 Oct 1767

WHITE, JOSEPH File no. 1579 (858); Gr. no. 95; Bk. 18, p. 360 (17, 394)

Plat: Surveyed for Joseph White 140 A on both sides S fork Packolett including mouth of Cub Creek between 2 tracts belong to James Hutchins . . . William Dickson, [nd] Anthoney, Hutchins, John Clark, CB Iss. 25 Apr 1767

WIDEMAN, JOHN File no. 2367; Gr. no. 127; Bk. 23, p. 207
Plat: May 27, 1767, Surveyed for John Wideman, 200 A on Packlet . . . Samuel Smiths line . . . Zach Bullock Phillip Wideman, John Wideman, Junr., CB Iss. 28 Apr 1768

WIDEMAN, JOHN File no. 2366; Gr. no. 126; Bk. 23, p. 207
Plat: Feb 9, 1767, Surveyed for John Wideman, 200 A in fork of Broad and Packlet . . . Za Bullock Samuel Smith, Phillip Wideman, CB Iss. 28 Apr 1768

WILLIAMS, JOHN File no. 0414
Plat: Surveyed for John Williams 300 A on S fork Packlet . . . near Alexander Kilpatricks . . . John Sertains line . . . 8 Feb 1768 Zach Bullock, Joab Mitchell, Alexr Kilpatrick, CB

WILLIAMS, THOMAS File no. 2146; Gr. no. 199; Bk. 23, p. 116
Plat: Aug 22, 1765, Surveyed for Thomas Williams 200 A on both sides a branch of Bullocks Creek . . . William Sims, S.M.C. Wm Burns, Thos Williams, CB Iss. 26 Oct 1767

WILLIAMSON, JOHN File no. 2253; Gr. no. 412; Bk. 23, p. 158
Plat: Surveyed for John Williams 250 A on S side S fork Packolet on Indian Camp Creek . . . 2 June 1767 Wm Dickson, Surv. Thomas Williamson, Joseph Dickson, CB Iss. 26 Oct 1767

WILLIAMSON, THOMAS File no. 1376 (649); Gr. no. 49; Bk. 18, p. 259 (17, 285)
200 A on Lawsons fork Packolet below Jones Waggon Road . . . 25 Sept 1766 Wm Tryon

WILLIAMS, THOMAS File no. 1618 (897); Gr. no. 142; Bk. 18, p. 370 (17, 404)
Plat: Surveyed for Thomas Williamson, 150 A on Packolate River between the forks including the Improvement he bought of James Green . . . 13 Dec 1766 Wm Dickson, Surv. Thomas Wmson, Elisha Wmson, CB Iss. 25 Apr 1767

WILLIAMSON, WILLIAM File no. 0416
Plat: Surveyed for William Williamson, 200 A on Burlesons & Loves forks of Turkey Creek . . . 22 May 1767 Peter Johnston, John Miller, James Martin, CB

WILSON, JOHN File no. 568 (1294); Gr. no. 297; Bk. 17, p. 248 (18, 225)

Plat: 11 July 1765, Surveyed for John Wilson, 150 A on a branch of Allisons Creek adj. McCord ... P William Sims, J.M.C. John Venables, Thos Dixon, CB Iss. 30 Oct 1765

WILSON, ROBERT File no. 239 (971); Gr. no. 49; Bk. 17, p. 41 (18, 35)
Plat: Surveyed for Robert Wilson 100 A on S side Broad River on a branch of Cane Creek including the place where Caled Dowd formerly lived, adj. Joseph Hollingsworth ... 10 Augt 1763 William Dickson, Surv. William Hollingsworth, Abraham Hollingsworth, CB Iss. 14 Feb 1764

WILLSON, ROBERT File no. 2528; Gr. no. 520; Bk. 23, p. 303
Plat: Surveyed for Robert Wilson 100 A on both sides Gawin Moores Creek ... near John McKinneys line ... Jno McK. Alexander, Surv. [nd] Abraham Smith, Wm Smith, CB Iss. 29 Apr 1768

WILLSON, SAMUEL File no. 869 (1590); Gr. no. 106; Bk. 17, p. 396 (18, 363)
Plat: Surveyed for Samuel willson, 180 A on N side Allisons Creek adj. William Davison, John Thomason, Joseph Carrold [sic] ... 19 Feb 1767 William Dickson, Surv. John Ross, John Gabby, CB Iss. 25 Apr 1767

WOFFORD, JOSEPH File no. 2461; Gr. no. 400; Bk. 23, p. 282
Plat: Surveyed for Joseph Wofford, 200 A on Packolet River including mouth of Richland Creek ... 20 Dec 1766 Wm Dickson, Surv. John Dennis, James Hammet, CB Iss. 29 Apr 1768

WILSON, WILLIAM File no. 1992; Gr. no. 416; Bk. 23, p. 32
Plat: Aug 29, 1765, Surveyed for William Wilson, 300 A on both sides Clarks fork Bullocks Creek ... Wm Sims, Surv. Thomas Black, Matthew Black, CB Iss. 25 Apr 1767

WORKMAN, JOHN File no. 2181; Gr. no. 240; Bk. 23, p. 124
Plat: Surveyed for John Workman, 200 A on So side Stoney fork Fishing Creek on the head of Lusks Creek [?] ... Elizabeth Lusks line ... 12 Jan 1767 Robt Lusk, Patrick Connely, CB Iss. 26 Oct 1767

WYLEY, MOSES File no. 2046; Gr. no. 476; Bk. 23, p. 42
Plat: Survey'd for Moses Wylie, 150 A on both sides Cowdens or the Dutchmans Creek falling into & on the No side Tygar River ... 2 or 3 miles above Thomas Fletchers land ... 25 Feb 1767 Wm Sharp, Surv. Robert Harris, Joseph Hall, CB Iss. 27 Apr 1767·

YOUNG, JAMES File no. 1131 (401); Gr. no. 18; Bk. 18, p. 137 (17, 152)
Plat: [nd], Surveyed for Jas. Young, 600 A adj. land he purchased of John McCulloh, main fork fishing Creek . . . Francis Beaty, DS Thomas McMurry, Moses Cotter, CB Iss. 6 Apr 1765

YOUNG, SAMUEL File no. 2056; Gr. no. 634; Bk. 23, p. 74
Plat: Jan 12, 1767, Surveyed for Samuel Young, 300 A on Gilkey Creek adj. Sims & Fannings line . . . Zach Bullock, [Surv.] John Russel, John Clark, CB Iss. 27 Apr 1767

YOUNG, SAMUEL File no. 2049; Gr. no. 484; Bk. 23, p. 44
Plat: Surveyed for Samuel Young 250 A on No fork of Paculet below Abraham Clements survey . . . Alexander Kirkpatricks [sic] line . . . [nd] Wm Dickson, Survr. Alexander Kirkpatrick [sic], James Howard, CB Iss. 27 Apr 1767

YOUNG, SAMUEL File no. 2048; Gr. no. 483; Bk. 23, p. 44
Plat: Surveyed for Samuel Young, 400 A on both sides of No fork of Packelot below John Wilsons land . . . Willm Dickson, Surv. [nd], Alexander Kirkpatrick [sic], James Howard, CB Iss. 27 Apr 1767

BOYD, JNO File no. 1387 (660); Gr. no. 60; Bk. 18, p. 261 (17, 287)
Plat: Survey'd for John Boyd 200 A on the Pinte branch between the two main fork of Fishing Creek adj. Samuel McCances line . . . 25 June 1765 William Dickson, Survr. Robt Lusk, Saml Porter, CB Iss. 25 Sept 1766

The following were found in N.C. Archives, S.S. 687, Sec. State Land Entries, Warrants, Surveys.

Plat: Mecklenburg, 3d Jan 1766, Surveyed for Robert Carr, by Virtue of a Re-Survey Warrant 408 A on both sides the middle fork of Fishing Creek . . . Kuykendalls corner . . . Henrys line . . . Ewarts line . . . McLearys line . . . P W Sims, Surv.

Plat: Surveyed for John Fondron and James Hanna 400 A in Mecklenburg County on waters of South Fork of Fishing Creek adj. Andrew McNabbs land . . . Davis's corner . . . Thomas Raineys line . . . 12 Augt 1767 Wm Dickson, Surv.

BYERS, JAMES File no. 1368 (641); Grant no. 41; Bk. 18, p. 258 (17, 283)
Plat: Survey'd for James Byers 300 A on the No side of Broad River on McDowells Creek a little above McDowells line . . . 21 March 1766 William Dickson, Survr. Hugh Berry, David Byers, Cha. Bear. Granted 25 Sept 1766

JONES, WYLIE and SOLOMON ALSTON & JOSEPH MONT-
FORT File no. 2594; Grant no. 270; Bk. 23, p. 361
Plat: Survey'd for Wylie Jones Solomon Alston & Joseph
Montfort 300 A on Shoal Creek about a Mile above Brights
New Place ... Novr 13th 1768. (No C.B.) Granted 22 Dec
1768

JONES, WYLIE and SOLOMON ALSTON & JOSEPH MONT-
FORT File no. 2596
Plat: Novem. the 13th 1768, Surveyed for Wylie Jones Solo-
mon Alston Joseph Montfort 200 A on Shoal or Smiths
Creek above their other Land Zac Bullock, Surv. Samuel
Bright, Charles Spencer, Chain Bearers. Granted 22 Dec 1768
Grant no. 272; Bk. 23, p. 361

[NO NAME GIVEN] File no. 909; Grant no. 406; Bk. 24, p. 18.
200 A on the No. side of Pacolet River...25 Novr 1771. Jo
Martin.

ADAMS, FRANCIS File no. 569; Grant no. 458, Bk. 22, p. 109
Plat: Surveyed for Francis Adams...500 A on the Head of
Fishing Creek...near William Watson line...Smith's line...Jno
Kirkconnell Survr. Joseph Harden & Samuel Adams, C.B.
[n.d.] Grant issued 23 May 1772.

ADEMES. SAMUEL File no. 276; Grant no. 155; Bk. 20, p. 602.
Plat: Surveyed for Samuel Adams 70 A on waters of So. fork
of Fishing Creek, joining Edward Lacey's land...Richard Sadlers line...Raineys corner...Hendersons line...June 16th 1770
Peter Johnston [Survr.] John Moore & Thos Rainey, C.B. Gr.
issued 11th Dec. 1770.

AKINS, ALEXANDER File no. 89; Grant no. 108, Bk. 20, p.437.
223 A on waters of Crowders and Allisons Creek including
his improvement...Wm Patricks line...4th May 1769 Wm.
Tryon.

ALLEY, JAMES File no. 394; Grant no. 46; Bk. 20, p. 698.
Plat: Surveyed for James Alley 200 A on both sides of Packe-
lott...March 21st 1771. Jno Kirkconell Survr. William Smith
& George Fair, C. B.
Grant issued 14th Nov. 1771.

ANDERSON, DENNIS File no. 549; Grant no. 424; Bk. 22, p.
101.
Plat: Surveyed for Denny Anderson 150 A on both sides of
So fork of Tygar River including the mouth of Ready fork...
16th Janry 1772. John Kirkconell, Surv. William Boullinger
& John Williams , C.B. Grant issued 22 May 1772.

ANDERSON, JOHN File no. 259; Grant no. 180; Bk. 20, p. 564.
150 A on So. side of So fork of Tygar river...both sides of
Bens Creek...David Lewis line...9th April 1770 Wm. Tryon.

ANDERSON, JOHN File no. 02, Entry no. 708
Warrant: 300 A on No side Indian Creek joining [torn] No
side of Moses Moores land & Thomas [torn] Land...19 May
1772 Jo Martin Saml Strudwick Su. (Returned Decem Court
of Claims 1772)

Two identical plats in package: Surveyed for John Anderson Two hundred A...on No side Indian Creek...Thomas Robisons corner...near Moores line...13th June 1772 Jno Kirkconell Sur. Jno Houstler & Jno Moore, C.B.

ARMSTRONG, MARTIN File no. 812; Grant no. 88; Bk. 23, p. 329

200 A on the branches of Fishing Creek including his own improvement...Corner of the Indian Land (claimed by the Catawba)...Peter Keykendalls line...22nd December 1768 Wm Tryon.

BARBER, JOHN File no. 949(740); Grant no. 450; Bk 24, p. 27 (Bk. 22, p. 312)

Plat: Surveyed for John Barber 250 A on head waters of Allisons Creek including the improvement he lives on...John Gordons corner...headwaters of Bullocks Creek...Peter Johnston Sur. William Henry, John Jordon [Gordon?] ,C.B. Grant issued 25 Nov. 1771.

BARNETT, HUGH File no. 873; Grant no. 274; Bk. 23, p. 362

Plat: Surveyed for Hugh Barnet 200 A in ____ County on the Middle fork of Tygar River joining the lower line of Jos. Jones place...near Alexander McCarters line on the No side of sd fork...12th Sepr 1768 by Wm Sharp Survr. [No CB]. Gr. issued 26 Dec 1768.

BARNETT, HUGH File no. 874; Grant no. 275; Bk. 23, p. 362

150 A on No side of the Middle fork of Tygar River on a branch falling at the upper end of Jones land...22d December 1768 Wm Tryon

BARNET, SAMUEL File no. 348; Grant no. 119; Gk. 20, p. 666

Plat: Surveyed for Samuel Barnet 65 A on both sides of Bullocks Creek including part of the improvement he now lives on...corner of the old survey...Gillhams line...Linion Fannans line...June 21st 1770. Peter Johnston Survr. John Dickey & Jacob Barnet, CB. Grant issued 18 Apr 1771.

BARROW, WILLIAM File no. 586; Grant no. 477; Bk. 22, p. 112

300 A on both sides of Sadlers branch of Broad River...So. side of Loves Road leading from Fishing Creek to Broad River...23d May 1772 Jo Martin

BARROW, WILLIAM File no. 498; Grant no. 118; Bk. 22. p. 29

Plat: Surveyed for William Barrow 250 A on So fork of Turkey Creek...James Stephensons corner...John Glovers line...1 January 1772 Jno Kirkconell, Surv. Drury Glover & Lowery Glover, C B Grant issued 15 May 1772.

BARROW, WILLIAM File no. 585; Grant no. 476; Bk. 22, p. 112
200 A on both sides of Owens Branch of Sandy River...Edward Crafts second corner...23d May 1772 Jo Martin

BARROW, WILLIAM File no. 586; Grant no. 477; Bk. 22, p. 112.
180 A on both sides of the So fork of Turkey Creek...Benjamin Philips's Corner...Robert Brattons line...Wm Garvirs Line 23rd May 1772 Jo Martin.

BERRY, ANDREW File no. 505; Grant no. 136; Bk. 22, p. 34
Plat: Surveyed for Andrew Berry 150 A on waters of Tygar River...March 18th 1771 Jno Kirkconnell Surv. Charles Moore & Alexr. Barron, CB Grant issued 15 May 1772

BIRD, WILLIAM File no. 392; Grant no. 44; Bk. 20, p. 698
Plat: Surveyed for William Bird 100 A on waters of Turkey Creek including the improvement he lives on...June 16th 1769 Peter Johnston Sur. Mathew Harper & Samuel Gay,C B Grant issued 14 Nov 1771.

BLACK, JOHN File no. 193; Grant no. 195; Bk. 20, p. 521
265 A on South side of Allisons Creek...Flemings Line... William Stevensons Line...John Flemings corner...16th Dec 1769 Wm. Tryon.

BRANDON, CHARLES File no. 05 Entry no. 391
Warrant: 200 A on Birlison's fork of Turkey Creek joining and between the Line of George Hogue senior & George Hogue Junior 3 May 1769 Wm Tryon Ben Heron Audr. Returned April Court 1770
Two identical plats: Surveyed for Charles Branden 200 A on Burlison's fork of Turkey Creek joining & between lines of George Hogg & William Ross's lands...George Hogg Junrs line ...Peter Johnston Sur January 20th 1770
George Hogg & Charles Branden, C B

BRICE, DANIEL File no. 121; Grant no. 336; Bk. 20, p. 476
200 A on the So side of the No fork of Tygar River on Jamies Creek including his improvement 5th May 1769 Wm. Tryon

BRICE, SAMUEL File no. 853; Grant no. 192; Bk. 23; p. 348
200 A on the middle fork of Tygar river about a mile and a half below the Indian path...about 2 miles below Jones' old place...22d December 1769 Wm Tryon

BRATTON, WILLIAM File no. 91; Grant no. 112; Bk. 20, p. 438
Plat: Surveyed for Wm. Bratton 200 A on waters of the south
fork of Fishing Creek, joining Robert Kers land...James Wil-
liamsons corner...joining Mchans[?] land...June 11, 1768
Peter Johnston Survr. Thomas Bratton & Samuel Gay, C B
Grant issued 4 May 1769

BROWN, JOHN File no. 84; Grant no. 101; Bk. 20, p. 436
Plat: Surveyed for John Brown 418 A on waters of the No
fork of Tygar river & both sides of Brown [Branch], joining
Millers land, joining Knox land...John Millers land...joining
McKlehenny['s land]...Peter Johnston Survr. Feb. 1, 1769
Francis Prince & John Rottan C B Grant issued 4 May 1769

BUCHANNAN, JOHN File no. 24; Grant no. 474; Bk. 20, p. 401
200 A on West side the Catawba River on both sides Allisons
Creek joining John McCormacks corner...23d December 1768
Wm Tryon

BYARS, DAVIS File no. 417; Grant no. 70; Bk. no. 20, p. 701
Warrant: No. 424...unto David Byars 400 A on the head of
Turkey Creek, joining his own land & including his own im-
provement 10th December 1770 Wm Tryon
Plat: Surveyed for David Byars 300 A on head waters of Tur-
key Creek...Samuel Porters land...Ishmael Vinyard's line...
July 20th 1771, Jno Kirkconell Survr.
William Byers, William Williamson, C B
Grant issued 14 Nov 1771

BULLION, THOMAS File no. 192; Grant no. 193; Bk. 20, p. 521.
200 A on the So side of Fair Forrest on both sides the Lick
branch about a mile below Millers Wagon road and joining
Giles Tillets land...16th December 1769 Wm Tryon

BULLOCK, LEONARD HENDLY File no. 55; Grant no. 538; Bk.
20, p. 413
400 A on both sides Tygar river...23d December 1768 Wm
Tryon

BULLOCK, ZACHARIAH File no. 096
Plat: Oct 1st 1770 Survey'd for Zachariah Bullock 640 A on
waters of Jumping Run...Milweans & Bullocks line...Randolph
Hames's line...Zacha Bullock
Thos Draper, John Haile Cha Bearer

BULLOCK, ZACHARIAH File no. 133; Grant no. 362; Bk. 20, p.
479
Plat: March 21st 1769 Survey'd for Zachariah Bullock 200 A

on both sides Gilkeys Creek...Zach Bullock [No CB]   Grant issued 5 May 1769

BULLOCK, ZACHARIAH File no. 132; Grant no. 361; Bk. 20, p. 479
Plat: Surveyed for Zachariah Bullock 298 A on both sides Gilkeys Creek of Thickety...his other line...Zach Bullock. John Nuckols & David Brown [CB]   Grant issued 5 May 1769

BULLOCK, ZACHARIAH File no. 698(907); Grant no. 404; Bk. 22, p. 305(Bk. 24, p. 15)
640 A on the Waters of Jumping Run...Melwins & Bullocks lines...Hamet's [Hamer's?] line...25th November 1771 Jo Martin

BULLOCK, ZACHARIAH File no. 700; Grant no. 406; Bk. 22, p. 305
Plat: September 2d, 1771 Survey'd for Zachariah Bullock 200 A on Noth side of Packlet...Zacha Bullock John Hamit & George Randolph, Cha Bearers
Grant issued 25 Nov 1771

BURCHFIELD, ADAM File no. 594; Grant no. 28; Bk. 28, p. 123
200 A on the Waters of thickety Creek...near Wm March-Banks line...Jany 23, 1773

BURCHFIELD, JOHN File no. 895(686); Grant no. 392; Bk. 24, p. 16(Bk. 22, p. 303)
Plat: Sept 1st 1771 Surveyed for John Burchfield 400 A on the waters of Thicketty...Zacha Bullock Jos Burchfield, Wm Marchbanks, Chain Bearers
Grant issued 25 Nov 1771

BURCHFIELD, JOSEPH File no. 097
Warrant: 250 A in County of Mecklenburg on the North fork of thickety joining Steen land...21st Dec 1768 Wm Tryon Bene Heron D Audr
Returned November Court of Claims 1771
Plat: Nov. 2d 1771 Surveyd for Joseph Burchfield 250 A on North fork of Thicketty...Millers line...Zacha Bullock(,Son) Vardry Mcbee, Wm Johnston Cha Bearers

BUTLER, JOHN File no. 698(898); Grant no. 395; Bk. 22, p. 304(Bk. 24, p. 16)
Plat: Sepr 1st 1771 Survey'd for John Butler 300 A on the North side of Packlet River on both sides of the Path that leads from Flanreys ford to thicketty...Zach Bullock Jas. Burchfield, Wm Marchbanks, Cha Bearers   Grant issued 25 Nov 1771

BYARS, WILLIAM File no. 384; Grant no. 238; Bk. 20, p. 686
Plat: Jan. the 4th 1767 Surveyed for William Byars, 130 A
on both sides a branch of Bullocks Creek...joining William
Byars Land he lives on...McLeans line...Williams Sims Surv.
Grant issued 18 Apr 1771

CAMPBELL, ANDREW File no. 19; Grant no. 464; Bk. 20, p. 399
150 A on Allisons Creek joining his own land near Robert
Adams land...22d December 1768 Wm Tryon

CARRAWAY, THOMAS File no. 022; Entry no. 492
Warrant: Thomas Conaway 200 A..the north side of Packolet
including the mouth of Bush Creek & his own improvement...
25th Nov 1771 Jo Martin Wm Palme D Surv.
Return July Court of Claims 1774

CARROL, JOHN File no. 105; Grant no. 134; Bk. 20, p. 442
100 A on waters of Fishing Creek including part of the improvement he lives on...Keykendalls line...4th May 1769 Wm
Tryon

CASE, JOHN File no. 500; Grant no. 120; Bk. 22, p. 30
Plat: Surveyed for John Case 200 A on So side Packlat River
including the mouth of Cases Creek...11th January 1771 Jno
Kirkconell Surv.
David Bartin & Thomas Conal [?], C B Grant issued 15 May
1772

CLARK, HENRY File no. 711(920); Grant no. 420; Bk. 22, p.
307(Bk. 24, p. 21)
Plat: June 5th 1770 Surveyed for Henry Clark 83 A on the
South side of thicketty...Zachariah Bullocks line...Stephen
Joneses line...Zach Bullock Josep Burchfield & James Burch-
field, Chain Bearers Grant issued 25 Nov 1771

COBURN, SAMUEL File no. 153; Grant no. 399; Bk. 20, p. 482
150 A on both sides the Long Branch of Allisons Creek...
Patricks line...5th May 1769 Wm Tryon

COLLINS, DANIEL File no. 422; Grant no. 75; Entry no. 429;
Bk. 20, p. 702
Warrant: unto Daniel Collins 200 A upon both sides of the
main fork of Bullocks Creek including the improvement on
which he now lives...land of John Laughlin and James Smith
...10th Dec 1770 Wm Tryon John London (Sur) Grant issued 14 Nov 1771

COLLINS, THOMAS File no. 114; Grant no. 147; Bk. 20, p. 444
124 A on the NO fork of Tygar river joining John Millers,
Alexander Vernons, Francis Dodds, and John McKelhenny's
land...4th May 1769 Wm Tryon

CONNELL, GILES File no. 570; Grant no. 459; Bk. 22, p. 109
Plat: Surveyed for Gills Connells 450 A on a Branch of Kelseys Creek...22nd of May 1772 Jno Kirkconell Jessey Connells & John Golightly, C B Grant issued 23 May 1772

CONNELL, GILES File no. 54: Grant no. 537; Bk. 20, p. 413
Plat: Mecklinburg County, February 20th, 1768, Surveyed for Giles Connell 300 A on a Reedy Branch of Fair Forest beginning at a RED Oak in Giles Telletts Line Zach Bullock... James Fillet, James Gibbs, C B Grant issued 20 Feb 1768

CONNELL, JESSE File no. 287; Grant no. 278; Bk. 20, p. 624
Plat: March 29th 1769 Surveyed for Jesse Connel 500 A on East side of fairforrest including his improvement...Zach Bullock Giles Connel, John Ford, Chain Bears. Grant issued on 20 Dec 1770

CONNELL, PATRICK File no. 494; Grant no. 114; Bk. 22, p. 28
Plat: Surveyed for Patrick Connell 200 A on waters of fishing Creek...Samuell Kelseys line...Samuel Wherrys line...18th April 1772 Jno Kirkconell Sur
Samuel Wherrey & Jno Moffett, C B Grant issued 15 May 1772

CRAVEN, JAMES File no. 1867; Grant no. 483; Bk. 22, p. 114
200 A on a branch of South Packolate about three Quarters of a Mile above Alexander Kilpatricks Land, where he now lives...23d May 1772 Jo Martin

DAVIES, WILLIAM File no. 102; Grant no. 127; Bk. 20, p. 114
50 A on the Beaverdam fork of Bullocks Creek joining or near the land he now lives on...below the Cabbin...4th May 1769 Wm Tryon

DICKEY, GEORGE File no. 260; Grant no. 40; Bk. 20, p. 581
Plat: Surveyed for GEORG DICKEY 150 A on the fourth branch of Turkey Creek...including his own improvement... crossing the fort branch...June 20th 1770 Peter Johnston Survr. William Hillis & George Dickey, C B Grant issued 11 Dec. 1770

DICKEY, JOHN File no. 261; Grant no. 41; Bk. 20, p. 581
Plat: Surveyed for John Dickey 175 A on waters of Bulocks Creek including the improvement he now lives on...near handles line...Hugh Willsons Corner...Jamisons line...Bryars line ..June 20th 1770 Peter Johnston Survr. George & John Dickeys, C B Grant issued 11 Dec 1770

DICKSON, EDWARD File no. 168; Grant no. 132; Bk. 20, p. 512
Plat: Surveyed for Edward Dickson 125 A on No side Broad

River about 2 miles below his own land being Elaps'd land formerly surveyed for William Willson above the mouth of McInties Creek...Wm Dickson Surv. Thomas Willson & John McIntie, Cha Bear. Grant issued 6 Dec 1769

DICKSON, EDWARD File no. 537; Grant no. 412; Bk. 22, p. 99
Plat: Surveyed for Edward Dickson 100 A on the So side of Lawsons fork of Packolet...joining the So side of his own formerly Alexander Dicksons land...Jany 14th 1772 Jo Dickson Sur. Grant issued 22 May 1772 [No CB]

DICKSON, WILLIAM File no. 115; Grant no. 177; Bk. 20, p. 449
200 A on both sides of the South fork of Packolet...4th May 1769 Wm Tryon

DICKSON, WILLIAM File no. 28; Grant no. 478; Bk. 20, p. 402
600 A on the South fork of Pacalet including Hutchins cabbin, land that was surveyed for Hutchins 23d December 1768 Wm Tryon

DICKSON, WILLIAM File no. 29; Grant no. 479; Bk. 20, p. 42
300 A on South fork of Pacalet, a place called the pretty meadows above Hutchins Cabbin 23d December 1768 Wm Tryon

DUFF, DAVID File no. 343; Grant no. 114; Bk. 20, p. 665
Plat: Surveyed for Duff 215 A on waters of Allisons Creek joining Alexander Akins land...William Patricks land...June 2d 1769 Peter Johnston Alexr Akins, Jeremiah Damus, C B Grant issued 18 Apr 1771

EARL, JOHN File no. 159; Grant no. 447; Bk. 20, p. 487
400 A on both sides of the main Lawsons fork of Packolet... 6th May 1769 Wm Tryon

ELLIOT, JOHN File no. 420; Grant no. 73; Bk. 20, p. 702
300 A on both sides of Pacolet...John Grindalls Line...14th November 1771 Jo Martin

FAVOUR, THEOPHILUS File no. 724(933); Grant no. 433; Bk. 22, p. 309 (Bk. 24, p. 23)
400 A on Albertons Creek...25th Novem 1771 Jo Martin

FIFER, JOHN File no. 27; Grant no. 477; Bk. 20, p. 402
500 A on the South fork of Pacalet above the Maidens meadow...corner formerly made for Hutchins...William Dicksons line...38th December 1768 Wm Tryon

FLEMMING, JOHN File no. 64; Grant no. 55; Bk. 20, p. 427
297 A on waters of Allison Creek joining John McKnit Alexrs and John Buchannans Land..John Blacks line...4 May 1769 Wm Tryon

FLEMING, ROBERT File no. 271; Grant no. 53; Bk. 20, p. 583
Plat: Surveyed for Robert Fleming 50 A on waters of Middle
Branch of So fork of fishing Creek joining the Land Hugh
Bratton now lives on...Robert Days Corner...Thomas Raineys
line...June 18th 1770 Peter Johnston Surv. Thomas Rainey
& Samuel Gay, C B Grant issued 11 Dec 1770

FONDERN, JOHN File no. 719(928); Grant no. 435; Bk. 22, p.
309 (Bk. 24, p. 23)
300 A on both sides of Cherokee Creek...25th Novem 1771
Jo Martin

FONDREN, JOHN File no. 726(935); Grant no. 425; Bk. 22, p.
309 (Bk. 24, p. 24)
Plat: August 7th 1770 Surveyed for John Fondren 198 A...
William Henry's corner...2 of Robert Carr's line...Zach Bullock Sur. John Conner & Edward Craft, Chain Bearers, Grant
issued 25 Nov 1771

FORD, JOHN File no. 714(923); Grant no. 423; Bk. 22, p. 308
(Bk. 24, p. 22)
Plat: Decemr 21, 1768 Surveyed for John Ford 300 A on
the second fork of Fair forrest joining the south survey of
said Fords, being the tract he now lives on...[No surv.] William Ford & John Ford, C B Grant issued 25 Nov 1771

FOSTER, JOHN File no. 131; Grant no. 360; Bk. 20, p. 479
200 A on the head of Harriss Creek, a branch of Fair Forrest
a little above John Davis...5th May 1769 Wm Tryon

FOWLER, JAMES File no. 888; Grant no. 383; Bk. 24, p. 13
170 A on the Waters of Turkey Creek including his own improvement...Thos Morrison line...Colbs line...Stevensons land
...Jno McKnitt Alexanders line...25 Novr 1771 Jo Martin

FULTON, JOHN File no. 216; Grant no. 311; Bk. 20, p. 537
100 A on the W side of Bullocks Creek...Samuel Fultons Line
...Thomas Brandons Line...Floyds line...Prices Line...Fultons
old line...16th December 1769 Wm Tryon

GARDNER, JACOB File no. 937(728); Grant no. 437; Bk. 24, p.
24(Bk. 22, p. 310)
200 A on both sides of Abbitons Creek...Robert Willsons line
...Moses Jones's line...25th Novem 1771 Jo Martin

GASTON, WILLIAM File no. 452; Grant no. 71; Bk. 22, p. 18
Plat: Surveyed for William Gaston 100 A on a Branch of Tur-
key Creek...13th July 1771
Jno Kirkconnel Sur. William Robbins & John Steen, C B
Grant issued 15 May 1772

GIBBS, JAMES File no. 486; Grant no. 106; Bk. 22, p. 26
  Plat: Surveyed for James Gibbs 640 A on waters of fareforest
  ...Zachariah Gibbs line...15 Jan 1772   Jno Kirkconell, Sur.
  George Fare, John Gibbs, C B
  Grant issued 15 May 1772

GIBBS, JOHN File no. 56; Grant no. 539; Bk. 20, p. 413
  300 A on Duggins branch of Fair Forest...Duggins corner...
  23d December 1768 Wm Tryon

GIBBS, JOHN File no. 57
  250 A on Kilceys Branch...joining Kilceys Line...23d December 1768 Wm Tryon

GIBBS, ZACHARIAH File no. 4; Grant no. 529; Bk. 20, p. 391
  400 A on both sides Fair forrest Creek...Duggins line...another
  of Duggins lines...23d December 1768 Wm Tryon

GOLIGHTLY, JOHN File no. 454; Grant no. 73; Bk. 22, p. 19
  Plat: Surveyed for John Golightly 400 A on both sides of Kel-
  seys Creek of fareforest...on So side Rich land hill...James
  Hamits line...15 January 1772 Jno Kirkconell, Sur. George
  Fare & James Hammett, C B Grant issued 15 May 1772

GOLIGHTLY, JOHN File no. 480; Grant no. 100; Bk. 22, p. 25
  Plat: Surveyed for John Golightly 500 A on Both sides of
  Denesses Creek of fareforast...William Wafford corner...Dick-
  son line...Cristopher Colmans line...16 Jan 1772
  Jno Kirkconell, Surv. James Hammitt & George Fare, C B
  Grant issued 15 May 1772

GOWDILOCK, ADAM File no. 285; Grant no. 276; Bk. 20, p. 623
  200 A on both sides the second Reedy branch of Thickety
  Creek...Collins Line...24th December 1770 Wm Tryon

GOLIGHTLY, JOHN File no. 573; Grant no. 464; Bk. 22, p. 110
  Plat: Surveyed for John Golightly 539 A on both sides of
  fareforast...Thomas Cases line...Robt McWherters line...Jiles
  Connells line...22d May 1772, Jno Kirkconell, Sur. Jilles Connells, C B Grant issued 23 May 1772

GOLIGHTLY, JOHN File no. 590; Grant no. 481; Bk. 22, p. 113
  Plat: Surveyed for John Golightly 200 A on both sides of
  fareforest including the improvement he bought of Willm
  Hammitt...fosters line...22 May 1772, Jno Kirkconell, Sur.
  Jills Connell & Jessey Connell, C B Grant issued 23 May 1772

GORE, MANNING File no. 869; Grant no. 230; Bk. 23, p. 355
  150 A on the W side of Broad River including his improvement and an Island in the river...23d December 1768 Wm
  Tryon

GOWDILOCK, ADAM File no. 394(725); Grant no. 434, Bk. 24, p. 24(Bk. 22, p. 309)
Plat: November the 1 1770, Surveyed for Adam Gowdilock 300 A on the Ridg between Packlet and Thickety...Zach Bullock John Nuckoles, John Goudelock, C B
Grant issued 25 Nov 1771

GRAHAM, ARTHUR File no. 067
Plat: Surveyed for Arthur Graham 200 A on No side of Pacolatt River including the improvement made by Caol which James Hammet now lives on...James Alleys corner Near a large Shoul...William Waffords line 3 July 1771, Jno Kirkconell, Surv.
John Steen & John Graham, C B Grant issued 14 Nov 1771

GRAHAM, ARTHUR & JOHN STEEN File no. 421; Grant no.74; Bk. 20, p. 702
Plat: Surveyed for John Steen 180 A on the Et side of Broad River...James Fannings corner...Joseph Woods's line...John Foster's line...July 11th 1771, Jno Kirkconell Surv. John Foster & James McLane, C B Grant issued 14 Nov 1771

GRANDAL, JOSEPH File no. 836; Grant no. 140; Bk. 23, p. 338
80 A on the No side of Pacolet joining his own line...22d December 1768 Wm Tryon

GUTHRY, FRANCIS File no. 194; Grant no. 116; Bk. 20, p. 439
Plat: Surveyed for Francis Guthrey 132 A on So side Allison Creek, joining John Henry & John Buchannons lands...Dec. 26th 1767, Peter Johnston [surv.] Wm. & Alexr Stevenson, C B Grant issued 4 May 1769

HALL, JOHN File no. 1866(1854); Grant no. 180: Bk. 22, p. 45
Plat: Surveyed for John Hall 100 A on both sides of Rocky Allisons Creek joining and between his own and Shaws land... Moffats open line...Moses Fergusons line...Augt. 3d 1771 Peter Johnston Survr. Alexr McWhorter & Wm. McMurray, C B Grant issued 19 May 1772

HAMMET, JAMES File no. 712(921); Grant no. 421; Bk. 24, p. 21
Plat: Surveyed for James Hammett 600 A on the Rich Hill of Fairforrest...Zach Bullock [Surv.] Wm Lee & Natt Dodd, C B Grant issued 25 Nov 1771

HAMMETT, JAMES File no. 713(922); Grant no. 422; Bk. 22, p. 308(Bk. 24, p. 21)
200 A on both sides of Lawsons Fork of Pacolet...including a Mill Seat...25th Novem 1771 Jo Martin

HAMSTON, RICHARD File no. 571; Grant no. 460; Bk. 22, p. 109
Plat: Surveyed for Richard Hamston 400 A on a branch of wards creek nearby his other survey...22d May 1772 Jno Kirkconell, Surv. Richard Hamstons & Jams Gibbs, C B Gr. issued 23 May 1772

HAMSTON, RICHARD File no. 568; Grant no. 457; Bk. 22, p. 108
Plat: Surveyed for Richard Hampston 400 A on a Branch of fareforast...22d May 1772 Jno Kirkconell Surv. Zachariah & James Gibbs, C B Grant issued 23 May 1772

HANNA, JAMES File no. 112; Grant no. 142; Bk. 20, p. 443
Plat: Surveyed for James Hanna 200 A on the west side of the middle fork of Tygar River, joining the land he bought of black Febry 2d 1769 Peter Johnston Survr. Thomas & John Pennys, C B Grant issued 4 May 1769

HANNA, WILLIAM JUNR File no. 876; Grant no. 322; Bk. 23, p. 369
180 A on the So side of the Stoney fork of Fishing Creek joining and between William Hannah Senr, William Dicksons, Edward Crofts and Thomas Blacks Lines...22d December 1768 Wm Tryon

HANNAH, WILLIAM File no. 185; Grant no. 179; Bk. 20, p. 518
Plat: Surveyed for William Hannah 45 A on Stoney fork of fishing Creek joining his own land...Culps line...William Hannah Junr corner...Hagertys line...Thomas Raineys line...Decr 11th 1767 Peter Johnston [Surv.] John Colwell & William Hannah Junr, C B Grant issued 16 Dec. 1769

HANNAN, WILLIAM File no. 704(913); Grant no. 412; Bk. 22, p. 306
250 A on Hannans Branch of Tyger River...Francis Willsons Line...Francis Princes Line...25th Novem 1771 Jo Martin

HARPER, MATHEW, Jr. File no. 011, Entry no. 404
Warrant: unto Mathew Harper Junior...200 A on both sides of a small branch North Side of So Packolet joining a tract first surveyed for Joseph White now in possession of Mathew Harper 10 Dec 1770 Wm Tryon
Two identical plats: Surveyed for Mathew Harper Junr 200 A on the waters of Packelott...N side river on or near Mathew Harper line...March 15th 1771, Jno Kirkconell, Sur. William Jamison & Robert Harper C B

HARPER, ROBERT File no. 101; Grant no. 126; Bk. 20, p. 440
Plat: Surveyed for Robert Harper 200 A on the Dividing
Ridge Between Turkey & fishing Creek...Peter Johnston Sur.
David Stevenson & Alexander Harper C B 27 Dec 1767 Gr.
issued 4 May 1769

HARPER, ROBERT File no. 265; Grant no. 47; Bk. 20, p. 582
Plat: Surveyed for Robert Harper 200 A on waters of fishing
Creek joining Davidsons...John Dennis's Corner...June 20th
1769...Peter Johnston Surv. John Dennis & William Harper
Grant issued 11 Dec 1770

HARRIS, ROBERT File no. 6; Grant no. 442; Bk. 20, p. 394
500 A on both sides of Harris Creek, waters of Fair Forrest
including James Harris old survey...James Mayes Corner...An-
drew Fosters corner...Bullocks corner...George Parks line...
22d December 1768 Wm Tryon

HENRY, WILLIAM File no. 183; Grant no. 177; Bk. 20, p. 518
Plat: Surveyed for William Henry, 100 A in Mecklenburg
(stricken) Tryon County on waters of Allisons Creek...John
Gordons corner...Febry 14th 1769 Peter Johnston, Survr.
Andrew Patrick, Alexr. Henry, C. B. Grant issued 16 Dec
1769

HOGAN, JOHN File no. 443; Grant no. 59; Bk. 22, p. 16
Plat: April the 8th 1772. Surveyd for John Hogan 300 A....on
McBee's fork of Thicketty Creek between Vardry Mcbee's
and Hannahs Cabin...P William Sims John Nuckols, Richard
Nuckols, S C Bearers Grant issued 15 May 1772

HOGE, GEORGE File no. 3; Grant no. 355; Bk. 20, p. 376
Plat: Surveyed for George Hogg , 200 A on Mecklenburg
County, on both sides of Burlisons Fork of Turkey Creek including his own improvement...8th March 1768. Joseph Dickson, D. S. Wm Williamson, George Hogg, Cha. Bear. Grant
iss 22 Dec 1768

HOGE, GEORGE JUNR. File no. 1; Grant no. 353; Bk. 20, p. 375
Plat: Surveyed for George Hogg Junior, 200 A Mecklenburg
County on Burlisons Fork of Turkey Creek including his own
improvement...May 19th 1767 Peter Johnston, Survr. Grant
issued 22 Dec 1768

HOWARD, PETER File no. 926(717); Grant no. 426; Bk. 24, p. 22
Plat: Novem the 7th 1769 Surveyed for Peter Howard 200 A
on Both Sides of Little Sandy Run...Zach Bullock William
Grant, William Williams, C B Grant issued 25 Nov 1771

HUNTER, SAMUEL File no. 552; Grant no. 427; Bk. 22, p. 102
Plat: Surveyed for Samuell Hunter 200 A on a Branch of Bullocks Creek of Broad River...John Laughlins corner...Frances Beatys line...26th July 1771 Patrick heney & Samuel Swann [?] , C B Grant issued 22 May 1772

INLOW, BENJAMIN File no. 579; Grant no. 470; Bk. 22, p. 111
200 A on the head waters of Allisons Creek...Barnhills corner ...Smiths line...Joseph Hardens corner...23d May 1772 Jo Martin

INLOW, ISAAC File no. 474; Grant no. 94; Bk. 22, p. 23
Plat: Surveyed for Isaac Inlow 150 A on a branch of Bullocks Creek...John Smith's line...Davis Watsons line...4 Feb 1772 Jno Kirkconell, Surv. John Wilson & Nathan Porter, C B Grant issued 15 May 1772

IRWIN, ROBERT File no. 80; Grant no. 94; Bk. 20, p. 435
Plat: Survey'd for Robt. Irwin 400 A on Tygar River about his former survey...Clayton's line...3 Apr 1769...Wm Sharp, Survr. [No C B] Grant issued 4 May 1769

JACK, JAMES File no. 268; Grant no. 50; Bk. 20, p. 583
Plat: Surveyed for James Jack 150 A on waters of fishing Creek joining John Boyds land...June 26th 1769 Peter Johnston [Survr.] John Nuly & Hugh White, C B Grant issued 11 Dec 1770

JOHNSTON, PETER File no. 98; Grant no. 123; Bk. 20, p. 440
Plat: Surveyed for Peter Johnston 92 A on the waters of Turkey Creek...Samuel Guyses land...Robert Harpers Corner... Febry 4th 1769. Peter Johnston James Hetherington & William Guyse C B Grant issued 4 May 1769

JOHNSTON, PETER File no. 34; Grant no. 506; Bk. 20, p. 407
300 A on both sides Fair forrest Creek...below Thomas Cases ...23d December 1768 Wm Tryon

JOHNSTON, PETER File no. 173; Grant no. 161; Bk. 20, p. 516
Plat: Surveyed for Peter Johnston 148 A on waters of the south fork of Fishing Creek joining Benjamin Phillips land... James Murpheys corner...October 30th 1769
Peter Johnston, Surv. Samuel Gay & William Bratton C B Grant issued 16 Dec 1769

JOHNSTON, PETER File no. 238; Grant no. 75; Bk. 20, p. 551
Plat: Surveyed for Peter Johnston 400 A on south side of the So fork of fishing Creek including the improvement he bought of George bounds, joining Alexanders land...Bounds corner

...June 19th 1769, Peter Johnston, Surv. John Sadler, John Dennis, C B Grant issued 9 Apr 1770

JOHNSTON, PETER File no. 263; Grant no. 45; Bk. 20, p. 582
Plat: Surveyed for Peter Johnston 170 A on waters of turkey creek joining the land Robert Bratton now lives on...June 19th 1770 Peter Johnston, Surv. Samuel Gay & Robt. Bratton, C B Grant issued 11 Dec 1770

JOHNSTON, PETER File no. 267; Grant no. 49; Bk. 20, p. 582
Plat: Surveyed for Peter Johnston 400 A on waters of fairforrest Creek joining John Thomas's land including part— Rich hill...joining Dodds' land...August 8th 177- Peter Johnston Sur. Grant issued 11 Dec 1770
John & Robt Thomass , C B

JOHNSTON, PETER File no. 359; Grant no. 130; Bk. 20, p. 668
Plat: Surveyed for Peter Johnston 175 A on So side of So fork fishing Creek joining & between James Murphys & Kids land...Rottons line...Febry 7th 1771 Peter Johnston John Kirkconnell & John Kid, C B Grant issued 18 Apr 1771

JOHNSTON, PETER File no. 737(946); Grant no. 447; Bk. 24, p. 26(Bk. 22, p. 311
200 A on the So side of Allisons Creek joining Robert McDowells land on both sides of the Waggon Road...John Blacks Corner...John Youngs land...25th Novem 1771 Jo Martin

KELLER, JOSEPH File no. 012
Plat: Surveyed for Joseph Keller 128 A on waters of No fork of Tygar River joing the So side of Joseph Jones Mill seat place & David Davis land...adj. line of a place surveyed for Saml. Neisbet...June 7th 1768 Peter Johnston Surv. Alexander McCostor & Joseph Thompson C B

KEMBROLL, JOHN File no. 190; Grant no. 190; Bk. 20, p. 520
Plat: Surveyed for John Kembro 100 A on both sides Allisons Creek joining Wm Patricks land...Decr 28th 1767 Peter Johnston Drury Cook & William McDowell, C B Grant issued 16 Dec 1769

KENEDY, ALEXANDER File no. 671(880); Grant no. 363; Bk. 22, p. 298(Bk. 24, p. 8)
Plat: Surveyed for Alexr Kenrud 113 A on waters of Rockey Allisons Creek joining Js. McCallan & Thomas Barrons land... Archibald Barrons line...January ye 8th 1770 Alexr. & James Stevenson, C B Peter Johnston Grant issued 22 Nov 1771

KENNADY, ALEXANDER File no. 557; Grant no. 433; Bk. 22, p. 103

Plat: Surveyed for Alexander Kennedy 300 A on a Branch of Fishing Creek...John Millers line...Colo. Palamer's land...19th July 1771 Jno Kirkconell Sur. Thomas Barron & Joseph Gabbey, C B Grant issued 22 May 1772

KER, JOHN JUNR File no. 62; Grant no. 113; Bk. 20, p. 438
Plat: Surveyed for John Ker Junior 150 A on waters of Allisons Creek, joining his own land...joining Watsons land... Peter Johnston Sur. Feby 10th 1769
Samuel Nisbet & Daniel Brice, C B Grant issued 4 May 1769

KERR, JAMES File no. 123; Grant no. 340; Bk. 20, p. 471
Plat: Surveyed for James Ker 160 A on the ridge between Loves and Burlisons fork of Turkey Creek & on both sides of the path that leads from Edmond Bishops to Loves old survey...Febry 9th 1769 Wm Williamson & Frances Ress, C B Peter Johnston, Su. Grant issued 5 May 1769

KERR, WILLIAM File no. 708(917); Grant no. 417; Bk. 22, p. 307(Bk. 24, p. 21)
William Keer...300 A on the Head of Loves Creek...near Wades line...John Mckennys line...25th Novem 1771 Jo Martin

GRAHAM, JEAN File no. 0100; Entry no. 316
Two identical plats: July the 4th 1769 Surveyed for Jean Graham 150 A on Turkey Creek joining her line...Michael McGarrity line...Zach Bullock. Frances Guttery & Michael McGarrity, S C B
Original grant in file envelope dated 16 Dec 1769, but not issued

HENDERSON, RICHARD File no. 62; Grant no. 545; Bk. 20, p. 414
Plat: Tryon County, March 12, 176-[8] Surveyed for Richard Henderson, 300 A on both sides south fork of Packlet... pine in John Croford's line on N side of sd. Creek...Zach Bullock. Alexander Kilpatrickt, Joab Mitchel, C. B. Grant issued 23 Dec 1768

KERKENNEL, JOHN [KIRKCONNEL] File no. 538; Grant no. 413; Bk. 22, p. 99
200 A on both sides of Lawsons fork of Packlot including Halkams Cabbin...John Millers corner...22d May 1771 Jo Martin

KERCONNEL, JOHN File no. 583; Grant no. 474; Bk. 22, p. 112
200 A on both sides of Susey Bolds Branch of Turkey Creek ...Edward Leaseys line...23d May 1772 Jo Martin

KIRKCONNEL, JOHN File no. 541; Grant no. 416; Bk. 22, p. 99
200 A on both sides of little Sandy Run of Packlett including

Hugh Pellims Cabbin...No side of Roches branch...22d May 1772 Jo Martin

KIRKCONNEL, JOHN File no. 542; Grant no. 417; Bk. 22, p. 100
200 A on both sides of Peters creek of Packlett River...22d May 1772 Jo Martin

KIRKCONNEL, JOHN File no. 543; Grant no. 418; Bk. 22, p. 100
Plat: Surveyed for John Kirkconnell 200 A on the No side of Packlatt...Youngs corner...26th April 1772 Jno Kirkconnel, Surv. Thomas Nicklos & John Elliott, C B Grant issued 22 May 1772

KIRKCONNEL, JOHN File no. 544; Grant no. 419; Bk. 22, p. 100
250 A on both sides of Lawson fork of Packlett...below a small island...22d May 1772 Jo Martin

KIRCONNELL, JOHN File no. 951; Grant no. 464; Bk. 24, p. 30
200 A on the N side of Paccolet River...upper side of John Portmans Land & including the improvement where Jno Williams now lives...Pillets Shoal...25th Nov 1771 Jo Martin

KIRKCONNELL, JOHN File no. 575; Grant no. 465; Bk. 22, p. 100
200 A on both sides Packlott River...23d May 1772 Jo Martin

KIRKCONNELL, JOHN File no. 582; Grant no. 473; Bk. 22, p. 112
300 A on a branch of Lawsons fork of Packelott...23d May 1772 Jo Martin

KIRKCONNELL, JOHN File no. 743; Grant no. 743; Bk. 22, p. 314
Plat: 26th Novemr 1771 Surveyd for John Kirkconell 200 A on No side of Packolet River on the upper side of John Portmans land and including the improvement where John Williams now lives...Pittets Shoull...Jno Kirkconell Survr Thomas Nicklas, John Elliott, C B Grant issued 25 Nov 1771

KNOX, DAVID File no. 196; Grant no. 198; Bk. 20, p. 521
300 A on the waters of the No fork of Tygar river joining and between John Miller, John Brown, and Samuel Knoxes Land...16th December 1769 Wm Tryon

KNOX, SAMUEL File no. 189; Grant no. 189; Bk. 20, p. 520
Plat: Surveyed for Samuel Knox 200 A on the waters of Lawsons fork of Packelot joining or near the Land See [Lee?] now lives on...Decr 23d 1767 Peter Johnston David Knox & John Knox Junr, C B Grant issued 16 Dec 1769

LAUGHLIN, WILLIAM File no. 710(919); Grant no. 419; Bk. 22,
p. 307(Bk. 24, p. 21)
Plat: July 5th 1770 Surveyed for William Lawlin 200 A on
both sides of Bullocks Creek...Saml Davises Line...Wrightes
line...P Zach Bullock William Scales, William Laughlin J, C B
Grant issued 11 Nov 1771

LEAMEY, THOMAS File no. 167; Grant no. 463; Bk. 20, p. 483
Plat: Surveyed for Thomas Learney 200 A on Mecklenburg
(stricken) Tryon on waters of Turkey Creek on the head of
Susy Bowls branch...John Dennis's line...7 May 1766 William
Dickson Survr. Edward Lacey & John Dennis Cha. Bear.
Grant issued 6 May 1769

LEECH, DAVID File no. 269; Grant no. 51; Bk. 20, p. 583
Plat: Surveyed for David Leech 200 A on Et side of tygar
River on both sides of the Waggon Road that leads from
Georg Stories to Nathaniel Mills...Millers Corner...Lawsons
corner...Augt 7d 1770 Peter Johnston Sur. Henry & John
Leechs, C B Grant issued 11 Dec 1770

LEECH, JOHN File no. 74; Grant no. 76; Bk. 20, p. 431
Plat: Surveyed for John Leech 167 A in Mecklenburg Coun-
ty on James Crek, joining Thomas Collins, John McKle-
hennys, and Alexander Vernons land...26 May 1767 Peter
Johnston Surveyor. Joseph Jones & Alexander Vernon, C B
Grant issued 4 May 1769

LEECH, JOHN File no. 275; Grant no. 154; Bk. 20, p. 602
Plat: Surveyed for John Leech 240 A on Jammies Creek
joining Sadlers land...near the meeting house...Augt 6d 1770
Peter Johnston Sur. David Leech & Richd Sadler, C B Grant
issued 11 Dec 1770

LINDSAY, ISSAC File no. 389; Grant no. 41; Bk. 20, p. 697
Plat: Surveyed for Isaac Lindsey 200 A on both sides of
Pacolat including a large Shoal & place called the Doctors
Bottom...bent of Lindsays branch...8th Novr 1770 Peter
Johnston Sur William Wafford & William Young, Chain
Bearers Grant issued 14 Nov 1771

LOGAN, JAMES File no. 109; Grant no. 139; Bk. 20, p. 442
Plat: Surveyd for James Logan 100 A on waters of Fishing
Creek, joining George Gills land he now lives on...Febry 16th
1769 Peter Johnston Survr. George Gill & Samuel Porter,
C B Grant issued 4 May 1769

LUNY, ADAM File no. 697(906); Grant no. 403; Bk. 22, p. 305
(Bk. 24, p. 18)

Plat: October 8th 1771 Surveyd for Adam Luny 300 A on North side of Packlett...Zach Bullock D S John Nuckoles and Wm Marchbanks, Cha Bearers/Grant issued 25 Nov 1771

LUSH, JAMES File no. 344; Grant no. 115; Bk. 20, p. 665
Plat: Surveyed for James Lusk 96 A on waters of fishing Creek joining his own & John Workman's lands...June 27th 1769 Peter Johnston John Downing, Robert Lusk, C B Grant issued 18 Apr 1771

McBEE, VARDRY File no. 741(950); Grant no. 453; Bk. 22, p. 312 (Bk. 24, p. 27)
Plat: Surveyed for Vardry Mcbee 300 A on thicketty Creek including Swoffords Camp...John Steens corner...Zach Bullock John Nuckols, Wm Marchbanks, Chain Bearers
Grant issued 25 Nov 1771

McBRAYER, WILLIAM File no. 100; Grant no. 125; Bk. 20, p. 440
Plat: Surveyed for Wm McBrayers 50 A on the watrey branch of Turkey Creek...near Rigs land...Wm Love's corner...Dec 5h 1767 Peter Johnston Survr. Grant issued 4 May 1769

McCURDY, ROBERT File no. 407; Grant no. 60; Bk. 20, p. 700
Plat: Surveyed for Robert McCurdy 140 A on both sides of Beaverdam Creek of Broad River...John Parress corner... James Dirivins line...April 23d 1771 Jno Kirkconell Sur. Patrick Lapherty & John Paris, C B Grant issued 14 Nov 1771

McDOWELL, WILLIAM File no. 76; Grant no. 78; Bk. 20, p. 432
233 A on waters of Allisons Creek including his improvement ...John McCullohs line...4th May 1769 Wm Tryon

McDOWELL, WILLIAM File no. 184; Grant no. 178; Bk. 20, p. 518
Plat: Surveyed for William McDowall 150 A on South sides of Allisons Creek joing Joseph Clarks land where he now lives ...Armstrong line...Willm McDowalls line...Febry 18th 1769 Peter Johnston Wm & Alexr Stevensons, C B Grant issued 16 Dec 1769

McKENNY, JOHN File no. 416; Grant no. 69; Bk. 20, p. 701
600 A on waters of Bullocks Creek...his own corner...14th November 1771 Jo Martin

McKLEKENY, JOHN File no. 86; Grant no. 104; Bk. 20, p. 437
Plat: Surveyed for John McKlekenny 100 A on south sides of the north fork of Tygar River, joining Thomas Collins, John Leech & his own land...27 May 1767 Peter Johnston, Surv.

Thomas Collins & Alexander Vernon, C B
Grant issued 4 May 1769, has Lucks corner instead of Leechs.

McKLEHANEY, JOHN File no. 77; Grant no. 70; Bk. 20, p. 432
200 A on the waters of the north fork of Tygar river on
BrownBranch joining John Princes land...4th May 1769 Wm
Tryon

McMURDIE, ROBERT File no. 32; Grant no. 493; Bk. 20, p. 404
300 A on the South side of Lawsons fork of Pacalet on both
sides Reedy Branch and both sides of Jones Waggon road...
John Millers corner...23d December 1768 Wm. Tryon.

McMURRAY, THOMAS File no. 853; Grant no. 191; Bk. 23, p.
348
150 A on the So side of Fishing Creek...Robert McClallonds
Line...Benjamin Philips line...22d December 1768 Wm Tryon

McNICE, JOSEPH File no. 358; Grant no. 129; Bk. 20, p. 668
Plat: Surveyed for Joseph McNice 200 A on So side of So
fork of fishing Creek, joining Peter Johnstons land...March
7th 1771 Peter Johnston Survr.
James Alcorn & Joseph McNice, C B Grant issued 18 Apr
1771

McNIGHT, THOMAS File no. 469; Grant no. 89; Bk. 22, p. 22
Plat: Surveyed for Thomas McNight...100 A on So side of No
Packlat. . .25 June 1772, Jno Kirkconnell, Survr. Charles Mc
Night, John Denkens, C B Grant issued 15 May 1772

McNEAR, RALPH File no. 896; Grant no. 393; Bk. 24, p. 16
300 A on Mays Creek...25 Novr 1771 Jo Martin

MACKELROY, JAMES File no. 805; Grant no. 75; Bk. 23, p. 327
350 A on both sides Lawsons fork of Pacolet including a
large shoal and mill seat...22d December 1768 Wm Tryon

MAHAN, JAMES File no. 846; Grant no. 184; Bk. 23, p. 346
250 A on the Stoney fork of Fishing Creek joining William
Hannah Junior and Culps Land...22d December 1768 Wm
Tryon

MARCHBANKS, WILLIAM File no. 094; Entry no. 400
Warrant: 640 A in County of Mecklenberg on Both sides of
the North fork of Packolet above Alexander Kilpatricks Line
and Below Clemmers Line...21 Dec 1768 Wm Tryon
Bena. Heron D Audr Returned Novr Court of Claims 1771
Plat: Septr 23d 1771 Surveyed for William Marchbanks 400
A on both sides Packlet...Zach Bullock John Golman, George
Marchbanks, Cha Bearers

MARCHBANKS, WILLIAM File no. 690(899); Grant no. 396; Bk. 22, p. 304(Bk. 24, p. 16)
400 A on both sides of Pacolet River...25th Novem 1771 Jo Martin

MATTHEWS, PHILIP File no. 706(915); Grant no. 414; Bk. 22, p. 306(Bk. 24, p. 20)
200 A on a large branch of Bullocks Creek of Thicketty... 25th Novem 1771 Jo Martin

MAYS, JAMES File no. 174; Grant no. 164; Bk. 20, p. 416
Plat: Surveyed for JAMES MAYS 80 A on waters of Fair Forrest Creek joining land he now lives on...George Parks line...Mr Tales line...June 14th 1769 Peter Johnston, Survr. George Park & Isaac Patton, C. B.

MILLAR, NATHANIEL File no. 858; Grant no. 197; Bk. 23, p. 349
100 A on both sides the mouth of north fork of Tygar River ...his uper line...John Nicholas land...22d December 1768 Wm Tryon

MILLER, ABRAHAM File no. 195; Grant no. 197; Bk. 20, p.521
Plat: Surveyed for Abraham Miller, 146 A...south side of Allisons Creek joining & between McDowell & Major Temples Land...June 21 [no year] Peter Johnston. Grant issued 16 Dec 1769 John Black & John Foster, C B

MILLER, JAMES File no. 834; Grant no. 138; Bk. 23, p. 338
100 A on the So side of the Middle fork of Tygar River joining Robert and John Millers line...22d December 1768 Wm Tryon

MILLER, JOHN File no. 674(883); Grant no. 375; Bk. 24, p. 11 (Bk. 22, p. 301)
Plat: Surveyed for John Miller 50 A on the waters of Turkey Creek joining and between his own and Robert Simintons land...August 23d 1770 Peter Johnston Sur. Robt. Siminton & John Miller, C B Grant issued 22 Nov 1771

MILLER, JOHN File no. 203; Grant no. 291; Bk. 20, p. 535
Plat: Surveyed for John Miller 200 A on the Dividing ridge between Love's fork and Burlinsons fork of Turkey Creek including the improvement William Williamson now lives on... George Rutledges line...August 5th 1769 Peter Johnston, Surv. William Williamson, George Waggoner, C B Grant issued 16 Dec 1769

MILLER, JOHN File no. 75; Grant no. 77; Bk. 20, p. 432
100 A on a branch of Turkey Creek where Hugh Sagriff now Lives...4th May 1769 Wm Tryon

MILLS, JESSE File no. 209; Grant no. 304; Bk. 20, p. 536
Plat: March the 3d 1769 Surveyed for Jesse Mills 150 A on So side of N fork of Packlet...James Howards line and Kilpatricks line...Zach Bullock Robert Moore, John Moore, C B Grant issued 16 Dec 1769

MOFFETT, JOHN File no. 546; Grant no. 421; Bk. 22, p. 100
Plat: Surveyed for John Moffett 180 A on the head branches of Bullocks Creek...10th April 1772 Jno Kirkconell Sur. John Hollon & John Johnston, C B Grant issued 22 May 1772

MOORE, CHARLES File no. 456; Grant no. 75; Bk. 22, p. 19
Plat: Surveyed for Charles Moore 200 A on So side of Tygar River...John Foard's line...near Neallys Corner...16th Jany 1772 Jno Kirkconell Sur. Andrew Berry, Alexander Barron C B Grant issued 15 May 1772

MOORE, HUGH File no. 699(908); Grant no. 405; Bk. 22, p. 305 (Bk. 24, p. 18)
Plat: October 10th 1771 Survey'd for Hugh Moore 100 A on Bullocks fork of Thicketty Creek...his old line...Zach Bullock D S George Underwood, Isham Saffold, Cha Bea. Grant issued 25 Nov 1771

MOORE, JAMES File no. 166; Grant no. 461; Bk. 20, p. 488
Plat: Surveyed for James Moore 300 A in Mecklenburg (stricken) Tryon County on the waters of the south fork of Fishing Creek on Laceys spring branch and on both sides of the Waggon Road...John Prices corner...Edward Laceys corner...Thomas Raineys line...John Walkers line...16 Feby 1767 Wm Dickson Sur. Samuel Rainey & Joshua Lacey, Cha. Bear. Grant issued 6 May 1769

MOORE, JOHN File no. 106; Grant no. 136; Bk. 20, p. 442
Plat: Surveyed for John Moore 50 A on the waters of the South fork of Fishing Creek...James Moores corner...Thomas Raineys line...June 10th 1768 Peter Johnston Surv. 'David Leech & Samuel Rainey, C B Grant issued 4 May 1769

MORGAN, THOMAS File no. 172; Grant no. 160; Bk. 20, p. 516
Plat: Surveyed for Thomas Morgan 90 A on Barnet Humphreys Branch of Fishing Creek, joining John Anderson's land... Peter Kuydendalls line...Decr 23 1767 Peter Johnston Sur.

Martin Armstrong & Meshah Stillions [Stillhous?], C B Grant issued 16 Dec 1769

MURPHEY, JAMES File no. 867; Grant no. 206; Bk. 23, p. 350
150 A on the So fork of Fishing Creek joining the land he now lives on...Edward Laceys corner...William Adairs corner.. 22d December 1768 Wm Tryon

NAVILL, WILLIAM File no. 503; Grant no. 134; Bk. 22, p. 34
Plat: Surveyed for William Navell 300 A on waters of Lawsons fork of Packelott...June 28th 1771 Jno Kirkconell Sur. Richard Halkam, Benjamin Thomson, C B Grant issued 15 May 1772

NEISBET, SAMUEL File no. 266; Grant no. 48; Bk. 20, p. 582
Plat: Surveyed for Samuel Neisbet Tree Hundred & fifty A... waters of No fork of Tygar River including a mill seat...McCree's line...Knox's corner...McCarters corner...August 2th 1770 Peter Johnston Surv. Saml Brice & John Penny,CB Grant issued 11 Dec 1770

NEISBET, SAMUEL File no. 240; Grant no. 77; Bk. 20, p. 551
Plat: Surveyed for Samuel Neisbet 200 A on No fork of Tygar River joining land Joseph Jones now lives on...Millers line ...Jones line...March 15th 1770 Peter Johnston John Jones & James Reynolds, C B Grant issued 9 Apr 1770

NEISBET, SAMUEL File no. 199; Grant no. 233; Bk. 20, p. 526
Plat: Surveyed for Samuel Neisbet 200 A on a south branch of the North fork of Tygar River known as reedy branch...so side of David Davis's land...Millers & said Davis's line...near Jean Knoxs land...July 24th 1769 Peter Johnston Sur. Daniel Brice & Thomas Penny[?], C B Grant issued 16 Dec 1769

NEISBET, SAMUEL File no. 532; Grant no. 322; Bk. 22, p. 78
176 A on the No side of the So fork of Tygar River joining his old Survey...22 May 1772 Jo Martin

NICHOLAS, THOMAS File no. 555; Grant no. 431; Bk. 22, p. 102
Plat: Surveyed for Thomas Nicklas 400 A on both sides of Thickety Creek...John Steens corner...James Wilkey's line... Robert Moores line...25 March 1771 Jno Kirkconnell Sur. John Sneed & George Hyed[?] C B Grant issued 22 May 1772

OZBURN, ADLAI File no. 445; Grant no. 61; Bk. 22, p. 16
Plat: April the 7th 1772 Surveyed for Adlai Osborn 300 A on a branch of Thicketty Creek near the Road that Leads from Vardry M:bees to the Cherokee Ford on Broad River... P William Sims John Nuckols, Richard Nuckols, S C Bearers Grant issued 15 May 1772

PALMER, WILLIAM File no. 052; Entry no. 172
Warrant: 640 A on the waters of fair forest joining Robert Harriss's Land including the Land formerly enter'd by Zach Bullock 11 Nov 1771 Jo Martin, Wm Palmer, D Sec Returned July Court of Claims 1774

PARK, JOSEPH File no. 181; Grant no. 175; Bk. 20, p. 518
Plat: Surveyed for Joseph Park 150 A on waters of fair Forrest Creek joing the Land John Parks lives on...William Mims line...June 14th 1769 Peter Johnston Joseph and John Parks, C B Grant issued 16 Dec 1769

PARKS, HUGH File no. 199; Grant no. 284; Bk. 20, p. 468
Plat: Mecklinburg (Stricken) Tryon March the 3rd 1766 Surveyed for MOSES FERGUSON (stricken) HUGH PARKS 400 A on the middle fork of Tyger River below David McKees land...Zach Bullock Sur. Hugh Barnet & James Carruth [C B] Grant issued 4 May 1769

PARRATT, JAMES File no. 739; Grant no. 449; Bk. 22, p. 312
200 A on both sides of Richardson Creek of Broad River... including the improvement John Neighbours made...25th Novem 1771 Jo Martin

PARRATT, JAMES File no. 563; Grant no. 441; Bk. 22, p. 104
200 A on a small branch of Thicketty Creek...22d May 1772

PATTEN, JOHN File no. 517; Grant no. 187; Bk. 22, p. 46
Plat: Surveyed for John Patten 14 A on So side Alisons Creek joining & between Ker's, Tygart's, and his own land... Dec 14th 1771 Peter Johnston Surv. John Patten & John Patten Jnr, C B Grant issued 19 May 1772

PETERSON, ISRAEL File no. 237; Grant no. 72; Bk. 20, p. 550
Plat: Surveyed for Israel Peterson 250 A on right & left hand Dry fork of Turkey Creek joining George Rutledges land including his own improvement he now lives on...Thor[?] Brysons line...James Brysons line...Waggoners land...August ye 4th 1769 Peter Johnston, Surv. George Waggoner & Andrew Peterson, C B Grant issued 9 Apr 1770

PORTER, MATHEW File no. 875; Grant no. 276; Bk. 23, p. 362
300 A on Turkey Creek beginning at David Byars corner... 22d December 1768 Wm Tryon

POLK, EZEKIEL File no. 468; Grant no. 88; Bk. 22, p. 22
Plat: Surveyed for Ezekiel Polk 200 A on the head branches of Bullocks and Allison's Creek and on Both sides of the waggon Road leading from the So fork of the Catawba River to

Charlestown...Charles McCleans line...20 April, 1772 Jno Kirkconell Surv. Samuel Wilson & John Moffett, C B Grant issued 15 May 1772

PRICE, JONATHAN File no. 90; Grant no. 109; Bk. 20, p. 437 150 A on the waters of Allisons Creek including his own improvement where he now lives...William Dicksons line...4th May 1769 Wm Tryon

PRINCE, FRANCIS File no. 947; Grant no. 448; Bk. 24, p. 26 Plat: Surveyed for Francis Prince 180 A on the North side of the North fork of Tygar River on both sides of Browns branch ...John Macklehenny's corner...John Princes line... John Millers corner...Collins corner...Dodds corner...Febry 14th 1770. Peter Johnston, Surv. William Prince, William Hannons, C B Grant issued 25 Nov 1771

QUINTON, SAMUEL File no. 273; Grant no. 55; Bk. 20, p. 632 Plat: Surveyed for Samuel Quinton 126 A between Allisons & Crowders Creek including the improvement he now lives on...William Patricks line...Neisonilles land...June 2d 1769 Peter Johnston John McCormick & Samuel Quinton, C B Grant issued 11 Dec 1770

RAINEY, THOMAS & BENJAMIN PHILLIPS File no. 326: Grant no. 391; Bk. 20, p. 643
Plat: Surveyed for Thomas Rainey & Benjamin Philips 200 A on waters of turkey Creek including the improvement Philips bought of Bull...Thomas Hillighs[?] line...William Barrons line...June 18th 1770 Peter Johnston Surv. Samuel Gay & Hugh Bratton, C B Grant issued 24 Dec 1770

RAINEY, THOMAS & JAS. WILLIAMSON File no. 324: Grant no. 388; Bk. 20, p. 642
Plat: Surveyed for Thomas Rainey & James Williamson 110 A on So fork of Fishing Creek...joining Raineys land...Harpers line...June 18, 1770 Peter Johnston, Surv. Oliver Wallace, Be. Phillips, C B Grant issued 24 Dec 1770

ROBISON, PATRICK File no. 349; Grant no. 120; Bk. 20, p. 666 Plat: Surveyed for Patrick Robison 250 A on South side of broad river & no side of Gilkies Creek...Febry 7th 1771 Peter Johnston Surv. John Kirkconnel & Patrick Robison, C B Grant issued 18 Apr 1771

RUTLEDGE, RUSSEL File no. 342; Grant no. 113; Bk. 20, p. 665 Plat: Surveyed for Russel Rutledge 150 A on waters of Turkey Creek including the improvement he now lives on... David Stevensons line...John Glovers Corner...Janry 18th

1770 Peter Johnston William Glover & Thomas Morris, C B Grant issued 18 Apr 1771

SADLER, GEORGE File no. 356; Grant no. 127; Bk. 20, p. 667
Plat: Surveyed for George Sadler 260 A on waters of Turkey Creek joining Edward Laceys Land...Feby 4th 1771 Peter Johnston Sur. Isaac Sadler & William Manahan, C B Grant issued 18 Apr 1771

SADLER, JOHN File no. 347; Grant no. 118; Bk. 20, p. 666
Plat: Surveyed for John Sadler 130 A on waters of Turkey Creek joining his own line...Kellys corner...Febry 4th 1771 Peter Johnston Surv. George Sadler & William Manahan, C B Grant issued 18 Apr 1771

SADLER, JOHN File no. 176; Grant no. 166; Bk. 20, p. 516
Plat: Surveyed for John Sadler 300 A on waters of Sandy River including his own improvement...Thomas Browns line... Peter Johnston sur. June 19, 1769
Samuel Gay & Josiah Citchons C B Grant issued 16 Dec 1769

SADLER, MARY File no. 68; Grant no. 64; Bk. 20, p. 429
100 A on waters of the No fork of Tygar river joining Samuel Nisbet, Daniel Brice, and Alexander McCarters Land...4th May 1769

SADLER, RICHARD File no. 327; Grant no. 392; Bk. 20, p. 643
Plat: Surveyed for Richard Sadler 45 A on waters of the middle branch of the So fork of fishing Creek, joinining the land he bought of David luck...John Moors corner on William Brattons line...Lacues land...June 16th 1770 Peter Johnston Surv. David Leech, Henry Ditts, C B Grant issued 24 Dec 1770

SADLER, RICHARD File no. 558; Grant no. 434; Bk. 22, p. 103
Plat: Surveyed for Richard Sadler (Carpenter) 150 A on waters of Turkey Creek including his own improvement... James Browns line...James Stevenson's corner...Febry 4th 1771 Peter Johnston Sur. George Sadler & William Manahan, C B Grant issued 22 May 1772

SAMPLE, JOSEPH File no. 830; Grant no. 128; Bk. 23, p. 336
200 A on both sides of Lawson fork of Pacolet joining John Alexanders lower line...22d December 1768 Wm Tryon

SIMS, WILLIAM File no. 298; Grant no. 289; Bk. 20, p. 625
Plat: Augt the 19th 1770 Surveyed for William Sims 240 A on the Branches of Turkey Creek of Broad River...Russels Line...Stinsons Corner...Sadlers line...P William Sims. Grant

issued 24 Dec 1770   William Glover, William Glover, Junr S C Bearers

SISSON, WILLIAM File no. 158; Grant no. 426; Bk. 20, p. 484
Plat: Surveyed for William Sisson 400 A in Mecklenburg (stricken) Tryon County on both sides of Packolet River including the Scull Shoal & bent of the River...Robert Bishops lower corner...21 Dec 1766 Wm Dickson Surv. Hugh Moore & Alexr Chissom, CHA. Bear.   Grant issued 5 May 1769

SPENCE, JOHN File no. 547; Grant no. 422; Bk. 22, p. 101
Plat: Surveyed for John Spence 176 A on the So side of Ellysons Creek of the Catawbaw River...McDowalls corner...20th July 1771 Jno Kirkconell John Black & William McDowall, C B Grant issued 22 May 1772

SMITH, JOHN File no. 30; Grant no. 487; Bk. 20, p. 403
200 A Wt side of Catawba and No side of main Fishing Creek ...Smiths Branch commonly called the Stil house Branch... Mary Smiths line...23d December 1768 Wm Tryon

SMITH, GEORGE File no. 31; Grant no. 488; Bk. 20, p. 403
160 A on Wt side the Catawba on the So side of Fishing Creek on both sides of Watsons Branch joining and between Isaac Smiths, Samuel Wherrys corner...23d December 1768 Wm Tryon

STEEN, JOHN File no. 396; Grant no. 48; Bk. 20, p. 698
Plat: Surveyed for John Steen 229 A on waters of Thickety Creek near his own line...Adam Luneys line...July 13th 1771 Jno Kirkconell Surv. Jno Graham, James Steen C B Grant issued 14 Nov 1771

STEEN, JOHN File no. 491; Grant no. 111; Bk. 22, p. 28
Plat: Surveyed for John Steen 190 A on Both sides Thickity Creek...his other line...2 April 1772 Jno Kirkconell Sur. James Steen & William Steen, C B Grant issued 15 May 1772

STEVESON, JAMES File no. 234; Grant no. 68; Bk. 20, p. 550
Plat: Surveyed for James Stevenson 60 A on waters of turkey creek joining his own and John Glovers land...William Glovers line...Janry ye 18th 1770 Peter Johnston Survr. Alexander & James Stevensons, C B Grant issued 7 Apr 1770

STOCKTON, NEWBERRY File no. 283; Grant no. 274; Bk. 20, p. 623
Plat: November 28th 1768 Survey'd for Newberry Stockton 300 A on both sides of Clarks fork of Bullocks Creek...Pott's line...Zac. Bullock Surv. [No CB] Grant issued 24 Dec 1770

STOREY, GEORGE File no. 178; Grant no. 168; Bk. 20, p. 517
Plat: Surveyed for George Storey 400 A on waters of Fair-
forrest Creek including his improvement he now lives on...
June 31th 1769 Peter Johnston Sur. Anthoney Storey,
Samuel Cluney, C B Grant issued 16 Dec 1769

TERRELL, ABEGAIL File no. 918; Grant no. 418; Bk. 24, p. 21
Plat: October 15th 1770 Surveyed for Abigal Terrel 150 A
on both sides of Beverdam fork of South fork of Packlet...
Solomon Alstons Line...Zach Bullock, Gilles Tilles, Saml
Tilles, C B Grant issued 25 Nov 1771

THACKSTON, JAMES File no. 699(897); Grant no. 394; Bk. 22,
p. 304(Bk. 24, p. 16)
Plat: Surveyed for James Thackston 300 A on Harris's Creek
...Zacha Bullock Joab Mitchel, John Hail, C Bearers September 10th 1771 Grant issued 25 Nov 1771

THACKSTON, JAMES File no. 33; Grant no. 494; Bk. 20, p. 405
200 A on So branch of Lawsons fork of Pacalet about four
miles No of Joseph Jones and above his Buffalow waggon
ford joining Moses Fergusons survey...23d December 1768
Wm Tryon

THOMAS, JOHN JUNR File no. 385; Grant no. 242; Bk. 20, p.
686
Plat: Surveyed for John Thomas Junior 250 A on both sides
of fairforrest Creek joining John Thomas land...Dugans...
Tillets corner...near Taits land...August 9d 1770 Peter Johnston Sur. John Thomas & Robt. Ditts, C B Grant issued 18
Apr 1771

THOMSON, BENJAMIN File no. 471; Grant no. 91; Bk. 22, p. 23
Plat: Surveyed for Benjamin Thomson 200 A on both sides
of fareforast...the Grenston Branch...holstons branch...Jno
Kirkconell Sur William Weck & William Thomson, CB Grant
issued 15 May 1772

THOMSON, JOSEPH File no. 095; Entry 442
Warrant: Joseph Tomption 200 A in County of Mecklenburg,
on the South Branch of the North fork of Tygar River joining Alexander McCarter, Joseph Jones and Alexander·Rayes
including his own improvement he Now Lives on...26th April
1768 Wm Tryon John London, Ben Heron D Aud. Returned
May Court of Claims 1769
Plat: April 1st, 1769, Surveyed for Joseph Thompson, 200 A
on the South Branch of the North fork of Tyger River...Mc-

Carters and Nesbitts line...Joseph Jones...Zach Bullock Alex. Ray, Alexr McCarty, Cha Bear

TILLET, GILES File no. 806; Grant no. 76; Bk. 23, p. 327
640 A on both sides Fair Forrest 22d December 1768 Wm Tryon

TILLET, JAMES File no. 729(938); Grant no. —; Bk. 22, p. 310 (Bk. 24, p. 24)
200 A on the So side of Fair Forrest...Tates line...Tillets old line...25th Novem 1771 Jo Martin

TOWNSEND, REPENTANCE File no. 272; Grant no. 54; Bk. 20; p. 583
Plat: Surveyed for Repentance Townsend 300 A on main fork of fishing creek including his own improvement...on the Indian line, Samuel Porters corner...Willm Smiths land...John Salers Corner...June 17th 1769 Peter Johnston Sur.
John Adams & John Saler, C B Grant issued 11 Dec 1770

TRAMMELL, JOHN File no. 219; Grant no. 314; Bk. 20, p. 537
Plat: Surveyed for John Trammill 200 A on both sides of the No fork of Packlet including his improvement...Zach Bullock James Howard, Wm Imrupton, C B Grant issued 16 Dec 1769

TRAVIS, DANIEL File no. 99; Grant no. 124; Bk. 20, p. 440
160 A on Susey Boles branch of Turkey Creek joining Seth Johnston & John McKnit Alexanders Land including the improvement he now lives on...4th May 1769 Wm Tryon

VINYARD, ISHMAEL File no. 434; Grant no. 102; Bk. 20, p. 76
Plat: Surveyed for Ishmael Vinyard 50 A on waters of Turkey Creek including part of his own improvement...16th July 1771 Jno Kirkconell, Survr. George Ross, William Erwin, C B Grant issued 14 Nov 1771

WADE, JOHN File no. 290; Grant no. 281; Bk. 20, p. 624
Plat: Novr the 26th 1769, Surveyed for John Wade, 400 A on the N fork of Thickety Creek...Zach Bullock. Grant issued 25 Dec 1770

WALLING, WILLIAM File no. 180; Grant no. 172; Bk. 20, p. 517
Plat: Surveyed for William Walling 70 A on the stoney fork of fishing creek...John McKnit Alexanders...Febry 16th 1769 Peter Johnston Hugh Neely & Wm Walling, C B Grant issued 16 Dec 1769

WATSON, DAVID File no. 565; Grant no. 443; Bk. 22, p. 165
100 A on the head of Bullocks Creek near his own land...22d May 1772 Jo Martin

WATSON, JOHN File no. 514; Grant no. 45; Bk. 22, p. 36
Plat: Surveyed for John Moffat (stricken) Watson 144 A on waters of Bullocks Creek joining and between James Templeton & James Watsons lands...Febry 9th 1771 Jno Kirkconell Surv. Gilbert Watson, Jno Lauchline, C B Grant issued 15 May 1772

WATSON, SAMUEL File no. 65; Grant no. 59; Bk. 20, p. 428
50 A on waters of Allisons Creek joining and between his own and Robert McDowalls land...4th May 1769 Wm Tryon

WATSON, WILLIAM File no. 116; Grant no. 178; Bk. 20, p. 449
Plat: Surveyd for William Watson 250 A on waters of Fishing Creek joining his own land...Gilespies corner...Febry 10th 1769 Peter Johnston, Sur. William Watson & John Gabbey, C B Grant issued 4 May 1769

WEDENMAN, JOHN File no. 137; Grant no. 353; Bk. 20, p. 637
Plat: Nov 15, 1769 Survey'd for John Widenman 100 A on Reedy Branch of Packlet...Zach Bullock Phillip Wedenman, Christopher Wedman, CB Grant issued 24 Dec 1770

WHITAKER, RICHARD File no. 559; Grant no. 435; Bk. 22, p. 103
Plat: Surveyed for Richard Whiteacker 140 A on a branch of Allysons Creek...on or near McNight Alexanders corner... David Duffs corner...17 April 1771 Jno Kirkconell Sur. Joseph Henderson & John Cooper, C B Grant issued 22 May 1772

WHILCHEL, FRANCIS File no. 936; Grant no. 436; Bk. 24, p.24
Plat: Surveyed for Francis Whilchel 100 A...on both sides of London Bridg branch...Zach Bullock. September 1st, 1769 John Whelchey, Joseph Forgerson, C B Grant issued 24 Dec 1770

WILLIAMS, JOHN File no. 288; Grant no. 279; Bk. 20, p. 624
Plat: Nov. 1, 1770 Surveyed for John Williams 500 A on both sides of Packlet including Clarks old Fields...Zach Bullock Adam Burchfield, George Marchbanks, C B Grant issued 24 Dec 1770

WILLIAMS, JOHN File no. 59; Grant no. 542; Bk. 20, p. 414
Plat: March 7th 1767, Surveyed for John Williams Jur. 300 A on both sides south fork of Packlet...in his own line...joines Twittys line...Zach Bullock [No C B] Grant issued 23 Dec 1768

WILLIAMS, JOHN JUNR File no. 58; Grant no. 541; Bk. 20, p. 414

Plat: Feb. 9th 1768 Surveyed for John Williams Jur 600 A on both sides of the south fork of Packlet Beginning...William Twittys corner...Zach Bullock...Alexr Kilpatrickt, Joab Mitchell, C B Grant issued 23 Dec 1768

WILLIAMS, JOHN JUNR File no. 60; Grant no. 543; Bk. 20, p. 414
600 A on both sides South fork of Pacalet...William Twittys corner...23d December 1768 Wm Tryon

WILLIAMSON, WILLIAM File no. 673(882); Grant no. 374; Bk. 22, p. 300 (Bk. 22, p. 11)
Plat: Surveyed for William Williamson 60 A on Burlisons fork of Turkey creek...George Hoggs land...Jany19th 1770 Peter Johnston Surv. John Millers, & John Donald, C B Grant issued 22 Nov 1771

WILLIAMSON, WILLIAM File no. 200; Grant no. 236; Bk. 20, p. 527
200 A on the Dividing ridge of Burlestons fork and loves fork of Turkey creek...16th December 1769 Wm Tryon

WILLSON, ROBERT File no. 730; Grant no. 403; Bk. 22, p. 310
200 A on both sides Abbertons Creek...Jacob Gardners line... Willsons old line...25th November 1771 Jo Martin

WILLSON, ROBERT File no. 939; Grant no. 439; Bk. 24, p. 24
Plat: March 4th, 1770 Surveyd for Robert Wilson 200 A on both sides Abbetons Creek...Jacob Gardners line...Wilsons old line...Zach Bullock Jacob Gardner, Will Smith, C B Grant issued 25 Nov 1771

WOOD, JAMES File no. 564; Grant no. 442; Bk. 22, p. 105
300 A on both sides of Lawson fork of Packlate including the mouth of Shoally Creek and his own improvement...22d May 1772 Jo Martin

WYLIE, MOSES File no. 9; Grant no. 453; Bk. 20, p. 397
Moses Wylie, Junr 80 A both sides Cowdens Creek joining his deceased fathers land...22d December 1768 Wm Tryon

YANCEY, JAMES File no. 902; Grant no. 397; Bk. 24, p. 17
300 A on the branch of the N of Tyger above Capt. Earls'... 25 Novr 1771 Jo Martin

YANCEY, JAMES File no. 693; Grant no. 399; Bk. 22, p. 304
300 A on the Branch of the North of Tyger above Capt. Earls ...25th Novem 1771 Jo Martin

YOUNG, JOHN File no. 103; Grant no. 128; Bk. 20, p. 441
Plat: Surveyed for John Young 100 A joining Charles Moors

land including his improvement where he now lives...Febry 2, 1769 James Young, Moses Coller, C B Peter Johnston Sur. Grant issued 4 May 1769

CLARK, NATHANIEL File no. 886; Grant no. 378; Bk. 24, p. 12
300 A on the Et side of Broad River...Ganym moore Line... Robt Palmers Corner...Jones's Line...22 Novr 1771 Jo Martin
[The Ganym moore is probably Guyan Moore.]

WARREN, HUGH File no. 597; Bk. 23, p. 123
100 A on both sides Buck Creek of Packlet...23 Jan ? Jo Martin
[S.C. Land Memorials, Vol. XII, p. 517, gives year as 1773.]

SWANN, ROBERT File no. 427; Grant no. 82; Bk. 23, p. 703
Plat: Oct 31, 1770, Surveyed for Robert Swann 240 A on both sides Kings Creek adj. Collins line, Wilsons line...William Sims. [No CB] Iss. 14 Nov 1771

SWANN, ROBERT File no. 435; Grant no. 103; Bk. 23, p. 706
Plat: Sept 24, 1771, Surveyed for Robert Swann, 300 A on both sides Floyds and Golds branch of Clarks Fork of Bullocks Creek...McKennys line...Joseph Clarks line...Pr William Sims, James Chamberlin, Jos[?] Harrison, C B Iss. 14 Nov 1771

SWANN, ROBERT File no. 207; Grant no. 302; Bk. 23, p. 536
Plat: March 30th 1769, Surveyed for Robert Swann, 200 A on both sides Bells branch of Kings Creek including Candles improvement...Wm Sims, Surv. Benjamin Rice, Wilkerson Turner, C B Iss. 16 Dec 1769

McDANIEL, DANIEL File no. 161; Grant no. 454; Bk. 23, p. 487
Plat: Survey'd for Daniel McDaniel 200 A on Suck Creek of Broad River including his own Improvement...Nov 30, 1768. Zach Bullock, Surv. [No CB] Iss. 6 May 1769

HENDERSON, RICHARD File no. 61; Grant no. 544; Bk. 20, p. 414
Plat: Surveyed for Richard Henderson, 300 A on both sides Cub Creek of South forke of Packlet 1st March 1767. Pr. Zach Bullock; Alexander Kilpatrick, Joab Mitchel, C B

PERSON, ANTHONY File no. 63; Grant no. 54; Bk. 20, p. 427
200 A on both sides James Creek, waters of No fork Tygar including his own improvement...adj. Alexr Vernon, Lucies line, Thomas Pennys line...4 May 1769.

STEVESON, ALEXANDER File no. 70; Grant no. 66; Bk. 20, p. 429

135 A on So waters of Allisons Creek adj. William Stevenson, John Henry & John Buchanan 4 May 1769.

KER, JOHN JUNIOR File no. 92; Grant no. 113; Bk. 20, p. 438
Plat: Surveyed for John Ker Junior, 150 A on waters of Allisons Creek adj. his own land, adj. Watson...10 Feb 1769, Peter Johnston, Surv. Samuel Nisbet, Daniel Brice, C B Granted 4 May 1769.

GUTHREY, FRANCIS File no. 94, Grant no. 116; Bk. 20, p. 439
Plat: Surveyed for Francis Guthrey, 132 A on S side Allison Creek adj. John Henry, John Buchanan...Dec. 26, 1767. Wm and Alexr Stevenson, C B Granted 4 May 1769.

McCULLOH, JOHN File no. 97; Grant no. 120; Bk. 20, p. 439
Plat: 126 A on the Dividing Ridge between Fishing and Allisons Creek, adj. John McKlemurrys...Feb. 11, 1769. Peter Johnston, Surv. Archibald Thompson, John Smith, C B Granted 4 May 1769.

McKINNEY, JOHN File no. 134; Grant no. 363; Bk. 20, p. 479
Plat: April 15, 1769, Surveyed for John McKeny, 271 A on Laffertys Creek including James Chambers improvement... Zach Bullock, Surv. Patrick Lafferty, William Little, S C B Granted 5 May 1769.

NEAL, JOSEPH File no. 135; Grant no. 364; Bk. 20, p. 479
Plat: February 3, 1769, Surveyed for Joseph Neal, 100 A on N side Broad River including the mouth of Kings Creek... Zach Bullock. John Loveletty, Marshal Loveletty, S C B Granted 5 May 1769.

PEE, GEORGE File no. 148; Grant no. 392; Bk. 20, p. 481
Plat: Surveyed for George Pee, 200 A on Abbertons Creek above Marshall Lovelettys...Zach Bullock, Surv. William Runolds, Marshel Lovelety, C B Granted 5 May 1769.

McDANIEL, DANIEL File no. 200; Grant no. 315; Bk. 20, p. 537
Plat: Surveyed for Daniel McDaniel 400 A on Buck Creek about 1 mile from the mouth on the North Side Broad River ...Zach Bullock. Charles Robertson, Wm McDaniel, C Bear. Granted 16 Dec. 1769.

YOUNG, JOHN File no. 231; Grant no. 59; Bk. 20, p. 549
150 A on Rockey Allisons Creek including the improvement he lives on...adj. Watson, 9 April 1770. Wm Tryon.

CHENEY, SAMUEL File no. 236(861); Grant no. 200; Bk. 20, p. 550 (23, 349)
Plat: Surveyed for Saml Cheney, 150 A on Panther Creek of Enoree River adj. Charles Moor...June 6, 1769. Peter Johns-

ton, Surv. David Anderson, John Williams, C B Granted 9 April 1770.

THOMPSON, ELISHA File no. 264; Grant no. 46; Bk. 20, p. 582
Plat: Surveyed for Elisha Thompson, 180 A on Jammies Creek, a SW granch of N fork Tygar including his own improvement adj. Alexr Vernon, James Miller...June 8, 1770; Peter Johnston, Surv. Thomas Penny, Elisha Thompson, C B Granted 11 Dec. 1770.

WOOD, JOHN File no. 277; Grant no. 156; Bk. 20, p. 602
Plat: Surveyed for John Wood, 300 A on N side N fork Packelet including his own improvement where he now lives... July 8, 1770. Peter Johnston, Surv. Arthur Rodgers, Hugh Moore, C B Granted 11 Dec. 1770.

DENNARD, JOHN File no. 286; Grant no. 277; Bk. 20, p. 624
Plat: April 11, 1769, Surv. for John Dennard, 200 A on Boaches Creek including his improvement...Zach Bullock; Patrickt Moore, Adam Burchfield, Ch. B. Granted 24 Dec 1770.

McBEE, JAMES File no. 293; Grant no. 284; Bk. 20, p. 625
Plat: Nov. 22, 1769, Surveyed for James McBee, 400 A on S side N fork Packlet, adj. Sam Youngs...Zach Bullock. Jas. Howard, Alexr Kilpatrick, C B Granted 24 Dec 1770

WEDENMAN, JOHN File no. 317; Grant no. 35; Bk. 20, p. 637
Plat: Surveyed for John Wedenman, 100 A on reedy branch of Pcklet...Zach Bullock, Surv. Phillop Wedeman, Christopher Wedman, C B Granted 24 Dec 1770.

DICKSON, JOSEPH File no. 336; Grant no. 67; Bk. 20, p. 657
Plat: Surveyed for Joseph Dickson, 200 A on W side Broad River, between Thickety & Packolet on both sides Gochers Creek...15 July 1770. Jo. Dickson, Surv. "Joseph Burchfield & Peak" Cha. Bear. Granted 18 April 1771.

TEMPLETON, JAMES File no. 433; Grant no. 101; Bk. 20, p. 706
Plat: Surveyed for James Templeton, 90 A on waters of Bullocks Creek. 20 April 1771, Jno Kirkconell, Surv. James Watson, John Givens, C B Granted 14 Nov 1771.

McKENNY, JOHN File no. 436; Grant no. 104; Bk. 20, p. 707
Plat: Surveyed for John McKenny, 176 A on both sides Lafertys Creek of Broad River, adj. Robert McCurdy, John McKnitt Alander (sic)...Goin Moore. July 25, 1771. Jno Kirkconell, Surv. Robert McCurdy, James Derwin, C B Granted 14 Nov 1771

GLOVER, DRURY File no. 465; Grant no. 85; Bk. 22, p. 21
Plat: Surveyed for Drury Glover, 200 A on both sides So
fork Turkey Creek adj. James Stephenson, 1 Jan 1772. Jno
Kirkconell, Surv. John & Lowry Glover, C B Granted 15
May 1772.

GRAHAM, JOHN File no. 466; Grant no. 86; Bk. 22, p. 22
Plat: Surveyed for John Graham 350 A on Griffen Branch of
Thickety Creek, 26 Mar 1771 Jno Kirkconell, Surv. William
Steen, John Steen, C B Granted 15 May 1772.

PATTERSON, ROBERT File no. 479; Grant no. 99; Bk. 22, p. 25
Plat: Surveyed for Robert Patterson, 100 A on both sides
Patterson Creek of Bullocks Creek 5 June 1771, John Kirk-
conell, Surv. James Black, Peter Patterson, C B Granted 15
May 1772.

GOLIGHTLY, JOHN File no. 480; Grant no. 100; Bk. 22, p. 25
Plat: Surveyed for John Golightly, 500 A on Dennesses
Branch of fareforast adj. William Wafford, 16 Jan 1772. Jno
Kirkconell, Surv. James Hammitt, George Fare, C B Granted
15 May 1772

ELLIOTT, JOHN File no. 550; Grant no. 425; Bk. 22, p. 101
Plat: Surveyed for John Elliott, 200 A on both sides Goo-
chers Creek of Thickety, 10 Jan 1772, Jno Kirkconnell;
Thomas Nicklas, David Allon, C B Granted 22 May 1772.

ROSSE, FRANCES File no. 561; Grant no. 439; Bk. 22, p. 104
Plat: Surveyed for Frances Rosse, 500 A on Naves Creek of
Lawsons fork of Packlatt adj. William Navels, 12 Jan 1772.
Jno Kirkconell, Surv. John Earles, William Naves, C B
Granted 22 May 1772.

ROSS, FRANCIS File no. 562; Grant no. 439; Bk. 22, p. 104
Plat: Surveyed for Francis Ross, 200 A on the Dividing Ridge
of Fishing and Turkey Creek. 16 July 1771. Jno Kirkconell,
Surv. George Rosse, Wm. Erwin, C B Granted 22 May 1772.

GLOVER, LOWARY File no. 580; Grant no. 471; Bk. 22, p. 111
150 A on a Branch of Turkey Creek adj. William Glover, 23
May 1772 Jo Martin

JEFFERS, NATHANIEL File no. 581; Grant no. 472; Bk. 22, p.
111
400 A on both sides Lusks branch of Thicketty Creek...23
May 1772

BARROW, WILLIAM File no. 584; Grant no. 475; Bk. 22, p. 112
300 A on both sides Sadlers branch of Broad River on So

side Love Road from Fishing Creek to Broad River 23 May 1772

BARROW, WILLIAM File no. 585; Grant no. 476; Bk. 22, p. 112
220 A on Owens branch of Sandy River, adj. Edward Crafts, 23 May 1772. Jo Martin.

BARROW, WILLIAM File no. 591; Grant no. 482; Bk. 22, p. 113
Plat: Surveyed for William Barrow, 600 A on Alexr Harpers Branch of Turkey Creek, below Phillips corner...Hacklens line...22 May 1772. John Kirkconell, Surv. Lowry Glover, Drury Glover, C B Granted 23 May 1772.

McKENNY, JOHN File no. 589; Grant no. 480; Bk. 22, p. 113
200 A on Stinson branch of Bullocks Creek adj. John Gardner, John Harkness. Granted 23 May 1772. Jo Martin

BURCHFIELD, JOSEPH Grant no. 399; Bk. 24, p. 16
250 A in the fork of Thicketty adj. Millers line. 25 Nov 1771 Jo Martin

BURCHFIELD, JOSEPH Grant no. 397; Bk. 22, p. 304
250 A in the fork of Thicketty, 25 Nov 1771 Jo Martin

MOORE, HUGH Grant no. 431; Bk. 22, p. 309
200 A on both sides of Gochers Creek including Dennard's and Ray's improvements. 25 Nov 1771 Jo Martin.

ROBERTS, OBADIAH Grant no. 440; Bk. 22, p. 310
200 A on both sides of Brulesse's branch 25 Nov 1771 Jo Martin

PRINCE, FRANCIS Grant no. 448; Bk. 22, pp. 311-312
180 A on N side of N fork of Tyger on both sides Brown branch adj. John McKlechenney's (sic) corner on John Princes line, John Millers corner, Collin's corner, 25 Nov 1771 Jo Martin

McMURRAY, Thomas Grant no. 191; Bk. 23, p. 348
150 A on S side Fishing Creek on Robert McClallond's Line adj. Benjamin Phillips, 22 Dec 1768 Wm Tryon

BUTLER, JOHN File no. 689; Grant no. 395; Bk. 22, p. 304
Plat: Survey'd for John Butler, 300 A on the North side of Packlet River on both sides of the Path that leads from Flanreys ford to thicketty...Sept 1, 1771. Zach. Bullock. Wm Marchbanks, Jas Burchfield, Cha Bearers. Granted 25 Nov 1771

CLARK, NATHANIEL File no. 677; Grant no. 378; Bk. 22, p. 301
Plat: Surveyed for Nathaniel Clark Three Hundred acres on

the Et side of broad river including his own improvement adj. Ganym Moors line, Robert Palmers corner, Jons's line, Augt 13th 1770. Peter Johnston, Surv. Nathaniel Clark, Jacob Vance, C B Granted 22 Nov 1771

FOWLER, JAMES File no. 679; Grant no. 383; Bk. 22, p. 302
Plat: Surveyed for James Fowler 170 A on the waters of Turkey Creek including his own improvement adj. Thos Morris, Colbs line, Stevensons land, John Mcknit Alexrs line...June 22d 1770. Peter Johnston, survr. James & Joseph Colbs, CB Granted 25 Nov 1771.

GOWDILOCK, ADAM File no. 934; Grant no. 434; Bk. 24, p. 24
Plat: November 1, 1770, Surveyed for Adam Gowdelock 300 A on the Ridg between Packlet and Thicketty...Zach Bullock. John Nuckoles, John Goudelock, C B Granted 25 Nov 1771.

PRINCE, FRANCIS File no. 705; Grant no. 413; Bk. 22, p. 306
Plat: Surveyed for Frances Prince 200 A on the Head of Hannons branch of Tygar River...Jno Kirkconell, Surv. Joseph Brown, William Hannon, C B Granted 25 Nov 1771.

WILLSON, HUGH File no. 675; Grant no. 376; Bk. 22, p. 301
Plat: Surveyed for Hugh Wilson 100 A on E side of Broad River adj. Archd Robisons land, Feb. 5, 1771. Peter Johnston, Survr. John Kirkconnel, Mathew Patterson, C. B. Granted 22 Nov 1771.

INDEX

166

Robert 60 (4), 78, 88, 95
Thomas 61
William 9 (3), 53, 61 (9), 62 (2),
  68, 84, 88, 90, 103, 118, 132
  (3), 136, 149
William (surv.) 42 (5), 43 (2), 44
  (3), 45, 46 (3), 47, 48 (4), 49
  (3), 50 (4), 51 (4), 54 (2), 55
  (2), 56, 57 (6), 58, 60 (3),
  61, 64 (3), 65 (2), 67 (2), 68
  (6), 69 (2), 70 (2), 71, 72 (3),
  73 (7), 74 (10), 75 (5), 78,
  81, 82, 83, 84 (3), 85 (3), 86
  (2), 88 (2), 90 (3), 92 (2), 93,
  94 (5), 95, 97, 98 (3), 99 (3),
  100 (5), 101 (3), 102, 103
  (4), 104 (3), 105, 106, 107
  (3), 108 (5), 109 (2), 110 (2),
  111 (4), 112 (5), 113 (2),
  114 (3), 115, 116 (2), 117
  (2), 118 (4), 119, 120 (5),
  121 (3), 122 (3), 123 (5),
  132 (2), 142, 146, 151
  See Dixon
Dill, John 62
  Phillip 10
Dinkins, ____ 10
  William 1
  See Denkens
Dirvins, James 143
Ditemore, Henry 113
Ditts, Henry 150
  Robert 152
Dixon, David 10
  Michael 10
  Thomas 122
  William 10 (2)
Dixson, John 9
  See Dickson
Dobbs, Francis 62 (3)
  George 11
Dodds, ____ 139, 149
  Frances 46
  Francis 56, 57 (2), 87, 100, 104,
  117, 130
  Nat 135
Donald, John 155
Donlop, Samuel 11
  See Dunlap
Dosson, Bartholomew 62, 103
Douds, Caleb 23
  See Dowd
Douglas, George 11

William 34
  See Dugloss
Dowd, Caled 122
  Richard 62, 98
  See Doud
Downing, John 143
Draper, ____ 95
  Thomas 52, 56 (2), 62, 67, 128
Duff, David 132, 154
Dugan, ____ 152
  Robert 54
Duggins, ____ 65, 134 (2)
Dugloss, John 11
  See Douglas
Dumas, Benjamin 11
Dunbar, Andrew 65
  David 23
Duncan, ____ 35 (2), 36
  James 117, 118
  Joseph 105 (2), 116
  Patrick 62, 117
  William 62
Dunham, John 113
Dunlap, ____ 48
  Charles 22
  Samuel 11
  William 83
  See Donlop
Dunlape, William 11
Dunlop, Robert 30
  See Dunlap
Dunn, James 16
Durroh, John 81
Durrumple, Thomas 10

E

Earle, Capt. 155 (2)
  John 109, 132
Earles, John 159
Easley, Robert 52
Edwards, Richard 57
Elliott, ____ 72, 94
  John 11, 63, 95, 132, 141 (2),
  159
  Solomon 84
Ervine, Thomas 11
Erwin, Christian 11
  Jno. 63
  Thomas 11, 12
  William 153, 159
  See Irwin
Evans, Jabes 63

Robert 64
Saml. 104
Humphries, John 57
Hunter, Samuel 138
Hutchins, _____ 61, 64, 85, 132 (2)
  Anthony 16, 57 (2), 73, 74, 75
    (2), 121
  James 73 (2), 74 (10), 75 (4),
    121
Hyde, George 147

I

Imrupton, William 153
  See Monrupty
Inlow, Benjamin 138
  Isaac 138
Irwin, John 75 (2)
  Nathaniel 75
  Robert 75 (3), 138
  William 75
  See Erwin
Islers, Frederick 24

J

Jack, James 138
Jackson, Banjamin 2
  Benjamin 16
Jameson, James 76 (2)
Jamison, William 136
Jarrot, John 76
Jeffers, Nathaniel 159
Jefferson, Nathaniel 76 (2), 114
Jeffress, _____ 63
Johns, _____ 111
  Lewis 10
Johnson, _____ 53
  John 53
  Seth 83, 153
  Thomas 99 (2)
Johnston, _____ 66
  Henry 116 (3)
  Isaac 50
  James 16
  John 51, 146
  Peter 76, 138 (4), 139 (4), 144
  Peter (surv.) 45 (2), 46, 49, 50,
    51 (2), 52, 54, 56, 57, 64, 67,
    69 (2), 72, 77 (2), 78, 83 (2),
    85, 86, 88, 90 (2), 93 (2), 94,
    96, 98, 99 (2), 102 (2), 105,
    106 (3), 109 (5), 113, 114,
    115 (2), 117 (2), 118, 119
    (2), 120, 125, 126 (2), 127
    (2), 128 (2), 131 (2), 132,

133, 135 (2), 136 (2), 137
(4), 138 (3), 139 (6), 140 (2),
141, 142 (5), 143 (4), 144,
145 (4), 146 (2), 147 (3),
148 (3), 149 (5), 150 (6),
151, 152 (2), 153 (2), 154,
155, 156, 157 (3), 158 (2),
161 (3)
Jolley, Joseph 66, 67
  William 66
Jolly, Joseph 76
Jones, _____ 61, 80, 94, 104, 121,
  126, 127, 144, 156
  Andrew 53
  John 21, 58, 147
  Jos. 43, 45, 54, 126
  Joseph 71, 76, 82, 89 (2), 90,
    93 (2), 99 (2), 100, 106, 111,
    115, 116 (2), 139, 142, 147,
    152 (2), 153
  Moses 45, 77, 133
  Stephen 100, 130
  William 58, 104
  Wylie 124 (2)
Jordan, John 77, 126

K

Keer, John 115
  See Care, Ker, Kerr
Keley, Hugh 35
Keilly, John 37
  See Kelly
Keller, Joseph 139
Kelley, _____ 89
  Jno. 77
  See Keilly, Kelly
Kellso, Joseph 25
  See Kelso
Kelly, _____ 150
  John 68 (2), 107
  Joseph 77
Kelsey, _____ 114, 134
  John 16 (2), 37, 65, 92
  Samuell 131
  See Kellso, Kelso, Kilcey
Kelso, John 17
  See Kellso, Kelso, Kelsey
Kembro, John 139
  See Kimbro
Kembroll, John 139
Kenedy, Alexander 139
Kennady, Alexander 139
Kennedy, Alexander 140
  George 17

172

174

John 26, 58, 73, 77, 79, 94, 97
  (2), 98 (2), 103, 105, 106,
  125, 126, 146 (2)
Moses 97, 125
Patrick 51, 73, 97, 98, 117, 158
Robert 146
Samuel 26
William 26, 28, 105, 109, 120
Morgan, Thos. 21, 146
Morris, ____ 45
  Garrot 69
  Robert 38
  Thomas 64, 98, 150, 161
Morrison, Thos. 133
Morrow, Samuel 86
Muldoon, James 80, 98, 120
Murphey, James 98, 138, 147
Murphy, James 139
Murray, James 27
Musketty, James 98 (2)

N

Navel, William 159
Navill, William 147
Neal, ____ 34
  Joseph 104, 157
  See Neel, Neil
Neale, Chrisr. (surv.) 15
Neally, ____ 146
Neel, David 99
  See Neal, Neil
Neeley, ____ 85
  John 85, 120
  Robert 82
  Samuel 82
  Thomas 82
  William 46, 99, 112
Neely, Hugh 86
  Robert 103
  Samuel 27 (5), 28 (2), 38, 72
  Thomas 27 (2), 28, 83
  William 27 (3), 28 (2), 38, 72,
    108
Neesbit, Alexander 3
  See Nesbitt
Neighbours, John 148
Neill, David 99 (2)
  Dd. 101
  John 71, 120
  Thomas 99, 100
  See Neal, Neel
Neisbet, James 99 (2), 109
  John 99
  Samuel 99, 100, 139, 147 (4)

See Nesbitt
Neisonille, ____ 149
Nelson, Hugh 59
Nesbet, Samuel 99
Nesbitt, ____ 153
  Alexander 3, 28
  John 62
  See Neesbit, Neisbit, Nisbet
Newman, Jonathan 59, 71, 83, 93,
  100, 115
Neyles, Samuel 81
  Thomas 81
Neysmith, Thomas 54, 100
Nicholas, John 145
  Thomas 147
  See Nicklas
Nichols, James 116
  John 93, 100
  See Nuckols
Nicklas, Thomas 141 (2), 159
  See Nicholas
Nisbet, Alexander 28 (2)
  John 104
  Samuel 140, 150, 157
  See Nesbitt
Nuckols, John 100, 129, 135, 137,
  143 (2), 147, 161
Nugent, Edward (surv.) 17
Nuly, John 138
Nutt, Andrew 28
  John 37
  William 28 (2)

O

Oarr, William 29
  See Orr
Oates, John 29 (3)
  Martin 94, 99
OCain, Daniel 35
Odell, John 60
Oneal, Cornelius 113
Ormond, Jacob 89 (2)
  James 25
Orr, John 100
  See Oarr
Osborn, Adlai 147
  Alexander 100
Osborne, James 60
  John 60
  Noble 60
  William 60
  See Ozburn
Otterson, James 13
Owen, ____ 127
Ozburn, Adlai 147

CPSIA information can be obtained at www.ICGtesting.com
Printed in the USA
LVOW130637110712

289552LV00007B/70/P